T0301545

PERSPECTIVES ON THE HISTORY OF
ECONOMIC THOUGHT
VOLUME IV

KEYNES, MACROECONOMICS AND
METHOD

Perspectives on the History of Economic Thought Volume IV

Keynes, Macroeconomics and Method

Selected Papers from the
History of Economics Society Conference,
1988

Edited by
D. E. Moggridge

Published for the
History of Economics Society
by Edward Elgar

Published by
Edward Elgar Publishing Limited
Gower House
Croft Road
Aldershot
Hants GU11 3HR
England

Eward Elgar Publishing Company
Old Post Road
Brookfield
Vermount 05036
USA

British Library Cataloguing in Publication Data
History of Economics Society *Conference* (1988: Toronto,
  Canada)
  Keynes, macroeconomics and method: selected papers from the
  History of Economics Society Conference, 1988. –
  (Perspectives on the history of economic thought; v. 4)
  1. Economics. Theory, history
  I. Title II. Moggridge, D. E. (Donald Edward) *1943*– III.
  Series
  330.1

ISBN 978 1 85278 294 3

Contents

Figures

Tables

Introduction
D. E. Moggridge

This volume and its companion (volume III) contain a selection of the over 135 papers presented at the annual conference of the History of Economics Society in Toronto in June 1988. Afterwards, those presenting papers were asked to submit either the version circulated at the conference or a revised version to the editor by the end of the summer of 1988. From those thus available, some sixty, the editor and Professor Mark Blaug made a final selection which, less a few unanticipated dropouts, appears here.

The papers in this volume cover a number of interrelated themes relating to the history of macroeconomics, particularly its Keynesian manifestation, and method. However, as many papers are devoted to both topics, rather than divide them by topic, I have listed them more or less chronologically – a hardly surprising way to treat historical topics.

The volume opens with a paper that straddles the boundary between the history of economics and economic history. There Arie Arnon takes us back to the Bullionist controversy of the Napoleonic Wars and asks what Thomas Tooke and David Ricardo could have learned about the trend in prices if they had applied some concept of indexation to the price data available at the time, particularly the data that Tooke himself would publish in 1823 as *On the High and Low Prices of the Last Thirty Years*. His conclusion is that, even though Tooke did not use indexation, in his debate with the Bullionists he accurately captured contemporary price trends, even if his position as to the causes of these movements was not completely correct.

The next papers also deal with matters arising from nineteenth-century monetary debates. Lawrence White and George Selgin provide a useful summary of the *laissez-faire* contributions to the 'free banking' debates in Jacksonian America, which had an important effect on the shape taken by the American monetary system after Jackson's veto of the attempt to re-charter the Second Bank of the United States in 1832, which they tie into more recent discussions. Thomas Humphrey traces the origins of Wicksell's cumulative process model of *Interest and Prices* (1898) back to its intellectual origins in Henry Thornton's contributions to the Napoleonic Wars discussions in his *An Enquiry into the Nature and Effects of the Paper Credit of Great Britain* (1802) and his first parliamentary speech on the

Bullion Report and Thomas Joplin's contributions to the currency debates of the 1820s and 1830s. In this paper he clearly shows that the model associated with Wicksell had its origins in this much earlier work and that Joplin introduced the savings-investment approach into English monetary economics a century before Robertson.

The next five papers deal with various aspects of Keynes's thought. The papers by R. M. O'Donnell and B. W. Bateman arose from a session which largely concerned itself with the question of whether Keynes's abandoned the logical theory of probability he had advanced in his *Treatise on Probability* in response to Frank Ramsey's 1926 critique. This question has recently generated a considerable literature, and one of the highlights of the Toronto meetings was the session in which all the younger scholars actively concerned with the question came together to discuss the issue, the excuse being the papers by Bateman and O'Donnell and the concluding chapter of Anna Carabelli's subsequently published *On Keynes's Method.*[1] As one can see from these papers, this discussion promises to continue for some time.

The other three papers concerned with Keynes all relate to the *General Theory*. Ingo Barens examines a piece of analysis that appeared in the drafts but did not survive to appear in the book: Keynes's taxonomy of types of economies in his monetary theory of production. He argues that Keynes sensibly scrapped the taxonomy because he found it would not give him analytically relevant results which he could not achieve more straightforwardly – a decision made easier by the appearance of a 'classical' model in Pigou's *Theory of Unemployment* (1933). In contrast, Amitava Dutt and Edward Amadeo tackle another puzzle, this time a part of the *General Theory* that did not pass into the subsequent mainstream literature – Keynes's denial that his theory had anything to do with wage-price stickiness. They suggest that, in this case, the profession did not follow the original model largely because it did not fit well into the simultaneously developing mainstream economic theory and because it did not fit contemporary academic fashions in theorizing. Finally, Victoria Chick comparatively examines Keynes's approach to speculation in the *General Theory* and the approach associated with Friedman–Baumol – Telser, and rational expectations. In doing so, she compares the methodology of each approach with methodological changes in physics and suggests that Keynes's methodology is the most modern.

The next three papers also have a strong inter-war flavour. Two have links back to Wicksell's cumulative process model discussed by Humphrey. Ivo Maes examines how Hayek's Austrian-oriented, neo-Wicksellian research programme in monetary theory at the London School of Economics was subverted by J. R. Hicks. Mario Seccareccia compares the neo-

Wicksellian model underlying Hayek's research programme with that developed by Wicksell's Swedish successors which had markedly different policy implications. Then Robert Dimand provides a useful survey of the mathematical models of the business-cycle developed in the late 1920s and early 1930s.

The final three papers echo concerns touched on earlier in the volume. Omar Hamouda provides a survey of Hicks's notion of dynamics between the 1930s and 1980s. Robin Rowley and Omar Hamouda take three instances in the area of production economics – the introduction of the Cobb–Douglas production function; the treatment of problems of heterogeneous capital inputs, and the contemporary problems in marrying evidence from fitted cost functions to 'well-behaved' production functions – to evaluate the evolution of research interests in the area and its relation to progress or rational science. Finally, J. Daniel Hammond returns to Milton Friedman's influential 'The Methodology of Positive Economics' and a gap in the subsequent interpretive literature – its few references to other works by Friedman, even from the same volume – to argue that on the evidence of the other primarily methodological chapters in *Essays in Positive Economics* the emerging consensus that Friedman's methodological point of view is instrumentalist is unfounded.

Note
1. Macmillan: London, 1988.

Contributors

Edward J. Amadeo, Department of Economics, Pontifical Catholic University, Rio de Janeiro, Brazil.

Arie Arnon, Department of Economics and Monaster Center for Economic Research, Ben Gurion University of the Negev, Israel.

B. W. Bateman, Department of Economics, Grinnell College, Grinnell, Iowa, USA.

Ingo Barens, Wirtschafts-Wissenschaft, Bergishe Universitat, Wuppertal, Federal Republic of Germany.

Victoria Chick, Department of Economics, University College, London, England.

Robert W. Dimand, Department of Economics, Brock University, St Catharines, Ontario, Canada.

Amitava Krishna Dutt, Department of Economics, University of Notre Dame, Notre Dame, Indiana, USA.

J. Daniel Hammond, Department of Economics, Wake Forest University, Winston-Salem, North Carolina, USA.

O. F. Hamouda, Department of Economics, Glendon College, York University, Toronto, Ontario, Canada.

Thomas M. Humphrey, Federal Reserve Bank of Richmond, Richmond, Virginia, USA.

I. Maes, Directorate General for Economic and Financial Affairs, Commission of the European Communities, and Brussels Business School (ICHEC), Brussels, Belgium.

D. E. Moggridge, Department of Economics, University of Toronto, Toronto, Ontario, Canada.

R. M. O'Donnell, School of Economic and Financial Studies, Macquarie University, Sydney, New South Wales, Australia.

Robin Rowley, Department of Economics, McGill University, Montreal, Quebec, Canada.

Mario Seccareccia, Economics, Faculty of Social Sciences, University of Ottawa, Ottawa, Ontario, Canada.

George A. Selgin, Department of Economics, University of Georgia, Athens, Georgia, USA.

Lawrence H. White, Department of Economics, University of Georgia, Athens, Georgia, USA.

1 What Thomas Tooke (and Ricardo) Could Have Known Had They Constructed Price Indices

Arie Arnon

Introduction

Many of the important debates during economic history have focused on prices: the determinants of prices in general and the reasons for changes in the price level in particular. These questions seemed of vital importance during the Restriction period in England (1797–1821), when notes were inconvertible and price levels unstable. During this period, two major schools of thought were formed – the Bullionists and the anti-Bullionists – who were distinguished first by their opposing recommendations *vis-à-vis* the preferred monetary regime. However, both the Bullionists's recommendation to return to convertibility and the anti-Bullionists's argument that England was not harmed by inconvertibility rested on their different analyses of the factors responsible for price rises. Who and what were, in fact, to be blamed for inflation? The Bullionists placed the blame on the Bank of England, maybe abetted by the other banks, who irresponsibly expanded the quantity of notes in circulation. They believed that convertibility would prevent the Bank from embarking on such an inflationary policy. In contrast, the anti-Bullionists considered price changes to be the result not of monetary but of real factors – such as the war with France and bad or good harvests. Thus in their view, neither the Bank of England nor the other banks were to be held responsible for unstable prices.[1]

In view of the centrality of the price level in these debates, it is surprising that the participants paid relatively little attention to empirical data on the timing and magnitude of price changes. This is surprising, first, because such data were in fact available. Thomas Tooke, later to be known as one of the founders of the Banking School, originally came to prominence for his exhaustive knowledge and publications of prices, which remain a major source of such information till the present day. Thus his later importance as a theoretician was preceded by his renown as a collector and interpreter of market prices. Ricardo, himself one of the foremost Bullionists, used Tooke's data and explanations for price changes in his defence of the return to convertibility in 1821, known as the Resumption (see Arnon, 1989). However, Tooke's explanations of price changes were on a different level from the deductive, abstract and general methodology which we usually associate with Ricardo. Tooke tended to provide specific explanations for each commodity based on the supply and demand in that particular market. It is surprising that not only Tooke but even Ricardo did not construct price indices from the huge data-base available, especially since rudimentary indexation had already been employed, for example by the Italian Carli in 1764 and by Sir George Schuckbury Evelyn in 1798 (see Mitchell, 1938; Gayer et al., 1953, pp. 517–27). This lacuna is all the more surprising since one might have expected that the shared interest of Tooke the 'empiricist' and Ricardo the 'theoretician' in price changes would have encouraged them to develop more general measures for evaluating the available data. Indeed, Tooke's failure to do so led Gregory (1928) to the far-reaching conclusion that 'he [Tooke] had no general picture in his mind of the trend of prices, largely owing to the fact that he did not employ index-numbers' (p. 21).

This paper will try to answer the question which neither Tooke not Ricardo asked: what could scholars of the time have learned about price trends had they applied some concept of indexation? – an endeavour which is expected to shed further light on the central debates of the time. The paper is organized in two main sections. The first constructs a series of alternative price indices, ranging from simple ones which scholars of the time could have employed, to the more complex ones of modern analysts. At this point, one may question the originality and contribution of this endeavour, since price indices based on Tooke's data have already been constructed by many scholars from Jevons in 1865 through Silberling in 1919 and 1923 to Gayer et al. in 1953. However, all these used Tooke's data as they appeared in his monumental *History of Prices*, published in six volumes between 1838 and 1857, i.e. seventeen years after the Resumption and fifteen years after Ricardo's death. To the best of my knowledge no studies have employed the data that Tooke published earlier, already in his 1823 work *On the High and Low Prices of the Last Thirty Years*.

These early data are important not only because they represent the information available to Ricardo, who died in 1823, and to Tooke prior to 1838, but also because they differ in certain important respects from those published in the *History of Prices*. In brief, in 1823 Tooke employed a rather idiosyncratic method, whereby the number of prices quoted for a particular commodity in a given year depended on the number of price fluctuations during that year. This method, which he later abandoned, generated extremely complex data, which are indeed difficult to interpret without some recourse to indexation. The present paper constructs various indices which can serve as a source of information also for modern students of economic history. In addition, I shall examine the compatibility of the present results with those yielded by the indices constructed by other writers from different data on the same period.

The second major aim of this paper will be to investigate the degree to which the information yielded by these indices can shed further light on the price trends and theoretical debates of the years under discussion. In other words, to what extent were the 'estimates' and interpretations of price trends among the political economists of the time compatible with the information contained in the then available data on prices. I shall address this general issue from two specific foci. One, did prices rise or fall in the years 1809–11, the years of the Bullion Committee? This question is of some importance, since while most scholars maintained that they rose, Tooke himself claimed that they fell. Thus the indices will first be employed to determine who was right. In addition, they will be used to shed further light on the ways in which the economists of the time reached conclusions about price changes. Were the Bullionists primarily influenced, as one might expect, by the price of gold, and Tooke, the champion of real factors, by the price of wheat? Could they have reached more accurate estimates using indexation? These questions lead us to the second major focus: how correct was Tooke in attributing price changes to real rather than to monetary factors in the economy? This old question was raised again by Bordo and Schwartz (1980; 1981), who attempted to demonstrate that Tooke and, of late, Rostow (1978) and Lewis (1978) were wrong in their support for real rather than monetary explanations of price changes. However, their analyses were based on data from 1870–1914, rather than of those of Tooke's own time. While, as Bessler (1984) notes, determination of causality in prices involves extremely complex methodological issues, this paper presents some preliminary analyses regarding the relative importance of seasons on the one hand, and of the quantity of money on the other in determining the price levels between 1797–1821. The results from these analyses suggest that, at least regarding the period under discussion, Tooke was not as wrong as Bordo and Schwartz claim.

The data
The data to be used appeared in the appendix to Tooke's book, *Thoughts and Details on the High and Low Prices of the Last Thirty Years,* 1823. This book analyses the years 1793 to 1822, but the appendix, compiled by Tooke's assistant A. Hinrichs, provides details on prices for 41 years, from 1782 to 1822. Prices are quoted for 41 commodities. The number of price quotations differs for each year. If the price of a commodity did not change in a particular year, Tooke quoted a single price. If the price of a commodity showed a certain trend (upward or downward) during the year

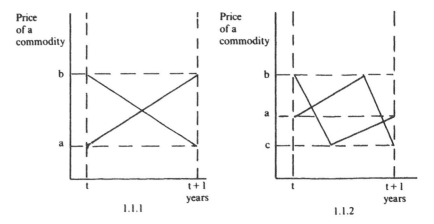

Figure 1.1   Prices of commodities

and the two extreme prices were a and b (see Figure 1.1.1), Tooke
informed us of (a,b) for that commodity – i.e. one cannot tell whether the
price rose or fell. If a commodity showed one maximum (or minimum)
and two trends through the year (upward or downward or vice versa)
Tooke quoted (a,b,c) (Figure 1.1.2). Thus the number of price quotations
for each commodity is not constant but ranges from one to ten, if there
were nine different successive trends for a particular commodity in a
certain year, as, for example, in the case of coffee in 1819. In addition,
Tooke sometimes reports separate data series according to the quality
(high or low) or origin (e.g. Russia or Sweden) of the commodity. The first
step of the present analysis was to compute an average price for each
commodity for each year over the various quotations and series provided.
This reduced Tooke's original data set from over 14,000 quotations to
1688.[2]

Indices1,2   Tooke and his comtemporaries had not developed ways of
quantifying the relative importance of different commodities. Indices 1
and 2 thus assign *equal weights* to each commodity, using arithmetic and
geometric means respectively while using 1782 as the base year.[3] These
indices are presented in Columns 1 and 2 of Table 1.1. Column 3 presents
the geometric averages for these years which were computed by Jevons in
1865 on the basis of Tooke's 1838 data. He too used equal weights. It
should be remembered that the 1838 data quoted a high and low price for
each commodity for a particular week in each quarter. This yielded eight
quotations for each year, regardless of the degree of variability in prices.
As revealed by Table 1.1, the results yielded by indices 1 and 2 show the

Table1.1 *'Tooke's' 1823 indices vs. Jevons's and Gayer's*

	(1) Index 1 Arithmetic	(2) Index 2 Geometric Equal Weights	(3) Jevons's Geometric	(4) Index 3 Arithmetic	(5) Index 4 Geometric Gayer's Weights	(6)* Gayer's et al Geometric
1782	100	100	100	100	100	
1783	93.16	93.18	100	93.00	91.77	
1784	86.97	86.76	93	90.23	88.50	
1785	83.84	83.25	90	86.35	84.42	
1786	84.46	83.41	85	89.72	87.28	
1787	89.46	87.49	87	93.77	91.47	
1788	87.45	83.98	87	92.69	90.33	
1789	82.35	79.43	85	93.41	89.28	
1790	83.82	81.39	87	94.87	90.71	89.3
1791	87.50	84.55	89	95.62	92.05	89.7
1792	91.95	88.89	93	101.32	96.87	88.1
1793	99.19	94.77	99	108.44	103.57	96.6
1794	99.08	95.57	98	108.12	103.66	98.5
1795	117.87	112.79	117	137.42	128.51	114.9
1796	118.77	114.33	125	134.72	128.18	116.1
1797	111.84	108.11	110	123.37	118.92	106.2
1798	116.88	112.16	118	118.60	113.58	107.9
1799	125.70	118.76	130	137.62	133.38	124.6
1800	130.22	119.96	141	161.78	149.20	151.0
1801	127.75	119.26	140	163.44	150.92	155.7
1802	115.48	107.81	110	128.34	121.88	122.2
1803	123.12	112.46	125	132.79	123.06	123.6
1804	120.48	110.11	119	142.69	133.53	124.3
1805	123.49	113.56	132	140.78	132.76	136.2
1806	120.94	110.82	130	137.47	129.10	134.5
1807	117.45	107.71	129	135.90	127.30	131.2
1808	143.84	129.74	145	162.06	150.68	144.5
1809	154.37	137.89	157	180.88	162.49	155.0
1810	145.08	134.70	142	172.13	157.65	153.4
1811	145.61	125.41	136	172.93	151.96	145.4
1812	158.21	133.92	121	195.17	167.93	163.7
1813	165.07	149.09	115	184.13	168.45	168.9
1814	156.27	148.74	114	172.03	162.10	153.7
1815	135.11	128.24	109	146.60	139.97	129.9
1816	118.95	110.00	91	141.04	131.07	118.6
1817	134.82	117.91	117	153.28	140.48	131.9
1818	136.77	123.22	132	151.58	140.85	138.7
1819	106.48	102.56	112	131.73	128.87	128.1
1820	92.79	89.12	103	122.34	114.46	115.4
1821	85.37	82.70	94	109.46	102.16	99.7
1822	87.17	83.38	88	98.15	92.20	87.9

Sources: Column 3 Jevons (1884/1964, pp. 144–5) (originally published in 1865).
Column 6: Mitchell (1962. p. 470).
Columns 1, 2 & 4, 5: see this paper.
*Base-average of 1821–5. Additional explanations in the text.

same general patterns as those yielded by Jevons's index. Figure 1.2 presents the arithmetic and geometric indices for the 1823 data together with Jevons's geometric index; it reveals an almost identical pattern for the years 1782–95. In later years, the peaks yielded by the two indices occur in almost the same years, except for the years 1811 to 1813 where the new index shows a rise in prices and Jevons's a fall in prices.[4]

Indices 3 and 4   It is, of course, unsatisfactory to ignore the relative importance of commodities. Tooke himself, when asked in 1840 about the unweighted indices computed by Porter, replied that he was opposed to unweighted indices which he saw as distorting and lacking significance (see Tooke, 1848, pp. 464–70). Gayer et al. (1953) computed weights for the commodities of the period, including 39 of the 41 covered by Tooke's data. The remaining two – hops and rice – were thus excluded from the present analyses.[5] They then computed a price index based both on Tooke's 1838 data and on additional sources. Indices 3 and 4 (see columns 4 and 5 of Table 1.1) present arithmetic and geometric indices respectively, incorporating Gayer's weights. Column 6 presents the Gayer–Rostow–Schwartz price index.

Figure 1.3 shows clearly the similar patterns yielded by Gayer et al.'s index and by the 1823 indices 3 and 4. This similarity was maintained also when 1821 was taken as the base year. In view of the similar results yielded by the arithmetic and the geometric indices (see Figures 1.2 and 1.3), only the arithmetic index was used for further analyses.

Indices 5–8   A major question of the present paper asks what political economists of the time could have known had they applied more general analyses to their data. Since the concept of weights had not been developed, they might have looked mainly at those commodities considered most important. At one extreme they might have looked at the price of gold or wheat or both as reflecting prices in general. Alternatively, they could have taken an average of some number of important commodities.

Index 5 assigns *equal weights* to those seventeen commodities reported by Tooke in 1823 which emerge as most important from Gayer et al.'s weights: those commodities with weights above 1 per cent of the total weights. Index 6 is based on those nine commodities to which Gayer et al. award the highest weights (above 4 per cent of the total weights). One should note that construction of these indices is relatively simple. Indices 7 and 8 are *weighted indices* for these same seventeen and nine commodities respectively.[6] These four indices are presented as columns 1–4 of Table 1.2. In general, the results for both unweighted (Figure 1.4) and weighted indices (Figure 1.5) suggest that in most years an index based even on nine commodities gives a fairly close approximation of prices over the 39 commodities. Not surprisingly, the approximation is better when indices

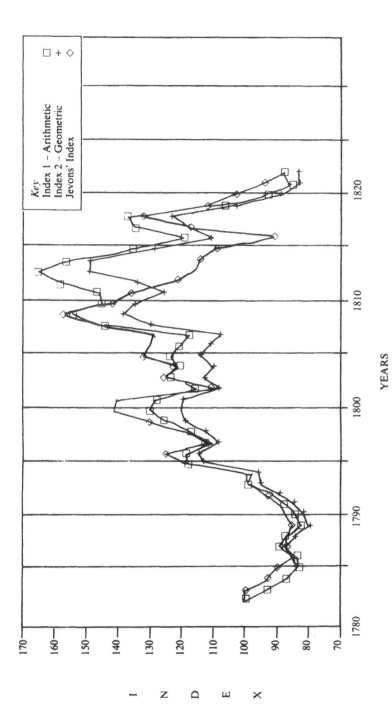

Figure 1.2 '*Tooke*' *vs. Jevons, equal weights (base-year 1782)*

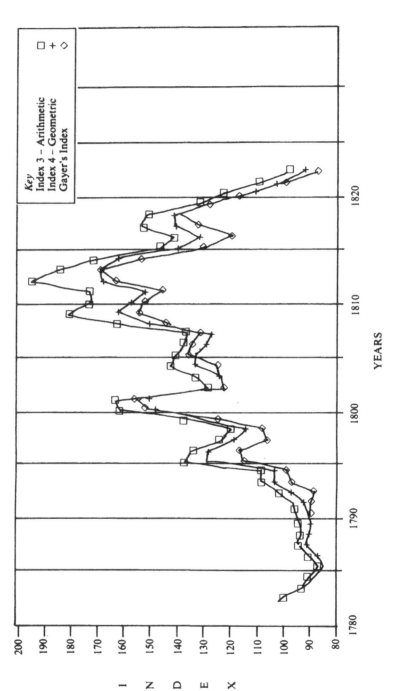

Figure 1.3 'Tooke' vs. Gayer, Gayer's weights

Table 1.2 'Tooke's' arithmetic indices for the 17 and 9 most important commodities

	(1) Index 5 17 Commodities Equal Weights	(2) Index 6 9 Commodities Equal Weights	(3) Index 7 17 Commodities Gayer's Weights	(4) Index 8 9 Commodities Gayer's Weights
1782	100.00	100.00	100.00	100.00
1783	93.22	85.59	86.94	73.33
1784	87.22	84.90	84.37	71.45
1785	82.68	83.59	81.04	68.33
1786	80.68	83.46	84.33	71.66
1787	87.39	85.02	87.76	74.90
1788	90.01	83.81	86.79	74.64
1789	83.34	78.19	87.29	75.82
1790	87.36	79.24	88.53	76.13
1791	95.08	83.56	88.67	75.72
1792	97.73	93.04	94.27	80.91
1793	108.24	98.53	100.80	87.25
1794	101.86	92.03	100.95	87.79
1795	113.23	103.22	128.25	113.03
1796	116.76	117.59	125.57	108.25
1797	120.22	119.791	114.74	97.59
1798	129.09	128.30	109.48	90.77
1799	134.64	123.67	128.52	109.61
1800	135.66	118.06	152.23	134.65
1801	131.88	127.18	153.58	134.94
1802	122.10	114.25	119.39	101.99
1803	127.69	125.70	123.24	105.10
1804	119.22	119.98	133.24	115.22
1805	120.58	120.03	131.02	113.35
1806	118.57	119.40	128.05	110.16
1807	114.58	114.09	126.85	109.28
1808	138.98	134.85	150.50	129.70
1809	150.29	167.22	169.64	148.65
1810	152.14	158.14	161.11	139.51
1811	157.67	130.73	159.60	139.38
1812	160.33	129.73	181.21	161.72
1813	173.64	154.11	171.29	150.85
1814	157.67	160.32	161.04	138.63
1815	131.34	127.23	137.94	119.18
1816	112.44	98.62	133.26	117.39
1817	145.67	108.42	144.16	128.24
1818	147.20	121.06	141.49	124.06
1819	103.13	112.87	124.80	107.94
1820	89.89	102.94	116.41	101.07
1821	83.37	92.28	103.55	89.96
1822	90.26	91.26	92.39	78.21

are weighted. Beyond noting these general patterns, this paper was specifically concerned with the degree to which indices can shed light first on price trends between 1809 and 1811, and second on Tooke's argument that prices were primarily affected by real rather than monetary factors.

Price trends: 1809–11

The first issue to be addressed using the above indices concerns actual price trends between 1809 and 1811. As noted above, there was wide consensus that prices rose during these years; however, Tooke maintained that they fell:

> The assumption by the framers of the Bullion Report and their partisans, of the relative state of prices at that period, so contrary to the actual facts of the case, is quite astounding; for, in reality, there had been a ruinous *fall* of prices in 1810, as compared with 1808 and 1809; and, so far from its being true, as affirmed in the Report, that 'the prices of all commodities have risen, and gold appears to have risen in price in common with them', – all commodities, provisions alone excepted (these being scarce from the effects of bad seasons, combined with obstructions to importation) were *actually falling, while gold was rising.* (Tooke, 1848, p. 110; emphasis in the original. See also Tooke, 1824, p. 370)

Examination of the relevant years in Tables 1.1 and 1.2 and Figures 1.4–5 reveals that all of the indices except for the unweighted index for seventeen commodities (Index 5), show prices *falling* between 1809 and 1811, and especially between 1809 and 1810. In other words, Tooke seems to have been right, and Ricardo, Huskisson and the Bullion Committee to have been wrong. As Tooke's quotation from their report implies, these latter may well have been misled by the market price of gold, which is presented as a proportion of the 1797 mint price of gold for each year in Table 1.3. Gold prices did indeed rise dramatically from 1809 to 1810. This was a source of considerable concern, especially for members of the Bullionist School, who thought the price of gold to be a measure of the depreciation of notes and thus of price changes. This concern was reflected in the creation of the famous Bullion Committee. It is beyond the scope of the present paper to provide a complete analysis of the unusual discrepancy between the price of gold and of commodities in general. However, one can speculate that gold did not function as the standard for prices during these years. The price of gold in terms of notes was measured in international financial centres and reflected supply and demand forces in the gold market (e.g. in Hamburg). This price may not have corresponded to the internal note purchasing power inside the British economy. In this case the discrepancy between the price of gold and the price level is consistent with Frankel's (1982) argument that the 1807–9 embargo against Great Britain was effective and reduced Great Britain to autarky. If we remember that there were almost no internal gold transactions during the Restriction, the discrepancy between the price of gold and the price level becomes less

Table 1.3   Selected prices and the money supply

	Index 9 (P_t)	Price of Wheat (P_w)	Quantity of Money (M)	Price of Gold (P_g)
1782	100.00	41.75	13,839	100
1783	90.26	41.82	12,276	100
1784	87.62	40.41	10,934	100
1785	88.73	34.07	12,708	100
1786	94.94	32.75	13,892	100
1787	94.24	39.03	14,775	100
1788	89.85	41.75	15,135	100
1789	85.45	46.95	16,435	100
1790	90.79	43.87	16,948	100
1791	97.33	38.67	17,957	100
1792	103.85	40.51	16,682	100
1793	108.60	45.96	17,272	100
1794	104.59	49.50	17,429	100
1795	116.96	78.00	19,504	100
1796	126.21	65.33	16,167	100
1797	128.14	47.42	16,722	100
1798	132.17	37.00	19,863	100
1799	130.60	64.75	20,062	100
1800	132.17	96.50	23,645	100
1801	136.74	94.42	24,825	109
1802	126.39	55.88	24,441	108
1803	139.67	49.42	24,586	103
1804	134.25	68.38	26,312	103
1805	132.85	67.21	30,196	103
1806	129.33	65.88	29,188	103
1807	129.06	63.83	30,124	103
1808	151.80	78.08	30,137	103
1809	170.84	85.75	30,179	103
1810	155.65	88.33	35,944	116
1811	152.25	92.63	34,585	109
1812	156.85	119.92	34,940	123
1813	169.99	91.25	35,234	130
1814	174.10	71.08	40,238	134
1815	148.24	61.00	39,454	120
1816	117.01	83.50	39,009	120
1817	127.25	90.07	38,426	103
1818	138.61	76.38	34,950	103
1819	121.05	65.63	31,549	105
1820	110.72	62.47	28,149	103
1821	100.58	54.50	27,811	100
1822	96.23	43.25	23,610	100

Sources: Column (1) & (2) - Tooke's 1823 data. Index 9 is a weighted arithmetic index which does not
include the price of wheat.
Column (3) from (Mitchell 1962, p. 447), the sum of Circulation and Deposits.
Column (4) from Tooke (1824, Appendix No. 1), also used by Jevons (1884, p. 139).

surprising and seems to be another facet of autarky during these years. In
all events, it is easy to understand why the theoretical position of the
Bullionists led them to concentrate on the price of gold and the exchanges

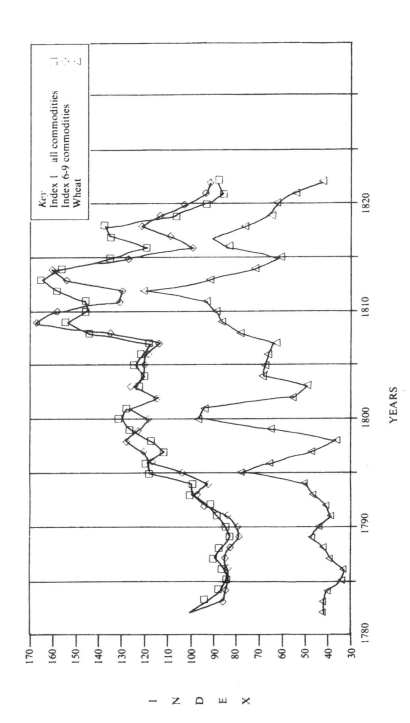

Key:
Index 1   all commodities
Index 6-9 commodities
Wheat

YEARS

I N D E X

Figure 1.4   'Tooke's' indices 1 and 6 vs. Wheat (Arithmetic equal weights)

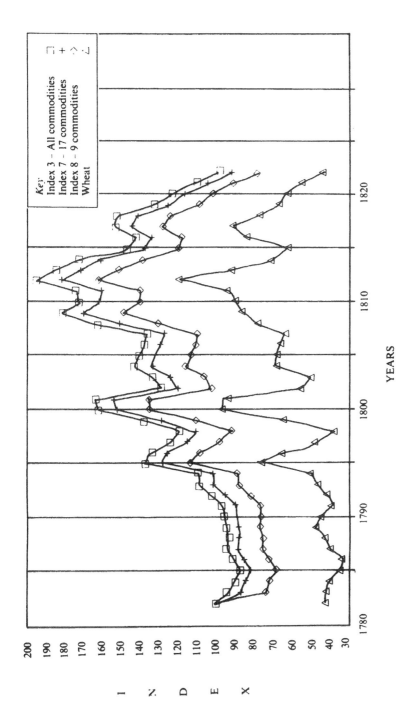

Figure 1.5 'Tooke's' indices 3, 7 and 8 vs. Wheat (Arithmetic, Gayer's weights)

and to misinterpret price trends in these years. Had they employed even the simplest indices, the actual price trends in these years would have emerged clearly.

Tooke, on the other hand, argued that the price of wheat was determined primarily by good and bad agricultural seasons, and that this price then determined the prices of other commodities. Thus we might hypothesize that his claim of falling prices between 1809 and 1811 was based on a fall in the price of wheat. However, as Table 1.3 and Figure 1.5 show, the price of wheat actually rose in 1809–11, continuing a trend which began in 1807, and of which Tooke seems to have been aware (see above. p.10). In fact, only in this period and in 1815–16 do the prices of wheat and of commodities in general show opposing trends. In this case, it is puzzling how Tooke arrived at his accurate conclusion and one can only offer the tentative suggestion that this was based on his far-reaching familiarity with actual price data. Thus, without the help of formal computation his intuition seems to have enabled him to capture the trends hidden in his data, even when these were not compatible with his general position on the determinants of prices. Thus Gregory seems to have erred in concluding that without indexation Tooke failed to estimate price trends.

As noted above, all the indices computed here yield the same trends with the exception of the unweighted index for seventeen commodities. A possible explanation for this discrepancy can be found by comparing these commodities with the nine commodities of Index 6. Of these nine commodities three (cotton, sugar, tea) were imported; of the eight additional commodities incorporated in Index 5, all but one kind of iron were imported. Since the prices of imports are more directly affected by the price of gold than local products, it is not surprising that this unweighted price index more closely follows the trends for gold. However, this is corrected by the use of weights (Index 7), since these same imported goods were relatively less important. While this is a minor point, it does illustrate the disadvantages of unweighted indices.

Was Thomas Tooke right?

In a recent article Bordo and Schwartz (1981) pose the question: was Thomas Tooke right? The reference is to interpretations of price changes as determined by real rather than monetary factors. Their main argument is with the position espoused, for example, by Rostow (1978) and Lewis (1978), (for further references, see Bordo and Schwartz, 1980, 1981). This position has clear affinities with Tooke's albeit later anti-quantity theory of money views (see Arnon, 1984). Bordo and Schwartz's (1981) conclusion that Tooke was wrong was based on analyses of data from 1870 to

1914; this section presents some preliminary analyses, which address the same question with reference to Tooke's own data, for the years 1782–1822, as reported in 1823.

As noted above, Tooke argued that the price of wheat is determined primarily by good and bad agricultural seasons, and that this price then determines the prices of other commodities. His rationale was that wheat prices importantly determine wages and thus the influence of wheat prices will be felt, sooner or later, throughout the economy. This argument, which implies real, rather than a monetary explanation for price changes was tested using procedures similar to those used by Bordo and Schwartz on a later data-set. An index was first computed for all the commodities which were both quoted by Tooke and given weights by Gayer et al., with the exception of wheat. Table 1.3 presents this index (P_ℓ) together with the price of wheat (P_w), a measure of the market price of gold over its pre 1797 fixed mint price (P_g) (both taken from Tooke's 1823 data), and a proxy for the quantity of money (M_ℓ).

If the monetary explanation is valid, the price level should be explained, to a large degree, by current and lagged quantities of money. The Bullionists argued that the price of gold is, in its turn, determined by the quantity of money. However, forces operating in the gold market such as trade deficits, the war (see Hueckel, 1973) and other non-monetary variables could also have an effect. If Tooke's real explanation is valid then the current and lagged price of wheat should explain the price level, at least to some degree. When the season is good, and the supply abundant, the price of wheat is low and the general price level, maybe with a lag, should be low as well.

Initially the hypothesis that the price level (P_ℓ) can be explained by current and lagged prices of wheat (P_w, P_{w-1}) and the quantities of money (M, M_{-1}) as well as by the price of gold (P_g) was examined for the Restriction period (1797–1821). A trend factor was included to capture the influence of changes in production and population, for which no reliable annual data exist. A preliminary analysis revealed a strong serial correlation, as is common in time-series. Thus a maximum likelihood procedure was adopted to deal with serial correlation. The first regression analysis revealed current prices of wheat and lagged quantities of money to be insignificant.[7]

Thus, the basic model used to test the real *vs.* monetary explanations included the lagged price of wheat and the current quantity of money as independent variables. The procedure utilized followed that of Bordo and Schwartz in order to enable comparison with their results.

Thus equations 1, 2 and 3 were estimated and the results obtained are reported in Table 4.

Table 1.4.   Regression results for the real vs. monetary explanation of price levels: England 1797–1821 (coefficients of independent variables (t values in parentheses))

Equation	B_0	B_1	B_2	B_3	Adjusted R^2	DW	ρ	F
A. Levels								
(1)	102.20	–1.44	0.30	1.83E-3	51.6	1.62	0.381	
	(5.542)	(–2.384)	(1.797)	(2.588)				
(2)	133.85	–0.69	0.27		25.9	1.59	0.710	$F_{(2\kappa1)}=12.70^*$
	(4.727)	(–0.756)	(1.661)					
(3)	115.62	–1.35		2.04E-3	43.8	1.57	0.460	$F_{(3\kappa1)}=4.56^*$
	(5.717)	(–1.960)		(2.704)				
B. Logs								
(1)	1.03	–0.34	0.12	0.44	50.0	1.63	0.408	
	(0.78)	(–2.549)	(1.414)	(2.729)				
(2)	4.78	–0.12	0.12		19.5	1.58	0.746	$F_{(2\kappa1)}=14.38$
	(6.855)	(–0.634)	(1.403)					
(3)	1.12	–0.32		0.47	45.3	1.58	0.468	$F_{(3\kappa1)}=3.06$
	(0.798)	(–2.244)		(2.906)				

Notes

P_t is a price index which excludes wheat.

P_{wt} is the price of wheat.

M_t is a proxy for the quantity of money which include Bank of England notes and deposits in millions of pounds (see Mitchell and Deane, 1962).

*$F_{(2\kappa1)}$ & $F_{(3\kappa1)}$ test the significance of including the missing independent variable in the regression in both cases the inclusion is statistically significant at the 5 per cent level. For further remarks see the text.

$$P_t = B_0 + B_1 \text{ trend} + B_2 P_{w_{t-1}} + B_3 M_t + e \qquad (1)$$

$$P_t = B_0 + B_1 \text{ trend} + B_2 P_{w_{t-1}} \qquad\qquad + e_1 \qquad (2)$$

$$P_t = B_0 + B_1 \text{ trend} \qquad\qquad\quad + B_3 M_t + e_2 \qquad (3)$$

This analysis indicates that while the quantity of money contributes more to explaining the price level, the price of wheat, which represents the real factor, also contributes significantly. Thus neither factor should statistically be dropped. Moreover, in this case, in contrast with the results reported by Bordo and Schwartz (1981, pp. 121–3) the adjusted R^2 remains quite high not only when the price of wheat is withdrawn but also when the quantity of money is excluded. Thus, while Bordo and Schwartz concluded on the basis of a similar analysis of aggregate data of the US and UK in 1881–1913 that the 'real' variable 'account[s] for only a small fraction of adjusted R^2', here the real factor accounts for a considerable proportion.

However, we should not forget that this analysis also emphasizes the significance of monetary factors. This emerged even more clearly when the above analysis was performed on log transformations of the variables. While real factors still explain far more than the 4–6 per cent reported by Bordo and Schwartz, they clearly contribute less than the monetary factor.

Similar results were received also when the price of gold represented the monetary factor.[8]

In other words, preliminary analyses, methodologically similar to those employed by Bordo and Schwartz on later data, suggest that, at least for those years with which he was familiar, Tooke's argument as to the role of real factors in determining prices cannot be discounted. However, examination of the relationship between P_w and M using simple regression analyses, explaining P_w in terms of the lag of M, and vice versa, yielded results compatible neither with a pure monetary nor a pure real explanation. Thus P_{w-1} explained 26 per cent of the variance in M, and M_{-1} 22 per cent of the variance in P_w. In view of the strong relations between the price of wheat and the quantity of money, Bessler's (1984) criticism of Bordo and Schwartz is relevant to the present analysis too. Simple regression analyses of interrelated variables is not strong enough to determine 'causal' relationships. Different techniques (causality and exogenity tests) should thus be utilized to improve our understanding of the causal relationships.

Summary

The present paper first presents indices constructed from a comparatively early data-set for the years 1782–1822. Comparison of the trends yielded by these indices with those yielded by indices from Tooke's later, and more straightforward, data suggest that the earlier data can be used by scholars of economic history as a reliable source of information as to prices during these years. This confirmation is of value in itself. In addition, the earlier data are more appropriate than the 1838 data for addressing certain questions. For example, since the earlier data report prices according to the number of changes in trends during each year, they can be used to clarify such modern concerns as the relationship between rates of change and variability in prices.

The present paper was concerned rather with the degree to which the trends yielded by indexation were congruent with the position of Tooke and his contemporaries regarding prices. In general, Tooke seems to have captured price trends, even though he did not use indexation. This is clear for the period 1810–11, where the Bullionists, possibly misled by the high price of gold, maintained that prices rose. Tooke, on the other hand, maintained that they fell, a position confirmed by the present analyses. Thus while in this particular controversy the Bullionists might have benefited from indexation, Tooke's estimates were accurate without this.

This accuracy is particularly interesting in view of the fact that the price of wheat during this period rose. Tooke's general position that prices are determined primarily by real factors was examined in a series of regression analyses. These revealed that neither the monetary nor the real explanation is sufficient in itself to explain absolute prices, at least for the period under discussion. These results seem to suggest that while Tooke was not completely correct, neither was he as wrong as Bordo and Schwartz claim, on the basis of similar analytic methods. However, Bessler's reservations as to the use of simple regression analyses for testing real versus monetary explanations of price changes may be relevant also to our results. Thus further research would do well to incorporate causality as well as exogenity tests.

Acknowledgement

I would like to thank Myra Gelbstein for her very able research assistance and Uri Regev for his helpful advice. The usual disclaimer certainly holds.

Notes

1. See Viner (1937) and Fetter (1965) for two comprehensive reviews, and Mokyr and Savin (1976) and Duffy (1982) for two more recent contributions. For a review of the historical research, see Bordo (1986).
2. Details of the data-set and preliminary computation available from author on request.
3. In all indices used the base year is 1782; analysis using a different base year (1821) yielded basically similar results.
4. The years 1787, 1795, 1800/1, 1805, 1809 and 1818 are all years of relatively high prices whereas prices were low in 1785, 1788, 1797, 1802, 1807 and 1816. In Index 1, 1811 is an additional minimum and 1813/14 another maximum.
5. One should note that Gayer et al. (1953) computed weights also for commodities, some of them important, for which Tooke did not provide price data (e.g. oats, mutton, coal). Thus, the present index is based on a sum of weights of 2463, as compared with Gayer et al.'s 3861. One should also note that Gayer et al.'s weights, which reflect the relative quantities produced of each commodity, were based on a slightly later period (1820–40). Thus they may not reflect the precise weights appropriate to the years under discussion, but clearly make an improvement over unweighted indices.
6. The nine most important are cotton, sugar, tallow, tea, wool, beef, pork, butter and wheat. To these flax, domestically produced iron, imported iron, silk, spirit (rum), tobacco, tin and woods, are added to form the seventeen most important.
7. The F test to test H_0: $\alpha_2 = \alpha_5 = \alpha_6 = 0$ in the general model:
    $P_t = \alpha_0 + \alpha_1 \text{ trend} + \alpha_2 P_u + \alpha_3 P_{u-1} + \alpha_4 M + \alpha_5 M_{-1} + \alpha_6 P_g + e$
    is 0.33 and is highly insignificant.
8. Since the Bullionists thought that the price of gold was wholly determined by the quantity of money, it follows that the price of gold can be used as a proxy for the monetary factor. As can be seen below, this is really the case. While M is a better explanatory variable than P_g the difference is small. Still, to facilitate comparisons with Bordo and Schwartz I used M in the test described above.

$$P_t = \beta_0 + \beta_1 \text{ trend} + \beta_2 p_{u-1} + \beta_3 M + \beta_4 P_g + e \qquad (1)$$

Equations 2 and 3 are the same as 1 assuming $\beta_3 = 0$ in 2 and $\beta_4 = 0$ in 3.

Regression results: Coefficients of independent variables (t values in parenthesis)

		β_0	β_1	β_2	β_3	β_4	$\bar{R}^2$	D.W.	ρ
(1)	P_t	83.78	-1.39	0.28	0.16E-2	23.96	51%	1.6	0.350
		(2.119)	(-2.279)	(1.531)	(1.765)	(0.498)			
(2)	P_t	83.65	-0.74	0.26	—	50.22	43%	1.72	0.564
		(1.946)	(-1.054)	(1.447)		(1.22)			
(3)	P_t	102.20	1.44	0.30	1.83E-3	—	51.6%	1.62	0.381
		(5.542)	(2.384)	(1.797)	(2.588)	—			

References

Arnon, A. 1984, 'The transformation in Thomas Tooke's monetary theory reconsidered', *History of Political Economy* 16, pp. 311–26.

Arnon, A. 1989, 'The early Tooke and Ricardo: a political alliance and first signs of theoretical disagreements', *History of Political Economy*, 21, pp. 1–4.

Bessler, D. A. 1984, 'Additional evidence on money and prices: U.S. data 1870–1913', *Explorations in Economic History* 21, pp. 125–32.

Bordo, M. D. 1986, 'Explorations in monetary history: a survey of the literature', *Explorations in Economic History* 23, pp. 339–415.

Bordo, M. D. and Schwartz, A. J. 1980, 'Money and prices in the nineteenth century: an old debate rejoined', *Journal of Economic History* XL, pp. 61–7.

Bordo, M. D. and Schwartz, A. J. 1981, 'Money and prices in the 19th century: Was Thomas Tooke right?', *Explorations in Economic History* 18, pp. 97–127.

Duffy, I. P. H. 1982, 'The discount policy of the Bank of England during the suspension of cash payments, 1797–1821', *Economic History Review* 35, pp. 67–82.

Fetter, F. W. 1965, *The Development of British Monetary Orthodoxy, 1797–1875*, Harvard University Press, Cambridge, Mass.

Frankel, J. A. 1982, 'The 1807–1809 embargo against Great Britain', *Journal of Economic History* 42, pp. 291–308.

Gayer, A., Rostow, W. W. and Schwartz, A. J. 1953/1975, *The Growth and Fluctuation of the British Economy 1790–1850*, Clarendon Press, Oxford.

Gregory, T. E. 1928, *An Introduction to Tooke and Newmarck's A History of Prices*, P. S. King, London.

Hueckel, G. 1973, 'War and the British economy,' 1793–1815. A general equilibrium analysis', *Exploration in Economic History* 10, pp. 365–96.

Jevons, W. S. 1884/1964, *Investigations in Currency and Finance*, A. M. Kelley, New York.

Lewis, W. A. 1978, *Growth and Fluctuations 1870–1913*, George Allen and Unwin, London.

Mitchell, B. R. and Deane, P. 1962, *Abstract of British Historical Statistics*, Cambridge University Press, Cambridge.

Mitchell, W. C. 1915/1965, *The Working and Using of Index Numbers*, A. M. Kelley, New York.

Mitchell, W. C. 1938, *The Making and Use of Index Numbers*, US Government Printing Office, Washington.

Mokyr, J. and Savin, N. E. 1976, 'Stagflation in historical perspective: the Napoleonic Wars revisited', in P. Uselding (ed.), *Research in Economic History* 1, pp. 198–259.

Rostow, W. W. 1978, *The World Economy: History and Prospects*, University of Texas Press, Austin, TX.

Silberling, N. J. 1919, 'British financial experience 1790–1830', *The Review of Economic Statistics*, 1, pp. 282–97.

Silberling, N. J. 1923, 'British prices and business cycles 1779–1850', *The Review of Economics and Statistics* 5, pp. 223–61.

Tooke, T. 1824, *Thoughts and Details on the High and Low Prices of the Last Thirty Years*, (2nd edition of the original 1823 edition), John Murray, London.

Tooke, T. 1838–48/1928, *A History of Prices and of the State of the Circulation from 1793 to 1837*, P. S. King, London (reproduction of the original with an Introduction by T. E. Gregory), Volumes 1, 2 and 4.

2 *Laissez-Faire* Monetary Thought in Jacksonian America
Lawrence H. White and George A. Selgin

In recent years there has been a noteworthy growth of literature on *laissez-faire* systems of money and banking.[1] The traditional view among economists, of course, has long been that the supply of money (including bank liabilities) will not behave properly without government control. But the contrary view that unregulated banking would work well is not new. Its early proponents included Adam Smith (1981, [1776], p. 329) and J. B. Say (1971 [1803], p. 271). Those who espoused the *laissez-faire* approach to money were in the intellectual minority even during the heyday of classical liberalism. Yet their ideas had an important influence on monetary legislation, as evidenced particularly in the United States by the Independent Treasury System and by the proliferation of state 'free banking' statutes.

Early writers in the tradition of *laissez-faire* monetary thought have recently begun to receive some attention from historians of economic thought, their views being now of obvious relevance to modern concerns. The important American proponents of unregulated money and banking in the first half of the nineteenth century, however, have never had their contributions critically surveyed.[2] This paper attempts to fill the gap. The next section sets the historical stage. Because of their small number, we then treat the leading *laissez-faire* monetary theorists individually. In treating individual writers we focus on four aspects of their thought:

1. the application of free-trade and spontaneous-order principles to money and banking;
2. the theory of restraints against over-issue in a free banking system;
3. the theory of business cycles or panics; and
4. proposed reform measures.

As many writers at that time did, we neglect questions relating to the deposit-taking and loan-making aspects of banking in order to focus on the more controversial questions regarding banknotes.

Monetary debates in the early Republic
The policy ideas on money and banking that dominated debate during the early decades of the Republic were, for various reasons, quite unsympath-

etic towards *laissez-faire* in money and banking. Advocates of strong central government, such as Alexander Hamilton, favoured mercantilist policies generally. But even among anti-mercantilist statesmen and intellectuals the area of money-issuing was considered an exception to the doctrines of free trade and open competition. Thus Pelatiah Webster (Krooss, 1977, pp. 221–9), a free-trade Whig, defended the exclusivity of the charter given to the Bank of North America in 1781 by the Continental Congress.[3]

In the debate over the chartering and attempted re-chartering of the First Bank of the United States (1791–1811), Thomas Jefferson (Krooss, 1977, pp. 273–7) and his followers such as John Taylor (1969, pp. 253–342) and James Madison (Krooss, 1977, pp. 262–70) advocated hard money and strict construction of the United States Constitution, which does not explicitly grant the Federal government any monetary powers beyond coinage. Pitted against them were Hamilton (Krooss, 1977, pp. 278–306) and other broad-constructionist proponents of a national bank. The concept of a *laissez-faire* monetary system was not introduced into the debate. The opponents of the exclusively chartered national bank, following Taylor and Jefferson, doubted the desirability of any note-issuing banks (as opposed to mere 'discount and deposit' banks). Although the Jeffersonians attacked the Bank as a monopoly, their view that any federal chartering of corporations was unconstitutional, mixed with their suspicion of note-issuing banks, prevented them from considering a system of *laissez-faire* based on federal charters available to all. The Hamiltonian advocates of banknotes, on the other hand, saw note issue as a government prerogative rather than as a common right. The debate in 1816, when the Second Bank of the United States secured a twenty-year charter, was similarly framed.

The strict-constructionist, anti-monopoly and anti-banknote strain of thought showed new life in the 1830s, being spread particularly by William Gouge (1833). Hard-money views dominated Jackson's party at the ideological level, though 'bank Democrats' more often held office. The national bank, of course, had its advocates in the Whigs. The conflict between hard money and national bank dominated the debate over Jackson's veto of the attempt to recharter the Second Bank in 1832, as it had dominated the earlier debates.

A third approach to the currency question was available, however, and came to play an important role in the debates of the 1830s and thereafter. The *laissez-faire* or 'free banking' approach, opposed to exclusive note-issuing privileges but not to banknotes *per se*, was first articulated in the United States in 1827 in a pamphlet by the Reverend John McVickar. It found its most consistent policy formulation in the writings of editorialist

William Leggett between 1834 and 1837. In the next few years *laissez-faire* banking was promoted by historian and journalist Richard Hildreth, who provided the best theoretical underpinning for its advocacy, and by economist Henry C. Carey. Hildreth (1840, p. 109) aptly characterized free banking opinion as one of the 'three opposite and hostile systems of opinion prevail[ing] at the present time in the United States, on the subject of banks and banking. One party is opposed to all banks whatever; a second party is in favor of the existing system of a monopoly of banking privileges; while a third paity desires to throw open in the business of banking, like all other mercantile business, to free competition.'

The free banking writers of this era shared with the hard-money school the fundamental tenet of Jeffersonian political economy that narrow limitation of government intervention was desirable. Both camps vigorously criticized the legislative chartering of banks with special privileges. But the *laissez-faire* camp diverged in recognizing note-issuing banks as natural creatures of commerce, rather than as products of government intervention. In Leggett's case a gradual evolution from hard-money to strictly *laissez-faire* policy recommendations can be seen.

Early writers: Butler and McVickar

Apart from the First and Second Bank of the United States, the chartering of banks of issue was the prerogative of the state governments. An early application of *laissez-faire* arguments to banking in America came in a brief pamphlet addressed to a member of the New York State legislature. New York's 'restraining act' of 1804 had outlawed non-chartered banking partnerships. The legislature in 1818 was considering a ban on non-chartered private banking by individuals as well.[4] Benjamin Franklin Butler, a private banker writing under the pseudonym of 'Marcus' (1818), protested that banking should be left as open as every other business, being 'the true and legitimate off-spring of commerce', and being able to trade its products only with members of a discerning public who voluntarily accepted them. The objections to private banking, Butler argued, came from established chartered banks 'desirous of monopolizing an employment which should ever be left open to the free exercise of all'. Prohibition of private banking by individuals 'would shackle the excursions, restrain the liberty, and abridge the rights of the citizen'. Butler was not entirely consistent with his professed principles, however. He disingenuously endorsed the legislature's restriction against private banking by partnerships, who were potential competitors with his own business.

A more important theoretical brief for freedom in banking came from the pen of a Columbia University professor, the Reverend John

McVickar. His anonymous pamphlet *Hints on Banking* appeared in 1827, the same year that the first major work of the Free Banking School in the British monetary controversies was published (see White, 1984, p. 62). McVickar (1827, pp. 5–7) clearly enunciated the *laissez-faire* idea that banking, like any other industry, would regulate itself if left free: 'the business of Credit, like every other business for which there is a demand in society, has its natural limits, and left to itself will regulate itself'. If it seems a relatively troublesome industry, that is because it has not been free: 'all the evils of banking, beyond those which exist in other modes of business, flow from needless or unwise legislation.' McVickar (1827, pp. 13–16) charged that the state legislature's process of bestowing monopoly banking charters on politically favoured applicants was rife with corruption, an extremely popular theme among both *laissez-faire* and anti-banking writers. Furthermore – and here again the argument was to be taken up by many others – chartering conferred a false and uniform respectability on all bankers which enabled the 'unprincipled and designing' among them to defraud the public. The power of granting special charters was an atavistic remnant of mercantilism, 'one, and almost the last of a long list of legislative powers, which one by one have been dropped into the lap of society, that real nursing mother of the rights of man, and there entrusted to the rights of individuals', because 'economical science' had shown that society is governed by laws other than statute laws. Free banking was thus presented as an integral part of the classical liberal programme for policy reform.

McVickar's account of the self-regulating character of banking consisted of a loosely expressed version of the needs of trade doctrine, which held that the quantity of monetary bank liabilities in circulation was and ought to be demand-determined. There is nothing fallacious in this doctrine provided that the 'needs of trade' refers to the demand to *hold* bank-issued money (rather than the demand for loanable funds), and provided that the purchasing power of money is determined exogenously to the banking system, as it is in a small open economy under a specie standard. Then the nominal quantity of money can and classically should vary endogenously. The needs-of-trade doctrine simply extends to specie-redeemable money the basic idea behind the price-specie-flow mechanism, that the quantity of specie in circulation conforms to the quantity demanded at a given level of purchasing power.[5] McVickar (1827, p. 10) explicitly analogized the demand-side determination of the quantity of a purely metallic currency in a small open economy to the similar determination of the quantity of a specie-redeemable currency: 'If [banks] issue a paper exchangeable on demand, like a metallic currency, it accommodates itself freely to every fluctuation from without, and the [individual] bank is governed imperatively in its issues, by the demand for specie that is immediately made upon it, whenever its paper is in excess.'

McVickar's statement, however, appeared in the context of an argument (1827, pp. 7–16) concerning 'the business of credit'. Under *laissez-faire*, credit 'left to itself will regulate itself, – will contract or expand with the varying demands of trade, and will be liable to no other fluctuations than those which arise out of trade itself'. Credit would be 'furnished to society at the cheapest rate, and in precisely that quantity which society demands'. By 'credit' McVickar seems to have meant the quantity of bank loans rather than the quantity of monetary bank liabilities. His reference to 'the cheapest rate', i.e. the lowest interest rate, suggests the furnishing of loanable funds rather than money balances. Because he blurred the distinction between money and credit, McVickar did not provide a clear account of the determination of the money stock.[6] He nonetheless showed some understanding of the principle that the circulation of any single bank is regulated by adverse clearings, i.e. that any bank expanding faster than its rivals would, assuming no change in note-holding demands, be forced to slow down by loss of reserves to the other banks as they accumulated and redeemed a greater number of its notes. McVickar (1827, p. 18) stated that if one bank contracts, every other bank must follow 'proportionately, under the penalty of becoming a debtor bank, and thereby losing a portion of the specie out of its vaults'. This statement is correct only under the assumption that the demand to hold notes has contracted generally.

McVickar (1827, pp. 24–33, 41) suggested that the bank chartering system made business cycles more severe because chartering reduced the number of independent decision-makers in the money market. The surplus profits in closed-entry banking, furthermore, tempted 'the needy and the speculating' to obtain charters through lobbying. This led to highly speculative banks whose actions increased the severity of fluctuations. In a less clear argument, McVickar attributed the speculativeness of chartered banks to their having excess capital, which they dumped on the market.

McVickar's reform proposal (1827, pp. 38–41) was animated by *laissez-faire* principles, but stopped short of full deregulation because of a fear of fraudulent banknotes. Were banking abuses limited to the commercial realm, 'the remedy would be as simple as it would be efficacious, viz. to cast off all restrictions, and to leave the business of banking to be regulated by the necessary laws of credit'. But notes pass into common circulation, substituting for coin. On this ground McVickar, like contemporary Currency School writers in England, justified 'the interference of the legislature, who, as the guardians of the coin of the country, acquire the right to regulate its substitutes'. McVickar accordingly proposed free entry into banking under a general statute, but with the restrictions (1) that 90 per cent of a bank's capital be invested in government bonds pledged for the redemption of notes, (2) that the volume of notes not exceed this 90 per cent of capital, and (3) that $5 be the minimum banknote denomination.

The bond-collateral requirement was to be a popular feature of proposals by American writers otherwise professing *laissez-faire* principles. It gave them a concrete answer to the fear of fraudulent banknotes, allowing them to argue more persuasively that the other aspects of banking (particularly entry) could be deregulated without danger. Collateral requirements became a central part of the 'free banking' legislation to be enacted by New York State in 1838 and by seventeen other states prior to 1860. The idea of compulsory bond-collateralization of notes was also advocated in the 1820s by several monetary reformers in England, including both Henry Parnell (1827, pp. 140–4) of the Free Banking School and his intellectual opponent J. R. McCulloch (1826, p. 280) of the Currency School. For Parnell, McVickar and later American free banking advocates such as Richard Hildreth, this restrictive measure became a token to be paid in order to secure the goal of free entry. From McCulloch, a devoted Ricardian, we can trace the bond-collateral idea back to David Ricardo (1951, pp. 72–3), who made it part of his *Proposals for an Economical and Secure Currency* in 1816. Ricardo argued that common folk who accept banknotes in everyday transaction are unqualified to judge the trustworthiness of the issuing banks, and suffer when the banks fail, so that for consumer protection the banks should be required to deposit with the government 'funded property or other government security in some proportion to the amount of their issues'.[7]

Soon after he had made his case for freer banking, McVickar (1830) curiously enough came out in favour of re-chartering the Bank of the United States. In an anonymous 1839 article he defended both the principles behind the New York State Banking Act of 1838 and the chartering of a national bank as a regulator of the various state banking systems. Two years later he published a formal plan for a national bank.[8] Far from affirming the self-regulating character of a free banking system, he now argued (1841, p. 2) that a national bank was necessary to end 'the *mad* experiment of attempting to *steer the ship without a rudder*, and to regulate, *without a regulator*, the vast and complex machinery of currency and exchanges' (emphasis in the original). The Ricardian element in his thinking had apparently crowded out the Smithian element, for McVickar (1841, pp. 16–17) proposed to give a monopoly over note-issue to a nonintermediating national bank of the sort Ricardo (1951, pp. 276–97) had advocated in his *Plan for the Establishment of a National Bank* (posthumously published in 1824). McVickar did not explicitly cite Ricardo, but he did cite the parliamentary testimony of Ricardo's followers, the Currency School opponents of free banking.

William Leggett

Andrew Jackson's message to the Senate in July 1832, vetoing the recharter of the Second Bank of the United States (Kroos, 1977, pp. 816–32), criticized the Bank primarily on strict-constructionist grounds. His opposition was seemingly only to its form and not to its substance, as Jackson held out the possibility that he could countenance a government bank of the right sort.[9] Yet Jackson concluded by denouncing the Bank as a privileged monopoly that infringed upon the just principle of equal treatment for all. This last theme – that legislative chartering of corporations (and particularly of banks) violated equal rights – was developed into a thoroughgoing programme for monetary reform by William Leggett. Editor of the New York *Evening Post* for 1834–6, and then author of his own New York newspapers the *Examiner* (daily) and the *Plaindealer* (weekly) in 1836–7, Leggett was the intellectual leader of New York's Equal Rights Party, a splinter group of radical young democrats more commonly known as the Loco-Focos.

Leggett (1984, p. 81) was unmistakably explicit in his desire to apply the *laissez-faire* principle to banking, expressing his hope 'to see the day when banking, like any other mercantile business will be left to *regulate itself*; when the principles of free trade will be perceived to have as much relation to currency as to commerce: when the maxim of *let us alone* will be acknowledged to be better, infinitely better, than all this political quackery of ignorant legislators, instigated by the grasping, monopolizing spirit of rapacious capitalists'. Leggett (1984, pp. 104, 130–1, 146, 164, 179–82) motivated the case for *laissez-faire* in currency in several ways. From political philosophy he derived the equal natural right of every citizen to open a bank and to issue any sort of promissory note that others would accept. On aesthetic grounds he appealed to the naturalness of a simple and parsimonious role for government. Most importantly for our purposes, he drew from his understanding of classical economics the concept of a spontaneous and self-regulating order: 'Enterprise would build up, and competition would regulate, a better system of banks than legislation ever can devise.'

Because he wrote a series of editorial essays rather than any extended monograph, Leggett never exposited at length his theoretical conception of the self-regulating processes at work in a free banking system. His various remarks (1984, pp. 118–19, 145–6, 174–5, 186–8) none the less sketch a definite picture of the system's operations. Under *laissez-faire*, in his vision, there would exist a plurality of well-capitalized banks. These banks would command 'the utmost public confidence', because competition for public patronage would force them to offer solid guarantees of security for their liabilities. The guarantees could take the form of pledged collateral property. Banknotes 'would, of course, be redeemable in specie', but the banks, immunized against panics by their solvency guarantees, would find small fractional reserves adequate. Competition would reduce the spread between loan and deposit interest rates to the smallest level compatible with the banks earning a normal rate of return on their capital. As Leggett (1984, p. 119, 130–31, 169) correctly insisted, these features were not merely figments of his imagination but could be observed in the contemporary Scottish banking system. In referring to the Scottish system, and in his theoretical remarks on banking, Leggett showed a distinct familiarity with the writings of the Free Banking School in the British monetary controversies of the day, though he did not explicitly refer to their works.[10] Leggett overlooked the Scottish experience, however, in suggesting that under *laissez-faire* the use of banknotes would dominate specie only in business-to-business transactions. A closer reading of Adam Smith (1981, p. 322), whom he was fond of citing, would have supplied him with evidence to the contrary.

The most important feature of free banking for Leggett, as for McVickar, was its automatic regulation of the currency supply. In an early essay Leggett (1984, p. 64) enunciated a normative version of the needs-of-trade doctrine. He was at best somewhat ambiguous on the source and measure of demand for bank-issued money, however, and at worst shaded off into the real-bills doctrine that Adam Smith (1981, pp. 304–8) had propounded and that John Fullarton (1844) of the British Banking School would come to endorse. The real-bills doctrine, interpreted as the belief that an excess supply of bank-issued money cannot be created by discounting 'real bills' (trade credit obligations in the form of commercial paper), is a fallacious version of the needs-of-trade doctrine in which the demand to hold bank-issued money is identified with the volume of 'real bills' offered to the banks.[11] A tinge of the Smithian real-bills doctrine may also be seen in Leggett's (1984, p. 157) later positive needs-of-trade argument that the currency would be self-regulating under free banking because, with hard money being used by the general public, 'banking will naturally confine itself to those operations which constitute its only legitimate field – the mere exchange of bank credit for mercantile credit, to the extent of actual commercial transactions'.

Leggett's (1984, pp. 82, 118) more emphatic statements, however, indicated a correct understanding of the adverse clearing and specie-flow mechanisms that prevent a sustained over-issue. Competition would lead banks to accept rivals' notes, and then to redeem them (presumably through a note-exchange system, although Leggett does not say so), confronting any over-expansive single bank with adverse clearings: 'The natural rivalry of trade would cause [a bank] to return the notes of other institutions for specie, whenever they accumulated beyond a certain point, and this would prevent overissue.'[12] The system as a whole would be checked by external drain if the actual quantity of currency exceeded the quantity demanded. Bankers knowing this would try to proportion their issues to the demand, taking the level of business activity as an indicator:

> when bankers are left to manage their own business, each for himself, they would watch the course of trade, and limit their discounts accordingly; because if they extended them beyond the measure of the legitimate business of the country, they could be sure that their notes would return upon them in demand for the precious metals, thus forcing them to part with their profits, in order to purchase silver and gold to answer such demand.

In examining the existing chartered banking system, on the other hand, Leggett (1984, p. 97) observed 'the banks ... striving, with all their might, each emulating the other, to force their issues into circulation, and flood the land with their wretched substitute for money'. An obvious question is why competition and prudence did not effectively constrain the chartered banks from over-issuing. Leggett (1984, p. 151) claimed that competition among the chartered banks was severely restricted, though in fact it seems to have been vigorous in the major cities (Schwartz, 1947). He also argued (1984, p. 162, 182–3) that chartered banks were able to over-issue 'by reason of the false character which their exclusive privileges give to the notes they issue'. The imprimatur of the state government upon the issuer, and the receivability of the notes by the government in taxes and other transactions, was apparently held to make the public less discriminating in its acceptance of notes. This would indeed slow the return of excess notes. If the public does not at all discriminate among banknotes according to bank of issue, then an excess supply of notes created by any issuer can be felt only as an excess supply of notes in general. The issuer at fault suffers no systematic adverse clearings against other banks. It only shares in the (relatively slowly acting) external drain that affects every bank in proportion to its circulation (Selgin, 1988, pp. 42–7).

Leggett's business-cycle theory strongly resembles the monetary mal-investment theory put forward by Robert Mushet (1826, pp. 152–8), Henry Parnell (1833, pp. 6–13), and other members of the British Free Banking School, and by some writers of the Currency School. In Leggett's (1984, pp. 65–70, 97–100, 113–14, 139) version, the cycle begins with an over-expansion of bank loans and note-issues that creates an investment boom. The boom raises prices generally and with a lag causes specie to leave the country. The loss of specie reserves forces the banks to stop expanding and even to start contracting. The contraction of loans leaves investment projects suddenly unsustainable and thereby instigates bankruptcies, panic and a crash. Leggett placed much more emphasis than the British writers on the malinvestment of capital and misdirection of labour during the boom period. The following passage (1984, p. 98) usefully encapsulates his account:

> What has been, what ever must be, the consequence of such a sudden and prodigious inflation of currency? Business stimulated to the most unhealthy activity; a vast amount of over production in the mechanick arts; a vast amount of speculation in property of every land and name, at fictitious values; and finally, a vast and terrifick crash, when the treacherous and unsubstantial basis crumbles beneath the stupendous fabrick of credit, and the structure falls to the ground, burying in its ruins thousands who exulted in the fancied security of their elevation.

The banks, forced to contract by dwindling gold reserves, could no longer finance 'the projects which would not have been undertaken but for the temptation they held forth'. As an example of misdirection of labour, Leggett (1984, p. 100) observed that fields lay untilled 'because the agricultural population has been drawn off to construct railroads and canals, or lay out sites for cities'. Later monetary business-cycle theorists, such as Hayek (1935) and Lucas (1975), have tried to account for malinvestments in long-term or capital-intensive projects of this sort.[13]

Consistent with his view that freer competition would allow the adverse-clearing mechanism to restrain over-issues more effectively, Leggett (1984, p. 118) came to view completely free banking as the remedy for monetary disturbances. In his earliest editorials, however, he showed more of a hard-money outlook.[14] He proposed (1984, pp. 71–3) a ban on small denomination banknotes, a measure Adam Smith (1981, p. 323) had endorsed for Scotland. Later, Leggett (1984, p. 82) urged this only as a transitional reform, and finally (1984, p. 152) he repudiated any attempt to institute a metallic currency 'by the force of artitrary government edicts'. Similarly, he first (1984, pp. 81–2) recommended free entry with a bond collateral system as a reform measure appropriate to 'the present temper of the times', which were not yet ready for full-blown *laissez-faire*. Later (1984, pp. 118, 146–8, 156–7, 174–5, 186), however, he insisted that competition by itself would induce banks to provide sufficient security to their liability-holders. His final proposal (1984, pp. 145–54) was simply that the state legislature repeal the law that restrained free entry into banking, replacing the chartering system by a law making incorporation freely available to all businesses. The federal government, in order to avoid unjust favouritism, was totally to disassociate itself from the banking system. The only statutes applying to banks, he believed, should be those concerning fraud, breach of contract, and incorporation, that applied to business in all fields.

In his arguments for 'separation of bank and state' Leggett provided a *laissez-faire* rationale for the Independent Treasury System which removed the federal government's money balances from the commercial banks. When President Van Buren in 1837 declared his support for such an idea, the mainstream Democratic Governor of New York, William Marcy (quoted by Sharp, 1970, p. 302), despaired of this seeming endorsement of ideas from the radical wing of his party: 'Is it reasonable to expect that the democrats of the state will range themselves under the banners of Ming, Leggett ... and others of better repute of Washington[?]'[15] As the acknowledged intellectual leader of the New York Loco-Focos (Byrdsall, 1967, pp. 15, 22–7), Leggett was also credited by his admirers with an important influence on the 'free banking' law enacted by New York State in 1838 (Bryant, 1839, p. 23; 'General Banking Law', p. 428). Fritz Redlich (1947, pp. 188–90), who provides the most thorough secondary account of the intellectual and political origins of the 'free banking' law, effectively concurs in concluding that 'Free banking was brought into being by the Loco-Focos'. Working against the mainstream Democrats who were allied with the chartered banks, the Loco-Focos generated a popular movement for free entry into banking to which Governor Marcy and the legislature (dominated by Whigs elected with the Loco-Focos's help) capitulated. Leggett's argument that free competition would itself suppress unreliable banknotes did not prevail, however. Instead, McVickar's bond-collateralization idea was adopted as a safety device.

Henry C. Carey and Condy Raguet
After its political success (qualified by the compulsory bond-collateral provision) in New York, the argument for free banking was addressed to the remaining states. The economist Henry C. Carey, a prolific author well known in his day, published two lengthy pamphlets (1838; 1840) favourable towards free banking. Carey's chief concern seems to have been the promotion of economic growth.[16] His earlier pamphlet offered little in the way of theory, but did make two noteworthy points in its discussion of Scottish banking. First, Carey (1838, p. 81) argued that *laissez-faire* in credit markets promoted economic growth. Scotland's rapid growth was attributed to the 'comparative absence of restraints upon the employment of capital. Were all restrictions abolished, her growth would be still more rapid.' Second, Carey considered unlimited liability for bank shareholders to be an important restriction on Scottish banking.[17] The lack of freedom to form limited liability corporations compelled risk-averse individuals to

become depositors rather than shareholders. He believed that New England had a superior banking system because the availability of limited liability there reduced 'friction', by which he meant impediments to enterprise.

Carey's second pamphlet repeated much of the detailed institutional discussion of the first, and added a more developed argument for free trade in banking. He began (1840, pp. 9–11) with a sweeping attack against restrictions on the application of capital and on freedom of trade. He concluded (1840, p. 75) with the argument that perfect freedom of trade in money is even more important than in other goods. Interference with trade produces irregularity in supply and price. Of all goods, money enters into the most contracts for delivery, so that irregularity of its supply and relative price causes the greatest inconvenience. Under *laissez-faire*, the currency would be self-regulating: 'by establishing perfect freedom of trade, we should permit the supply and demand to regulate each other, thus giving a safe and steady currency'.

Carey did not spell out any self-regulating mechanisms that would prevent over-issue by competing banks; nor did he develop a clear business-cycle theory. But he did argue (1840, pp. 7–11, 65) that 'unsteadiness is produced by restriction, causing capital to accumulate while the owners are seeking their means of investing it'. In contrast to restrictions that caused idle funds to be left temporarily on deposit, freedom to employ capital (particularly to form adequately capitalized banks) promoted soundness and steadiness. He cited as evidence (1840, pp. 41, 50) the relative mildness of business-cycles in Scotland, where banks could more freely be formed, in contrast to England. Carey (1840, pp. 16–17, 51–61) saw the unlimited liability statutes of bank shareholders in both countries, however, as a restriction that discouraged equity-holding and was therefore destabilizing. The recent introduction of unlimited liability to Rhode Island, Carey (1840, p. 61) claimed, had led at once to an increase in the holding of currency and deposits and a reduction in economic stability.

In the way of reform Carey (1840, pp. 55–7) explicitly rejected both higher tariffs (later in his career he switched sides on this question) and hard-money remedies. Higher tariffs would create idle capital and hence instability, while the substitution of specie for banknotes and checks similarly entailed 'a diminution of the facilities of trade ... Restrictions cannot give steadiness.' Repeal of usury laws would have a limited, though positive, effect. In order to employ the capitals of small savers, freedom to form limited-liability banks was paramount. Like Leggett, then, Carey (1840, pp. 69–72) favoured the enactment of a general law of incorporation to replace the legislative chartering of banks. He also rejected the bond-collateral requirement of the New York State law, though on grounds that it would discourage employment of capital in banks and thereby produce unsteadiness. He offered his own model statute allowing free banking with either limited or unlimited liability, requiring only that the balance sheets of limited-liability banks be made public. Carey characterized his proposal as one to 'ABOLISH ALL RESTRICTIONS, AND ESTABLISH PERFECT FREEDOM OF TRADE'.

Yet Carey's understanding of the ideal of free trade in money was different from Leggett's. Carey (1840, pp. 63–4) condemned the Independent Treasury system as a source of instability. Later in his career, Carey's enthusiasm for stimulation of enterprise led him to support the issue of greenbacks together with free banking (Carey, 1865a, 1865b, 1866) as means to an 'adequate' supply of money. Together with his eventually ardent support for protectionism, these views indicate (if there is any consistency to be found) that Carey's support for free banking was not (like Leggett's) based on a normative commitment to *laissez-faire*, but stemmed instead from his belief that free banking would promote economic growth.

Like Carey, Condy Raguet was an influential author who has been cited by historians of thought (Redlich, 1947, p. 202; Dorfman, 1966, p. 659) as a supporter of 'free banking'. Raguet favoured a national bank, however, and opposed Jackson's veto of the re-charter and removal of the federal deposits from the Bank of the United States.[18] Raguet (1839) did support the New York 'free banking' law, but principally because of its scheme for collateralizing banknotes. His book made no argument for the application of the *laissez-faire* principle to banking.

Richard Hildreth

Like Leggett and the early McVickar, Richard Hildreth grounded his argument for open competition in banking clearly on *laissez-faire* principles. Hildreth (1840, pp. 172, 149) insisted that the principle of free trade was just as applicable to banking as it was to other industries: 'As open competition has been found to be the best and safest regulator of all other kinds of trade, so it will no doubt prove the best and safest regulator of the trade of banking.' To establish open competition meant that '[t]he monopoly of bank charters must be abolished altogether ... Capitalists must be left as much at liberty to invest their money in a bank as in a cotton mill.' As especially relevant evidence of the virtues of open competition, Hildreth (1840, pp. 143–4) pointed to the free market for a product he thought quite similar to banknotes, namely bills of exchange. It would obviously be 'absurd and fatal' to grant a monopoly in that market, yet monopolies have curiously been thought proper in the supply of banknotes. Hildreth (1840, p. 165n) found it particularly anomalous that J. R.

McCulloch, 'a most uncompromising, and somewhat extravagant advocate of free trade in every thing else', was among the advocates of banknote monopoly.

Hildreth's (1840, p. 171) case against monopoly of note-issue recalls both the Hayekian idea that centralized economic control requires an unattainable degree of centralized knowledge, and the public choice idea that government officials have their own interests: 'This idea of creating one great bank to superintend and control all the other banks ... supposes a superior degree of knowledge and of disinterestedness on the part of the men who may happen to be chosen directors of the great bank, quite superhuman.' The mistakes of the Bank of England during the suspension period, and of the Second Bank of the United States early and late in its career, provided evidence of 'how they may be deluded, and how readily they may become the instruments to delude others'. Hildreth (1840, p. 167) dismissed the notion, propounded by the Currency School in England, that a fixed artificial rule could be laid down for dictating to all banks appropriate expansions and contractions of the currency. The proper control of any individual bank's issues instead required practical knowledge gained through experience with actual decentralized conditions. Similar views were being expressed at the time by Free Banking School writers in England (White, 1984, pp. 130–6). A public-choice orientation may clearly be seen in Hildreth's account (1840, pp. 123–4) of the rent-seeking and log-rolling processes associated with the procurement of exclusive charters.

In ascribing self-regulating properties to a convertible currency with plural issuers, Hildreth (1840, p. 88) exposited the needs-of-trade doctrine with unusual clarity. Banknotes cannot be kept in circulation unless 'demanded by the business wants of the community', these wants being identified as 'demand in the country for a circulating medium'. Or again (1840, p. 157): 'The amount of notes, payable on demand, that can be kept in circulation, is and must be limited by the demand of the community for a circulating medium.' Variations in the quantity of bank-issued money were the endogenous result of exogenous movements in the price level or real activity. These movements altered the nominal demand for money proportionally, the equilibrium ratio of nominal transactions to money (what we today call 'velocity') being assumed constant:

> The rise in prices, the activity of trade, the spirit of speculation, create a new use and a new demand for the circulating medium, the amount of which is increased accordingly. ... These fluctuations in the amount of the circulation are absolutely necessary to keep up a due proportion between the medium of trade and the amount of trade.

Hildreth (1840, p. 158) gave an unusually clear explanation of the adverse clearing mechanism that would check over-issues, even noting that increased gross clearing balances would cancel out in the event of a concerted system-wide over-issue:[19]

> If a number of banks issue a quantity of notes beyond what are needed for the operations of trade, those notes soon come into the possession of other banks, and when they are presented for payment, unless those other banks have also issued an extra quantity of notes, which having fallen into the hands of the first set of banks, will serve for the redemption of theirs, – the issuers will be obliged to redeem their excessive issue in specie, a process which will soon compel them to put a stop to that issue.

The greater the number of issuing banks, Hildreth added, the less likely is a system-wide over-issue: 'With a single great bank, or a small number of banks, an excessive issue may easily happen; but with the increase of banks the improbability increases of any such concert of action as would make it possible.' Thus a free banking system is more strongly self-regulating than a monopoly or restricted-entry system.

A system-wide over-expansion in the currency would also be self-correcting in Hildreth's view, but by a different route: the price-specie-flow mechanism. A fall in the purchasing power of domestic currency would cause an external drain of reserves, forcing corrective contraction by the bank(s). Unlike Leggett or the British Currency and Free Banking Schools, Hildreth (1840, p. 198) thought this self-correction would operate so promptly that 'the direct power of banks to raise prices is very limited'. Consequently he rejected the monetary theory of business cycles, developed by those writers, in favour of the British Banking School views that macroeconomic fluctuations grew naturally out of speculative economic activity, and that any cyclical role played by banks derived from variations in their intermediational activity (1840, pp. 159–65). Unlike the Banking School, however, Hildreth derived implications favourable to free banking from this cycle theory.[20] He argued that bank loans based on deposits were far more liable to fluctuate in volume than loans based on equity, because the volume of deposits varied cyclically. A greater number of banks, as would exist under free entry, implied to Hildreth an increase both in total banking equity and (the total sum of deposits apparently assumed unchanged) in the ratio of equity to deposit liabilities, and therefore an increase in 'the ratio which the stable portion [of loans] bears to the unstable portion'. This greater stability in loans would 'give a comparative stability to trade'.

With respect to reform measures, Hildreth, in his first book on banking (1837), argued only for open competition and against a national bank. An expanded version was published in 1840, just two years after the passage of the New York State Free Banking Act. He had now become a supporter of the compulsory bond-collateral idea embodied in that act, and even reprinted the act's text in an appendix (1840, pp. 200–9). Hildreth (1840, pp. 154–5) justified compulsory collateralization in the now-standard way as an effective means of protecting banknote recipients who were unable to judge every note's solidity.[21] Once the notes were thus secured, he insisted, no other legislative interference was warranted. Stockholders and depositors could look out for themselves. The measure 'completely does away with that plausible argument in favor of monopoly' that free entry would mean unsafe notes. Likewise, Hildreth (1840, p. 184) concluded, it removed the safety rationale for banning small notes. Hildreth thus warrants being called a *laissez-faire* monetary theorist, though the *laissez-faire* part of his message (that compulsory security for notes was a sufficient regulation) was somewhat obscured by the interventionist part (that such a restriction was desirable).

Conclusion

'Free banking' legislation in the New York State sense, providing free entry for new banks but with a bond-collateral restriction on their issue of banknotes, spread to a majority of the states prior to 1860. The National Currency Act of 1863, which provided federal sanction for notes collateralized by federal bonds, may be viewed as 'a sort of national free banking act' (Rockoff, 1974, p. 142). The success of the movement for such legislation had two important effects. First, it defused for the time being any incipient movement for truly *laissez-faire* banking. Enthusiasm was directed towards winnable legislative battles for freer entry rather than toward developing a more idealistic position. There were no noteworthy American contributions to *laissez-faire* monetary theory in the next few decades after 1840, though briefs on behalf of state 'free banking' legislation continued to appear. Second, the bond collateral restriction of the National Currency Act proved to be far from innocuous. This restriction made the supply of currency notoriously 'inelastic', and thereby contributed importantly (along with other provisions of the Act) to the banking panics of the late nineteenth century (Noyes, 1910; Vera Smith, 1936, pp. 133–4). In having this impact, the regulatory provisions of the National Currency Act themselves set the stage for a *post-bellum* revival of the *laissez-faire* approach to money and banking.[22]

Acknowledgement
The authors thank the Scaife Foundation for research support. Valuable comments on an earlier version were received from Milton Friedman, Thomas F. Huertas, Bala Subrama-

nian, Larry Schweikart, Richard H. Timberlake and participants in the Austrian Economics colloquium at New York University.

Notes

1. See for example Black (1970), Rockoff (1974), Klein (1974), Hayek (1978), Fama (1980), Greenfield and Yeager (1983), Rolnick and Weber (1983; 1984; 1986), White (1984), and Selgin (1988).
2. Nataf (1984a, b) has recently discussed French writers; White (1984) the British literature; and Cowen and Kroszner (1987) writers who associated *laissez-faire* with separation of the unit of account from the medium of exchange (anticipating a particular strain of the recent literature). The most important older secondary account of *laissez-faire* banking thought is Vera Smith (1936), who surveys the monetary regime debates in several nations but neglects the US debate before the Civil War. Redlich (1947) discusses the American opposition to a national bank and the movement for bond-collateralized 'free banking' legislation in New York State, but says little about theoretical economic arguments. Madeline (1943) discusses events rather than theories. Mints (1945, pp. 138–41) and Miller (1927, pp. 159–65) discuss views on competition in note-issue only briefly and unappreciatively.
3. Wilhite (1958) discusses Webster and his contemporaries.
4. On the early history of New York State banking legislation, see Hammond (1936, pp. 184–96).
5. An early British monetary writer to make this extension explicitly was Lord King (1804, pp. 116–20). On the needs-of-trade doctrine in the British literature see White (1984, pp. 90, 122–6). The proposition of a demand-determined currency stock was present in Adam Smith (1981, p. 300).
6. The confusion between money and credit, and consequent misunderstanding of the money supply process, persists today. For a critique, see Greenfield and Yeager (1986).
7. On the similarity of McVickar's views to those of McCulloch and Ricardo see Redlich (1947, p. 294, n. 47). Redlich notes that the same combination of Smithian free banking with Ricardian bond-collateral found in McVickar is also found in Parnell (1827). Ricardo and McCulloch both eventually advocated banknote monopoly, however, while Parnell advocated free entry.
8. Dorfman's (1966, pp. 516–22, 713–20) secondary account of McVickar's works fails to note the inconsistency in McVickar's views. The same inconsistency exists in the writings of McVickar's student William Beach Lawrence, who proselytised both for 'free banking' and recharter of the Second Bank of the United States (see Dorfman, 1966 pp. 720–31).
9. Madeline (1943, pp. 45–51) discusses Jackson's plans for a new national bank more favourable to his political interests.
10. Explicit evidence that Jacksonians were following the British free banking literature may be found, however, in Senator Thomas Hart Benton's (1854, pp. 188–9, 262) citation of Henry Parnell's and others' speeches and writings. Benton himself took a hard-money line, but occasionally (e.g. 1854, pp. 226, 248) made statements favourable towards Scottish-style free banking. See also Redlich (1947, pp. 295,n. 62) on citation of Parnell by Samuel Young, sponsor of an early New York State free banking bill.
11. For an elaboration of this critique, see White (1984, pp. 120–2). The real-bills doctrine as a guideline for prudent lending is another matter. Adam Smith argued that lending on real bills had both virtues.
12. Elsewhere, Leggett (1984, pp. 146, 187) argued that depreciation of over-issued notes would provide the check against excessive issues by any single bank. This is consistent with the adverse clearing check if depreciation makes it profitable for other banks and brokers to acquire and redeem the notes.
13. There are linkages here: the British Currency and Free Banking School writers influenced both Leggett and later Wicksell, Mises and Hayek. Lucas, in turn, has acknowledged an affinity with Hayek's work.

14. The evolution of Leggett's monetary reform proposals is treated at greater length by White (1986). The same evolution may be seen in the Loco-Foco movement more generally; see Redlich (1947, pp. 189–90), who surprisingly does not cite Leggett.
15. Alexander Ming was a prominent Loco-Foco.
16. Dorfman (1966, pp. 789–805) and Sharkey (1959, pp. 153–71) discuss Carey's thought and influence. Carey's greatest renown in America was later gained, incongruously, as a protectionist. In France, however, he was well known among economists as a free banking advocate (Nataf, 1984b).
17. The same conclusion has been reached recently (on different grounds) by Carr and Mathewson (1988).
18. Dorfman (1966, pp. 363, 376, 607–12, 659) provides an intermittant secondary account of Raguet's evolving banking views. Another spurious 'free banking' advocate was Charles Duncombe (1841).
19. In fact, cancellation would take place only in the mean. Concerted over-issue would still increase the variance of daily clearings against each bank, rendering its reserves inadequate and prompting it to retreat to its original level of issues. See Selgin (1988, pp. 80–2).
20. John Stuart Mill (1848, pp. 675–6), James Wilson (1847, pp. 30–35, 97–104) and Thomas Tooke (1844, pp. 44–5) of the Banking School all defended competition in note-issuing, but not because they thought it would moderate business cycles. Tooke had earlier (1840, pp. 202–7) been quite hostile to free banking. On the evolution of Tooke's policy views, see Arnon (1984).
21. Hildreth (1840, p. 155) suggested indirectly that the acceptance of notes was in some sense involuntary.
22. A companion piece, Selgin and White (1990), discusses this *post-bellum* literature.

References

Arnon, A. 1984, 'The transformation of Thomas Tooke's monetary theory reconsidered', *History of Political Economy* 16 (2) (Summer), pp. 311–26.
Bagehot, W. 1873, *Lombard Street*, Henry S. King, London.
Benton, T. H. 1854, *Thirty Year's View*, vol. I, D. Appleton, New York.
Black, F. 1970, 'Banking and interest rates in a world without money: the effects of uncontrolled banking', *Journal of Bank Research* 1(3) (Autumn), pp. 9–20.
Bryant, W. C. 1839, 'William Leggett', *US Magazine and Democratic Review*, 6 (July), pp. 17–28.
Byrdsall, L. 1967, *A History of the Loco Foco or Equal Rights Party*, Burt Franklin, New York.
Carey, H. C. 1838, *The Credit System in France, Great Britain, and the United States*, Carey, Lea, & Blanchard, Philadelphia.
Carey, H. C. 1840, *Answers to Questions: What Constitutes Currency? What are the Causes of Unsteadiness of the Currency? and What is the Remedy?* Lea & Blanchard, Philadelphia.
Carey, H. C. 1865a, *The Currency Question*, Collins, Philadelphia.
Carey, H. C. 1865b, *Letters to the Hon. Schuyler Colfax*, Collins. In Carey (1875), Philadelphia.
Carey, H.C. 1866, 'The National Bank Amendment Bill', reprinted from *The North American and United States Gazette*, April. In Carey (1875).
Carey, H. C. 1875, *Miscellaneous Papers on the National Finances, the Currency, and Other Economic Subjects*, Henry Carey Baird and Co., Philadelphia.
Carr, J. and Mathewson, F. 1988, 'Unlimited liability as a barrier to entry', *Journal of Political Ecomony* 96(4) (April), pp. 766–84.
Cowan, T. and Kroszner, R. 1987, 'The Development of the New Monetary Economics', *Journal of Political Economy*, 95(3) (June), pp. 567–90.
Dorfman, J. 1966, *The Economic Mind in American Civilization*, vols I and II, 1606–1865, Augustus, M. Kelley, New York.

Duncombe, C. 1841, *Duncombe's Free Banking*, Augustus M. Kelley, New York (1969 reprint).

Fama, E. 1980, 'Banking in the theory of finance', *Journal of Monetary Economics* 6(1) (January), pp. 39–57.

Gouge, W. 1833, *A Short History of Paper Money and Banking*, T. W. Ustick, Philadelphia.

Greenfield, R. L. and Yeager, L. B. 1983, 'A laissez-faire approach to monetary stability', *Journal of Money, Credit and Banking* 15(3) (August), pp. 302–15.

Greenfield, R. L. and Yeager, L. B. 1986, 'Money and credit confused: an appraisal of economic doctrine and Federal Reserve procedure', *Southern Economic Journal* 53(3), pp. 364–73.

Hammond, B. 1936, 'Free banks and corporations', *Journal of Political Economy* 44(2) (April), pp. 184–209.

Hayek, F. A. 1935, *Prices and Production*, 2nd edn, Augustus M. Kelley, New York (1967 reprint).

Hayek, F. A. 1978, *Denationalisation of Money*, 2nd edn, Institute of Economic Affairs, London.

Hildreth, R. 1837, *The History of Banks, to which is Added a Demonstration of the Advantages and Necessity of Free Competition in the Business of Banking*, Hilliard, Gray, Boston, Mass.

Hildreth, R. 1840, *Banks, Banking, and Paper Currencies*, Greenwood Press, New York (1968 reprint).

Joplin, T. 1826, *An Essay on the General Principles and Present Practice of Banking in England and Scotland*, 5th edn, Baldwin, Cradock & Joy, London.

King, Lord P. 1804, *Thoughts on the Restriction of Payments in Specie*, 2nd edn. In Earl Fortescue (ed.), *A Selection From the Speeches and Writings of the Late Lord King*, Longmans, 1844, London.

Klein, B. 1974, 'The competitive supply of money', *Journal of Money, Credit, and Banking* 6(4) (November), pp. 423–53.

Krooss, H. E. (ed.) 1977, *Documentary History of Banking and Currency in the United States*, Chelsea House, New York.

Leggett, W. 1984, *Democratick Editorials: Essays in Jacksonian Political Economy*, ed. L. H. White, Liberty Press, Indianapolis.

Lucas, Jr, R. E. 1975, 'An equilibrium model of the business cycle', *Journal of Political Economy*, 83(6) (December), pp. 1113–44.

Madeline, Sister M. G. 1943, *Monetary and Banking Theories of Jacksonian Democracy*, n.p., Philadelphia.

Marcus [pseud., for Benjamin Franklin Butler] 1818, *Remarks on Private Banking*, E. & E. Hosford, Albany.

McCulloch, J. R. 1826, 'Fluctuations in the supply and value of money', *Edinburgh Review* 43(86) (February) pp. 263–98.

McVickar, J. 1827, *Hints on Banking, in a Letter to a Gentleman in Albany: by a New Yorker*, Vanderpool & Cole, New York.

McVickar, J. 1830, *Introductory Lecture to a Course of Political Economy, Recently Delivered at Columbia College, New York*, J. Miller, London.

McVickar, J. 1841, *A National Bank: its Necessity, and Most Advisable Form*, n.p., reprinted from an article in the *New York Review*, New York.

Mill, J.S. 1848, *Principles of Political Economy*, Augustus M. Kelley, [1973 reprint], New York.

Miller, H. E. 1927, *Banking Theories in the United States Before 1860*, Harvard University Press, Cambridge, Mass.

Mints, L. 1945, *A History of Banking Theory*, University of Chicago Press, Chicago.

Mushet, R. 1826, *An Attempt to Explain from Facts the Effects of the Issues of the Bank of England upon its Own Interests, Public Credit, and Country Banks*, Baldwin, Craddock & Joy, London.

Nataf, P. 1984a, 'Business cycle theories of mid-19th-century France', Unpublished ms., University of Paris.

Nataf, P. 1984b, 'Competitive banking and the cycle', Unpublished ms., University of Paris.

Noyes, A. D. 1910, *History of the National Bank Currency*, Government Printing Office, Washington.

Parnell, H. 1827, *Observations on Paper Money, Banking and Overtrading*, James Ridgeway, London.

Parnell, H. 1833, *A Plain Statement of the Power of the Bank of England and the Use it has Made of it*, 2nd edn, James Ridgeway, London.

Raguet, C. 1839, *A Treatise on Currency and Banking*, Grigg & Elliot, Philadelphia.

Redlich, F. 1947, *The Molding of American Banking: Men and Ideas*, (Part I, 1781–1840), Hafner, New York.

Ricardo, D. 1951, *The Works and Correspondence of David Ricardo*, vol. 4, *Pamphlets and Papers, 1815–1823*, ed. P. Sraffa, Cambridge University Press, Cambridge.

Rockoff, H. 1974, 'The free banking era: a re-examination', *Journal of Money, Credit, and Banking* 6(2) (May), pp. 141–67.

Rolnick, A. J. and Weber, W. E. 1983, 'New evidence on the free banking era', *American Economic Review* 73(5) (December), pp. 1080–91.

Rolnick, A. J. and Weber, W. E. 1984, 'The causes of free bank failures: a detailed examination', *Journal of Monetary Economics* 14(3) (October), pp. 267–91.

Rolnick, A. J. and Weber, W. E. 1986, 'Inherent instability in banking: the free banking experience', *Cato Journal* 5(3) (Winter), pp. 877–90.

Say, J. B. 1971, *A Treatise on Political Economy*, Augustus M. Kelley, New York.

Schwartz, A. J. 1947, 'The beginning of competitive banking in Philadelphia: 1782–1809', *Journal of Political Economy* 55(5) (October), pp. 417–31.

Selgin, G. A. 1988, *The Theory of Free Banking: Money Supply Under Competitive Note Issue*, Rowman & Littlefield, Totowa, NJ.

Selgin, G. A. and White, L. H. 1990, 'Laissez faire monetary theorists in late nineteenth century America', *Southern Economic Journal* 56(3) (January), pp. 774–87.

Sharkey, R. P. 1959, *Money, Class, and Party: An Economic Study of Civil War and Reconstruction*, Johns Hopkins University Press, Baltimore, MD.

Sharp, J. R. 1970, *The Jacksonians versus the Banks: Politics in the States after the Panic of 1837*, Columbia University Press, New York.

Smith, A. 1981, *An Inquiry into the Nature and Causes of the Wealth of Nations* eds R. H. Campbell, A. S. Skinner, and W. B. Todd, Liberty Classics, Indianapolis.

Smith, V. 1936, *The Rationale of Central Banking*, P. S. King, London.

Taylor, J. 1969, *An Enquiry into the Principles and Policy of the United States* (ed. L. Bartiz), Bobbs-Merrill, New York.

Tooke, T. 1840, *A History of Prices*, vol. 3, Longmans, London.

Tooke, T. 1844, *An Inquiry into the Currency Principle*, 2nd edn, Longmans, London.

White, L. H. 1984, *Free Banking in Britain: Theory, Experience, and Debate, 1800–1845*, Cambridge University Press, Cambridge.

White, L. H. 1986, 'William Leggett: Jacksonian editorialist as classical liberal political economist', *History of Political Economy*, 18(2) (Summer), pp. 307–24.

Wilhite, V. G. 1958, *Founders of American Economic Thought and Policy*, Bookman Associates, New York.

Wilson, J. 1847, *Capital, Currency, and Banking*, The Economist, London.

3 Cumulative Process Models from Thornton to Wicksell

Thomas M. Humphrey

The celebrated Wicksellian theory of the cumulative process is a landmark in the history of monetary thought. It gave economists a dynamic, three-market (money, credit, goods) macro-model, capable of showing what happens when banks, commercial or central, hold interest rates too low or too high. With it one could trace the sequence of events through which money, interest rates, borrowing, spending and prices interact and evolve during inflations or deflations. The prototype of modern interest-pegging models of inflation, it influences thinking even today. It also confirms the adage, well known to historians of science, that no scientific discovery is named for its original discoverer. For, as documented below, it was not Knut Wicksell but rather two British economists, writing long before him in the first third of the nineteenth century, who first presented the theory.

The cumulative process analysis itself attributes monetary and price level changes to discrepancies between two interest rates. One, the market or money rate, is the rate that banks charge on loans. The other is the natural or equilibrium rate that equates real saving with investment at full employment and that also corresponds to the marginal productivity of capital. When the loan rate falls below the natural rate, investors demand more funds from the banking system than savers deposit there. Assuming banks accommodate these extra loan demands by issuing more notes and creating more demand deposits, a monetary expansion occurs. This expansion, by underwriting the excess demand for goods generated by the gap between investment and saving, produces a persistent and cumulative rise in prices for as long as the interest differential lasts. As stressed by Wicksell, the differential vanishes once banks raise their loan rates to protect their gold reserves from depletion by cash drains into hand-to-hand circulation. Unlike external drains, which become inoperative when banks worldwide expand in unison, such internal drains are always a threat. For given that the public transacts a certain proportion of its real payments in gold coin, these drains occur when price increases necessitate additional coin for such payments. The differential also vanishes when a loan rate set *above* the natural rate produces falling prices, a reduced coin circulation and a consequent reversal of the cash drain. In this case, the resulting excess reserves induce banks to lower their rates towards equilibrium in an effort to stimulate borrowing. These adjustments, however, may occur too late to prevent substantial changes in prices.

From this analysis it follows that the monetary authority must strive to keep the money rate equal to the natural rate if it wishes to maintain price stability. To do this, it must raise or lower its own lending rate as soon as prices show the slightest tendency to rise or fall and maintain that rate steady when prices exhibit no tendency to move in either direction. By following this rule, it eradicates the two-rate disparity that generates inflation or deflation.

The foregoing model and its policy implications are well known. Not so well known, however, is that the model was already more than 70 years old when Wicksell presented it in his *Interest and Prices* in 1898. Long before then, Henry Thornton (1802; 1811) and Thomas Joplin (1823; 1828; 1832) had already constructed versions of the model and had employed it in their policy analysis. The model's two-rate, saving-investment, loanable-funds framework was as much their invention as Wicksell's. The same is true of their demonstration that inflation stems from usury ceilings and bankers' attempts to peg loan rates at levels other than those that clear the market for real capital investment. Even the model's famous equilibrium conditions – two-rate equality, saving-investment equality, loan-saving equality, aggregate demand-supply equality, monetary and price stability – were recognized by them. All they lacked was an automatic stabilizing mechanism that brings the cumulative process to a halt by the convergence of the loan rate on the natural rate. And this was provided by Wicksell in the form of the feedback effect of price changes on the loan rate. In an attempt to correct some misconceptions about the theory's origins and to give these pioneers their due, the paragrpahs below outline the model and its components to show what the three contributors had to say about each.

The model and its components
To identify the specific contributions of Wicksell and his predecessors, it is useful to have some idea of the model they helped create. As presented here, that full-employment model consists of seven equations linking the variables investment I, saving S (both planned or *ex ante* real magnitudes), loan rate i, natural rate r, excess aggregate demand E, money-stock change dM/dt, and price-level change dP/dt.[1] Of these, saving and investment are taken to be increasing and decreasing linear functions of the loan rate, the presumption being that higher rates encourage thrift but discourage capital formation.

The first equation states that real investment I exceeds saving S when the loan rate of interest i falls below its natural equilibrium level r (the level that equilibrates saving and investment),

$$I-S = a(r-i), \tag{1}$$

where the coefficient a relates the investment-saving gap to the rate differential that creates it. The second equation states that the excess of investment over saving equals the extra money dM/dt created to finance it,

$$I-S = dM/dt \tag{2}$$

That is, assuming banks create money by way of loan, monetary expansion occurs when they lend more to investors than they receive in deposits from savers. To see this, denote the (investment) demand for loans L_D as $L_D = I(i)$, where I(i) is the schedule relating desired investment spending to the loan rate. Similarly, denote loan supply L_S as the sum of saving S(i) – all of which is assumed to be deposited with banks – plus new money dM/dt created by banks in accommodating loan demands; in short, $L_S = S(i) + dM/dt$. Equating loan demand and supply ($L_D = L_S$) yields equation 2 above.

The model's third equation says that an excess of investment over saving at full employment generates an equivalent excess demand E for goods,

$$I-S = E \tag{3}$$

as aggregate real expenditure outruns real supply. The fourth equation says that this excess demand bids up prices, which rise by an amount dP/dt proportionate to the excess demand,

$$dP/dt = kE \tag{4}$$

Substituting equations 1 and 3 into 4, and equation 1 into 2, yields

$$dP/dt = ka(r-i) \text{ and} \tag{5}$$

$$dM/dt = a(r-i). \tag{6}$$

Together, these equations state that price inflation and the money growth that underlies it both stem from the discrepancy between the natural and market rates of interest. This, of course, is the model's most famous prediction.

Finally, the seventh equation closes the model by linking loan rate changes di/dt to price changes dP/dt. It states that bankers adjust their rates upward in proportion to the price rises so as to protect their gold reserves from inflation-induced cash drains into hand-to-hand circulation.[2] That is, assuming the public makes a certain proportion of its real payments in the form of coin, rising prices increase the quantity of coin required for that purpose. To arrest the resulting drain of coin reserves into hand-to-hand circulation, bankers raise their loan rates by an amount di/dt proportionate to price changes dP/dt

$$di/dt = b \, dP/dt \tag{7}$$

This equation ensures that the loan rate eventually converges to its natural equilibrium level, as can be seen by substituting equation 5 into equation 7 and solving the resulting differential equation for the time-path of the loan rate.[3] At this point, saving equals investment, excess demand vanishes, money and prices are stable, and bank lending equals saving – these results obtaining when one sets the two rates equal to each other in the model. These, of course, are the famous Wicksellian conditions of monetary equilibrium. Given the model and its components, one can identify what Wicksell and his precursors contributed to it.

Henry Thornton

The origins of the cumulative process model are to be found in chapter 10 of Henry Thornton's classic *An Enquiry into the Nature and Effects of the Paper Credit of Great Britain* (1802) and in the first of his two parliamentary speeches of 1811 on the Bullion Report. In those works he contributed four ideas that together constitute the central analytical core of the model. He also demonstrated the model's power as a tool of policy analysis.[4]

First, he noted that the quantity of loans demanded depends upon a comparison of the loan rate of interest with the expected rate of profit on the use of the borrowed funds. He says (1802, pp. 253–4),

> In order to ascertain how far the desire of obtaining loans at the Bank may be expected at any time to be carried, we must enquire into the subject of the quantum of profit likely to be derived from borrowing there under the existing circumstances. This is to be judged of by considering two points: the amount, first, of interest to be paid on the sum borrowed; and, secondly, of the mercantile or other gain to be obtained by the employment of the borrowed capital ... We may, therefore, consider this question as turning principally on a comparison of the rate of interest taken at the bank with the current rate of mercantile profit.

He continues: 'The borrowers, in consequence of that artificial state of things which is produced by the law against usury, obtain their loans too cheap. That which they obtain too cheap they demand in too great quantity' (p. 255). Thus a loan rate equal to the profit rate limits loan demands to non-inflationary levels. But a loan rate below the profit rate induces additional – and inflationary – loan demands.

Second, he explained how the rate differential, through its effect on loan demands, translates into money and price-level changes. As noted above, the rate differential induces an expansion of loan demands. Assuming that bankers accommodate these loan demands by increasing their note issue – an assumption that implies a willingness to let reserve-to-note and -deposit ratios fall – the money stock expands. The resulting money-induced rise in aggregate expenditure puts upward pressure on prices. It also, because of an assumed sluggish adjustment of wages and other costs to rising prices, stimulates output and employment. Given that the economy normally operates close to its full-capacity ceiling, however, the price-effect predominates. It follows that price inflation as well as the money growth that underlies it stems from the differential between the loan and profit rates as indicated by the expressions $dP/dt = ka(r-i)$ and $dM/dt = a(r-i)$. Here is the first model to show that inflation occurs when bank rates are pegged at inappropriate levels.

Third, he stressed that the rate differential, if maintained indefinitely, produces cumulative (continuing) rather than one-time changes in money and prices. This is so, he said, because as long as the loan rate remains below the equilibrium rate, borrowing will continue to be profitable ('the temptation to borrow will be the same as before') even at successively higher price levels. The results will be more borrowing, more lending, more monetary expansion, still higher prices and so on without limit in a cumulative inflationary spiral. Under these conditions, 'even the most liberal extension of bank loans' will fail to have the slightest 'tendency to produce a permanent diminution of the applications to the bank for discount' (p. 256). On the contrary, loan demands will be insatiable while the rate differential lasts.

Fourth, from the foregoing considerations, Thornton derived his fundamental equilibrium theorem, namely that monetary and price-level stability obtain when the loan rate equals the profit rate. Such two-rate equality, he said (p. 254), would allow the banking system to 'sufficiently limit its paper' to non-inflationary levels 'by means of the price [i.e. rate] at which it lends'. For with the two rates equal, their differential would vanish and with it the inducement to borrow and lend that produces inflationary money growth. Money and prices would stop rising and stabilize at a constant level. Having described the two-rate equilibrium, however, he did not explain what forces would drive banks to attain it. His model lacked the automatic equilibrating mechanism through which inflation induces banks to raise their loan rates to equilibrium in order to protect their reserves from cash drains into hand-to-hand circulation.

Thornton's policy conclusions

Thornton's fifth contribution was his demonstration of the model's usefulness as a tool of policy analysis. He used his model to determine the cause of the paper pound's depreciation on the foreign exchanges during the Napoleonic Wars when Britain had suspended the convertibility of her currency into gold at a fixed price upon demand. He attributed the depreciation to note over-issue caused by the Bank of England's discount rate being too low. Usury ceilings, he noted, constrained the Bank's rate to a 5 per cent maximum at a time when, owing to the boom conditions of the war, the expected rate of profit was well in excess of 5 per cent. The result of this differential was a loss of Bank control over the volume of its loans and its note issue, both of which had expanded to produce inflation. To give the Bank a firm grip on the money supply, he urged removing the usury ceiling and requiring the Bank to set its discount rate equal to the profit rate. As a second-best alternative, he endorsed the Bank's policy of rationing loans. Apart from such direct credit rationing, however, he saw no end to inflation as long as the differential persisted. In this connection, he noted that no amount of monetary expansion could lower the profit rate to the level of the discount rate. The profit rate, he said, is a real variable determined by the demand for and supply of real capital. As such, it is invariant with respect to changes in nominal variables like the money stock. Somewhat inconsistently, he admitted that money growth could stimulate capital formation through *forced saving* – the inflation-induced redistribution of purchasing power from fixed-income receivers to capitalist investors. But he thought such effects to be quantitatively unimportant. For that reason, he made no mention of the resulting capital accumulation's impact on the profit rate.

He also employed his model to refute the real bills doctrine according to which inflationary over-issue is impossible as long as banks lend only on sound commercial paper arising out of real transactions in goods and services. He contended that the real bills test provided no check to over-issue when the loan rate is below the profit rate. For the resulting price rise emanating from the differential would, by raising the nominal value of real transactions, increase the nominal volume of eligible bills coming forward for discount. Since these bills would pass the real bills test (i.e. they are backed by an equivalent value of goods) banks would discount them and the money stock would therefore expand. This monetary expansion would validate a further rise in prices thereby resulting in more bills being presented for discount leading to further monetary expansion and still higher prices and so on ad infinitum in a never-ending inflationary spiral. These examples show that, for Thornton, the cumulative process model was not a theoretical toy but a key component of his policy analysis.

Thornton's contemporaries

Thornton's two-rate analysis was accepted by at least four of his contemporaries. Thus J. R. McCulloch (1828, p. 235), in his refutation of the real bills doctrine, argued that loan demands depend primarily on 'the rate of interest for which those sums can be obtained, compared with the ordinary rate of profit that may be made by their employment'. Similarly, Lord King (1803, p. 22) warned that such loan demands 'may be carried to any assignable extent' if the rate differential persists. John Foster (1804, p. 113) put the point even more forcefully. He said that if the directors of the Bank of England were to expand the note issue in an effort to accommodate all loan demands arising at the disequilibrium rate, they 'might at length reduce the value of their notes to that of the paper on which they are engraved'. But perhaps the clearest and most succinct statement came from David Ricardo (1817, p. 364) who wrote that:

> The applications to the bank for money, then, depend on the comparison between the rate of profits that may be made by the employment of it, and the rate at which they are willing to lend it. If they charge less than the market [i.e. natural] rate of interest, there is no amount of money which they might not lend, – if they charge more than the rate none but spendthrifts and prodigals would be found to borrow of them. We accordingly find that when the market rate of interest exceeds the rate of 5 per cent at which the Bank uniformly lend, the discount office is besieged with applicants for money; and, on the contrary, when the market rate is even temporarily under 5 per cent, the clerks of that office have no employment.

Missing from the analysis of Thornton and his contemporaries was any mention of the model's real saving and investment schedules. These components were largely overlooked before the appearance of Thomas Joplin's *Outlines of a System of Political Economy* (1823), *Views on the Currency* (1828) and *An Analysis and History of the Currency Question* (1832).

Thomas Joplin

Joplin incorporated saving and investment schedules into Thornton's model and defined the natural rate as the rate that equilibrates the two.[5] He then argued that an increase in the demand for capital, by raising the natural rate above the loan rate, will open a saving-investment gap and a corresponding excess demand for goods that bids up prices progressively as long as the rate differential lasts. He likewise noted that money growth would accompany and validate the price increases as bankers (who have no way of knowing what the natural rate is and so charge their customary rate) honour all credit demands at the going loan rate. These considerations led him to conclude with Thornton that monetary and price level changes stem from disparities between the two rates. He also concluded that monetary equilibrium and its attendant balance conditions – saving-investment equality, loan-saving equality, aggregate demand-supply equality, monetary and price-level stability – obtain only when the two rates are equal.

Joplin's observations are so Wicksellian that they must be read to be believed. On the relation I-S = dM/dt between the investment-saving gap and the monetary change that finances it, he (1832, p. 101) wrote, 'When the supply of capital exceeds the demand, it has the effect of compressing [the money stock]; when the demand is greater than the supply, it has the effect of expanding it again'. On the expression dM/dt = a(r-i) connecting money-stock changes with the natural rate-loan rate disparity, he remarked (pp. 109, 111) that since bankers 'never can know what the true [natural] rate of interest is' they 'charge a fixed [loan] rate', with the consequence that the currency 'expands and contracts, instead of the interest of money rising and falling'.

Likewise, on the mechanism through which deviations of the loan rate from the natural rate produce inflation, he (1823, pp. 258–9) observed, 'Money comes into the market ... from the banks ... in consequence not of a demand for currency, but of a demand for capital, determined by the interest which the banks charge proportioned to the market [i.e. natural] rate. And in all cases the influx of money into the market ... is not the effect, but the cause of high prices.' Here is an explicit recognition of (1) the two-rate disparity, (2) the investment demand for loans, (3) a loan-determined money stock, and (4) the money-price relationship – all key ingredients of Wicksell's analysis. Finally, on pegging the loan rate above the natural rate so that saving exceeds investment and loans, money, and prices all fall, he said (pp. 209–10):

If it [the fall of prices] proceeded from the interest charged by the banks, being too high, the economy [saving] of the country, instead of reducing the interest...would find vent in discharging the debts due to the banks, at the high rate of interest they imposed; and the value of money and profits of trade would thus be kept up to that level which rendered the general economy [saving] greater than the general expenditure [investment].

Here is perhaps the first application of the cumulative process model to the deflationary case in which a loan rate above the natural rate spells an excess of saving over investment, a deficiency of aggregate demand, a contraction of borrowing and the money stock, and a consequent fall of prices. In other words, Joplin recognized that interest-rate pegging can lead to deflation as well as inflation.

Like Thornton, he (1828, p. 146) saw forced saving as one effect of the price inflation produced by banks' willingness to lend more than the savings voluntarily deposited with them.

If the issues of the bank are not increased by any loan it makes at interest, an equal amount of money must have been previously saved out of income, and paid into the bank, in which case, the party borrows the income previously saved; but if not, and the issues of the bank are increased by the loan, prices rise, and the party who has borrowed the money obtains value for it by depriving the holders of the money in previous circulation, of a proportionate power of purchasing commodities. An economy is thus created, though a forced economy, but it answers all the purpose of a voluntary one.

He opposed forced saving on the grounds that it involved a fraud and an injustice on the pre-existing money holders.

From his analysis (pp. 152–3) he concluded that interest-rate pegging is an important cause of price-level fluctuations:

> One effect, no doubt, would be produced by the bank regulating its issues by the demand for [loans] at a particular rate of interest, namely, that the rate of interest would be kept steady. Instead of the savings of income rising above four per cent [following, say, an upward shift in the loan demand schedule], the enlargement of issues would create an additional quantity sufficient to supply, at four per cent, the increased demand. On the other hand, when the savings of income were not in such request, and the demand at four per cent fell off, the notes of the bank would be withdrawn, and the supply of such savings, to a corresponding extent, would be cancelled, by which the rate of interest would be kept up [above its natural level]. The alteration in the [loan] demand for capital would not affect its value. The supply of it by means of the enlargement and contraction of the currency, would be created and cancelled as it was required. Prices would fluctuate instead of the interest of money.

He contended that these price fluctuations occur because banks possess the power of creating and destroying paper money at will by varying their reserve ratios. Take away this power, he said, and banks would become pure intermediaries, lending only the savings entrusted to them. In this case, saving would equal investment, loan rates would equal the natural rate, excess demand would be zero, and price stability would prevail. To make these equilibrium conditions a reality he proposed a policy of 100 per cent required gold reserves behind note issues.

To summarize, Joplin gave the model its most complete formulation up to Knut Wicksell. His inclusion of saving and investment schedules allowed him to show how gaps between the two produced by deviations from the natural rate translate into money-stock changes and excess demand that bids up prices. In short, he recognized all the model's components except the price-induced interest-adjustment mechanism that ensures the stability of monetary equilibrium.

Knut Wicksell
When Wicksell presented his cumulative process model in 1898, he thought he was the first to do so.[6] At that time he was totally unaware of the earlier work of Thornton and Joplin. Not until 1916 did he discover

from his colleague David Davidson that Thornton had foreshadowed him by almost 100 years. But he apparently never learned about Joplin, whose saving-investment version of the model was virtually identical to his.

One finds in his model all the elements developed by Thornton and Joplin. The two-rate disparity is there, as are the saving-investment gap, the excess demand for goods that bids up prices cumulatively, and the accompanying money growth resulting from banks' willingness to accommodate all credit demands at the going rate. His conclusion – that monetary and price-level changes stem from the two-rate disparity – is the same as theirs. So too is his list of monetary equilibrium conditions, including two-rate equality, saving-investment equality, loan-saving equality, aggregate demand-supply equality and monetary and price-level stability. True, he differed from Joplin on how these conditions should be achieved. He preferred a policy of promptly moving the discount rate in the same direction as prices are changing, stopping only when price movements cease. By contrast, Joplin preferred a policy of 100 per cent required gold reserves. But both believed that there existed a workable policy rule to keep money rates in line with the natural rate. Like his predecessors, he even used his model as a tool to explain British price movements in the nineteenth century, although he focused on secular rather than cyclical changes.

He differed from Thornton and Joplin chiefly in his inclusion of the stabilizing feedback effect of price-level changes on the loan rate. By adding this element to the model he was able to show that the cumulative process is self-limiting provided banks maintain some desired level of gold reserves and provided the public transacts a certain proportion of its real payments in gold coin. Since inflation increases and deflation decreases the need for coin in circulation to effectuate these given real payments, banks, he argued, will find their reserves being depleted in the former case and augmented in the latter. To arrest these price-induced reserve drains or accumulations they will adjust their rates upward or downward. In this way those price changes bring their own cessation as the loan rate converges on the natural rate.

He also demonstrated that the cumulative process is *not* self-correcting in hypothetical 'cashless' or pure credit economies using no metallic money, all payments being made by bookkeeping entries. Since specie drains are not a threat in such economies, banks need hold no reserves and are free to maintain indefinitely any money rate they choose. As a result, there exists no reserve constraint in the cashless society to limit the cumulative process. Thus any spontaneous disturbance that upsets the initial equality between the two rates will set in motion an inflation or deflation that can continue indefinitely. He further argued that the same may be true even in pure cash societies if technological innovations, wars and other real shocks cause the natural rate to change before the loan rate can ever catch up with it. In this case, the loan rate's lag behind the moving natural rate spells incomplete adjustment, persistent disequilibrium and ceaseless price changes.

This last insight, which combined the notions of an active or leading natural rate and a passive or trailing loan rate, enabled him to resolve what Keynes was later to call the Gibson paradox. This paradox, which neither Thornton nor Joplin addressed, holds that prices and interest rates historically move together in the same direction when, according to standard monetary theory, they should move inversely as excess issues of money temporarily depress interest rates while raising prices. In resolving the paradox, Wicksell agreed that prices and loan rates would move inversely if those rates fell below a given natural rate. For example, if loan rates fell to 4 per cent when the natural rate was 5 per cent, prices would rise. On the other hand, prices and loan rates would tend to move together if the natural rate itself moves and the loan rate lags behind (i.e. adjusts incompletely to the changing natural rate). In this case, loan rates, though rising or falling, would still be too low or too high relative to the natural rate to prevent a cumulative rise or fall in prices. Indeed, this was precisely Wicksell's explanation of long-term price changes in nineteenth-century Britain. These changes he saw as emanating from movements of the active natural rate about the lagging loan rate. Except for these applications, Wicksell's use of the model was the same as Thornton's and Joplin's.

Concluding comments
That Wicksell at best only rediscovered or reinvented the model now universally associated with his name is hardly surprising. It merely confirms the validity of Stigler's (1980) Law of Eponymy according to which no scientific discovery is named for its original discoverer. Still this finding, though completely unexceptional, is nevertheless at odds with some recent interpretations of the model's history. Certainly it is not true, as suggested in Axel Leijonhufvud's recent (1981) essay on the 'Wicksell Connection', that the model derives solely from Wicksell. Nor is it true, as Leijonhufvud contends, that Wicksell originated the saving-investment approach to macroeconomics. For, as documented above, the cumulative process model together with its implied conditions of monetary equilibrium originated not with Wicksell but rather with Thornton and Joplin. Of these two pioneers, Joplin deserves at least some credit for initiating the saving-investment approach since it was he who first introduced saving and investment schedules into the model.

These findings also cast doubt on Robert Nobay's and Harry Johnson's recent (1977) attempt to distinguish between classical and Wicksellian phases in the evolution of monetary thought. The classicals, according to this distinction, concentrated on establishing the proposition of the long-run neutrality of money. Wicksellians, by contrast, focused on the dynamic implications of monetary responses and disturbances as well as on the conditions of monetary equilibrium. What is overlooked is that at least two classical monetary theorists, namely Thornton and Joplin, were Wicksellians as far as their monetary analysis was concerned. True, they accepted the neutrality proposition. But their main concern was investigating the dynamics of money's response to deviations of the loan rate from the natural rate. They also sought to eliminate those deviations so that prices could be stabilized. To that end they spelled out the conditions of monetary equilibrium and prescribed policies to achieve them. In these ways they largely anticipated Wicksell.

Notes

1. For similar models, see Eagly (1974, pp. 86–9) and Laidler (1975, pp. 104–5, 117).
2. External drains would also force banks to raise their rates. But such drains, unlike internal ones, would be inoperative if all banks expanded in unison worldwide.
3. Solving the differential equation $di/dt = bka(r-i)$ obtained by substituting equation (5) into equation (7) yields the expression for the time-path of the loan rate i,
   $$i(t) = (i_0-r)\,e^{-bkat} + r$$
   where t is time, e is the base of the natural logarithm system, i_0 is the initial disequilibrium level of the loan rate, and r is the (constant) natural rate. This expression states that the loan rate will converge on the natural rate with the passage of time if the coefficients b, k, and a are each positive, as is assumed in the model in the text.
4. On Thornton, see Hayek (1939; 1935, pp. 12–14) and Schumpeter (1954, pp. 720–4). Thornton (1811, pp. 335–6) also described expected inflation's 'Fisher effect' on nominal and real interest rates.
5. On Joplin, see Corry (1962, pp. 54–6, 60–1, 110), Hayek (1935, pp. 15–17), Link (1959, pp. 73–102), Schumpeter (1954, p. 723), Viner (1937, pp. 190–2), and Warburton (1967, pp. 125, 290).
6. On Wicksell, see Jonung (1979), Laidler (1972), Leijonhufvud (1981, pp. 151–61), Patinkin (1972; 1965, pp. 587–97) and Uhr (1962).

References

Corry, B. A. 1962, *Money, Saving and Investment in English Economics: 1800–1850*, St Martin's, New York.

Eagly, R. 1974, *The Structure of Classical Economic Theory*, Oxford University Press, New York.

Foster, J. L. 1804, *An Essay on the Principles of Commercial Exchanges*, J. Hatchard, London.

Hayek, F. A. v. 1935, *Prices and Production*, 2nd edn, Routledge, London.

Hayek, F. A. v. 1939, *Introduction to Thornton* (1802).

Jonung, L. 1979, 'Knut Wicksell and Gustav Cassel on secular movements in prices', *Journal of Money, Credit and Banking* 11 (May), pp. 165–81.

Joplin, T. 1823, *Outlines of a System of Political Economy*, Baldwin, Craddock & Jay, London, Reprint, Kelley, New York, 1970.

Joplin, T. 1828, *Views on the Currency*, J. Ridgway and Baldwin & Craddock, London.

Joplin, T. 1832, *An Analysis and History of the Currency Question*, J. Ridgway, London.

King, P. 1803, *Thoughts on the Effects of the Bank Restriction*, Cadell and Davis, London.

Laidler, D. 1975, 'On Wicksell's theory of price level dynamics', chapter 5 of his *Essays on Money and Inflation*. University of Chicago Press, Chicago.

Leijonhufvud, A. 1981, 'The Wicksell connection: variations on a theme', chapter 7 of his *Information and Coordination: Essays in Macroeconomic Theory*, Oxford University Press, New York.

Link, R. G. 1959, *English Theories of Economic Fluctuations 1815–1848*, Columbia University Press, New York.

McCulloch, J. R. 1828, Notes to A. Smith's *Wealth of Nations*, vol. 4, Edinburgh.

Nobay, A. R. and Johnson. H. G. 1977, 'Monetarism: a historic-theoretic perspective', *Journal of Economic Literature*, 15 (June), pp. 470–85.

Patinkin, D. 1965, *Money, Interest, and Prices*, 2nd edn, Harper & Row, New York.

Patinkin, D. 1972, 'Wicksell's cumulative process in theory and practice', *Studies in Monetary Economics*, Harper & Row, New York.

Ricardo, D. 1817, *The Principles of Political Economy and Taxation*, ed. P. Sraffa, Cambridge University Press, London, 1951.

Schumpeter, J. A. 1954, *History of Economic Analysis*, George Allen & Unwin, London.

Stigler, S. 1980, 'Stigler's law of eponymy', *Transactions of the New York Academy of Sciences*, 2nd ser., 39 (24 April), pp. 147–58.

Thornton, H. 1802, *An Enquiry into the Nature and Effects of the Paper Credit of Great Britain*. Together with his evidence given before the Committees of Secrecy of the two Houses of Parliament in the Bank of England, March and April, 1797, some manuscript notes, and his speeches on the Bullion Report, May 1811. Edited with an introduction by F. A. v. Hayek, Rinehart and Co., New York.

Uhr, C. 1962, *Economic Doctrines of Knut Wicksell*, University of California Press, Berkeley and Los Angeles.

Viner, J. 1937, *Studies in the Theory of International Trade*, Reprint Kelley, New York, 1965.

Warburton, C. 1967, *Depression, Inflation, and Monetary Policy: Selected Papers 1945–1953*. Johns Hopkins University Press, Baltimore, MD.

Wicksell, K. 1898, *Interest and Prices*, trans. R. F. Kahn, Reprint Kelley, New York, 1965.

4 Continuity in Keynes's Conception of Probability[1]

R. M. O'Donnell

The question addressed in this paper is whether, during his lifetime, Keynes changed his fundamental position in the philosophy of probability. Most commentators have answered in the affirmative, contending that 1931 saw Keynes abandon the logical conception of probability that was central to his earlier philosophical reflections and the *Treatise on Probability* of 1921 (hereafter *TP*), and that he adopted the subjective conception associated with that other Cambridge philosopher-economist, F. P. Ramsey. This paper opposes the conventional view and advances reasons for holding that Keynes retained a basic commitment to the logical conception throughout his life. It will not deny that Ramsey's thought exerted *some* influence on Keynes, but it will suggest that this involved an internal shift *within* the framework of the logical theory rather than the apostasy of the conventional viewpoint. The question is not merely of biographical interest. It impinges directly upon the interpretation of Keynes's stances in economics – his conceptions of uncertainty, of behaviour under uncertainty and of econometrics being salient instances. It is one of the arguments favouring the 'continuity thesis' advanced here that it is capable of providing a coherent explanation of *all* of Keynes's later writings, whereas the conventional viewpoint encounters difficulties.[2]

Conceptions of probability

It will assist discussion if comment is briefly made on two points:

1. the central characteristics of the three main philosophies of probability – the relative frequency, subjective and logical interpretations; and
2. certain *particular* features of Keynes's version of the logical theory.[3]

The *relative frequency* conception views probability as a property of nature, measured by the proportion of relevant instances in a given population. On this view, all probabilities are objective, numerical and independent of belief. The *subjective* account opposes the notion that probabilities are inherently objective, but accepts that they can all be expressed numerically. In this approach, probability is defined as the actual degree of confidence or belief that an individual has in a given proposition. Probabilities may vary between individuals without any reflection on their rationality, the only constraint on a person's freedom being conformity to the rules of the probability calculus. The usual method for converting such apparently incommensurable degrees of belief into numerical form is Ramsey's betting method. The *logical* theory also views probabilities as expressing degrees of belief, but insists that they are also objective. It conceives of probability as a unique logical relation between virtually any pair of propositions. Keynes writes this as a/h, where a is the proposition whose probability is sought and h is the proposition representing all the relevant information possessed by the individual. Such probabilities are said to be objective because they are grounded in logic which, being immutable and independent of individuals, transcends merely personal belief. Knowledge of such relations gives rise to *rational* degrees of belief in the proposition a, as distinct from purely psychological or subjective degrees of belief about a.

Keynes's development of the logical theory in the *TP* has certain notable characteristics, three of which are relevant to the present debate. The first is that along one line of division, his theory classifies probabilities into two classes – a quite small class of *numerical* probabilities comprising a single cardinal series, and a far larger class of *non-numerical* probabilities composed of many ordinal series. In general, the latter series are incommensurable in the sense that a probability in one series cannot be compared with a probability in another series, subject to the qualifications that all probabilities are comparable to 0 and 1, and that in certain cases cross-comparisons between series are possible. As regards the first class, numerical values are assignable to probabilities only under certain conditions – chiefly when the conditions of application of Keynes's principle of indifference are satisfied, of which the most important is the existence of a number of mutually exclusive alternatives. It was a point of frequent insistence by Keynes that this occurs in a minority of cases, and that non-numerical probabilities are consequently the predominant type. The possibility of irreducibly non-numerical probabilities is not admitted by the frequency theory, nor is it seriously entertained by the subjective theory.

Secondly, in Keynes's theory, knowledge of probabilities is conditional on individuals having sufficient intuition, mental power or reasoning ability to perceive the logical relation between the propositions a and h. If the individual has insufficient intuitive power for the task, say because the connection between a particular a and h is too difficult to discern, then the probability remains unknown. This creates a second important line of division in Keynes's theory – the distinction between a class of *known*

Probability theory	Objective	Complete numericalization	Belief
Relative frequency	Yes	Yes	No
Subjective	No	Yes	Yes
Logical	Yes	No	Yes

Figure 4.1 Probability

probabilities where the individual has sufficient mental insight to detect the logical relation, and a class of *unknown* probabilities where the individual does not have sufficient power (even though the probability always exists independently in the sphere of logical relations).

The final characteristic relates to Keynes's usage of relative frequency information in the formation of probabilities. All relevant statistical information, including relative frequencies, enters into the data h upon which the probability a/h depends, and in certain circumstances, this logical probability may be said to equal the relative frequency. In this way, the relative frequency theory may be regarded as a special case of the general logical theory of probability, and the objectivity of the logical conception can in some sense be brought into alignment with the objectivity of the frequency conception. But the question of when it was legitimate for a logical probability to be expressed in terms of a relative frequency was regarded by Keynes as a difficult one.

Many of the points in the preceding account are summarized in Figure 4.1. The second column refers to whether probabilities are claimed to be objective, the third to the contention that they are all capable of numerical expression, and the fourth to the proposition that there is a connection, of some fundamental kind, between probability and belief.

Ramsey's critique and Keynes's response
In an essay written in 1926, but published posthumously in the *Foundations of Mathematics* of 1931, Ramsey criticized Keynes's theory of probability and laid down part of the foundation of the modern subjectivist theory.[4] Keynes reviewed the Ramsey volume in October 1931 under the heading of 'Logic' in the *New Statesman and Nation*. The review is brief and spends almost as much time relating Ramsey to Cambridge philosophy as in actually discussing the work,[5] but it does contain a very striking passage which apparently signals repudiation by Keynes of the logical conception of probability.

Ramsey argues, as against the view which I had put forward, that probability is concerned not with objective relations between propositions but (in some sense) with degrees of belief, and he succeeds in showing that the calculus of probabilities simply amounts to a set of rules for ensuring that the system of degrees of belief which we hold shall be a *consistent* system. Thus the calculus of probabilities belongs to formal logic. But the basis of our degrees of belief – or the *a priori* probabilities, as they used to be called – is part of our human outfit, perhaps given us merely by natural selection, analogous to our perceptions and to our memories rather than to formal logic. So far I yield to Ramsey – I think he is right. But in attempting to distinguish 'rational' degrees of belief from belief in general he was not yet, I think, quite successful. It is not getting to the bottom of the principle of induction merely to say that it is a useful mental habit. (*X*, pp. 338–9)

Taken in isolation, these significant remarks seem to support the conventional view that Keynes abandoned the theory of probability of the *TP* in 1931, and became converted to, or at least sympathetic towards Ramsey's theory. While many commentators have adopted this intepretation, there has nevertheless been disagreement over what exactly Keynes is supposed to have retracted. Good's (1965, p. 7) contention is that 'in his biography of Ramsey, Keynes nobly recanted ... and admitted that subjective probabilities are primary and that credibilities [logical probabilities] might not exist'. Jeffreys (1961, p. *v*) understood Keynes to have withdrawn his 'distinctive' assumption that probabilities are only partially ordered, an interpretation which is agreeable to Jeffreys' own theory, but has been criticized by both Good (1965, p. 7) and Hicks (1979, p. 105, n2). Lindley (1968, p. 376) pressed on further: '[Keynes] withdrew his objections and admitted the correctness of Ramsey's view of probability as expressed in terms of bets. He also admitted Ramsey's argument that the rules of probability are logical deductions from proper betting behaviour, and not primitive axioms.' Schumpeter (1946, p. 502n) even went so far as to suggest that 'Ramsey's sayings became indicative of Keynes's philosophy'. Braithwaite (1975, p. 241; *VIII*, p. xxii) took a more cautious line, concluding that 'Keynes might not be unsympathetic' to the betting-quotient theory, a view echoed in an earlier work (1946, p. 284): 'Later [Keynes] was to find Ramsey's pragmatic approach sympathetic.' Although Braithwaite entered a qualification regarding induction, this does not disturb the impression left with the reader that the review marks a significant shift in Keynes's position on probability.

The remarks of these commentators, however, are mostly in the nature of *obita dicta*. They offer virtually no argument and rely almost entirely upon the construction which, *prima facie*, seems the obvious one to place upon Keynes's paragraph. Bateman (1987), however, proposes a more sophisticated variant of the conventional view and seeks somewhat more detailed analysis. In his account, Keynes changed his probability allegiance not once but *twice* – first the conversion in 1931 to Ramsey's subjective concept, and then later (during or before 1938) an acceptance of a dual position embracing both the subjective and relative frequency concepts. Bateman's position is discussed in a later section.

The case for continuity

At first blush, Keynes's paragraph does seem to support the conventional viewpoint and to pose difficulties for those who suggest close connections between Keynes's philosophy and his economics, in particular, between the *TP* and the *General Theory* (hereafter *GT*). I shall, however, advance a variety of reasons for thinking that the conventional inferences are incorrect. The necessary and sufficient indicators of what *actually* happened in Keynes's thought after 1931 are *all* his subsequent writings and not merely a brief paragraph in a single review. Once this post-1931 output is taken into account, a contrary picture emerges in which literal interpretations of the review are revealed to be superficial. Keynes's concession to Ramsey, whatever it amounts to, did not constitute a radical shift in the foundations of his thought.[6]

There are two general problems with the conventional view. The most important is that it fails to take account of Keynes's voluminous post-1931 writings. The above commentators, a majority of whom are philosophers, have not delved into Keynes's later writings, traditionally the preserve of economists, to test their hypotheses. If they had, they would have discovered that far from being sympathetic to the subjective theory, he frequently expressed views that were not only contrary to it, but were *directly descended* from the *TP*. Bateman is the notable exception here, but his arguments are restricted to only a small part of Keynes's later writings. The second problem is that the conventional view assumes that no alternative reading of Keynes's text is possible. Proof of what Keynes intended to say is now clearly impossible, but the existence of a different interpretation of his remarks (outlined below) is certainly relevant to the discussion.

To substantiate the claims of the continuity thesis – that Keynes neither threw over his particular conception of probability nor abandoned his general philosophical position in favour of Ramsey's ideas – the following seven arguments, covering a wide terrain, are marshalled.

To begin with, it is highly significant that *none* of Keynes's later writings makes any mention of Ramsey's theory, or of any reconsideration that Keynes felt compelled to undertake in the area of probability. Not a word, line or paragraph anywhere in his prolific output. This is especially true of 'My Early Beliefs' (*X*, pp. 433–50), his memoir of September 1938 in which he recalled the principal impacts on his virgin mind and wondered whether he still held by them. Although the memoir contains some inaccuracies as regards Keynes's recollections of the past, there is no reason to doubt the *basic* message he conveys regarding his present convictions, that of a *qualified reaffirmation* of his early beliefs. And while it is true that Moore rather than probability is placed at the centre of his discussion, he nevertheless mentions probability and gives no indication whatsoever that he later changed his mind in this area. Surely if Ramsey's criticisms had actually caused a fundamental shift in Keynes's views on probability or in philosophy, it would have merited recollection, at least to the extent of an aside if not a paragraph.

That Keynes did, in fact, remain committed to the logical analysis of the *TP* is indicated by his correspondence with Townshend from July to December 1938 (*XXIX*, pp. 288–94). He accepted Townshend's presupposition of a link between the *TP* and the *GT*, repeated various non-subjectivist ideas of the *TP*, and nowhere thought it necessary to suggest to Townshend, a highly sympathetic reader, that he had later abandoned its analysis. Consider the following excerpt:

> But a main point to which I would call your attention is that, on my theory of probability, the probabilities themselves, quite apart from their weight or value, are not numerical. So that, even apart from this particular point of weight, the substitution of a numerical measure needs discussion. (*XXIX*, p. 289)

Here Keynes returns to his basic concept of non-numerical probabilities, a concept in conflict with both the subjective and frequency approaches. On this issue, he never submitted to Ramsey's universal numericalization of probabilities, a point to which I shall subsequently return.

Furthermore, it is evident that Keynes retained the *TP*'s fundamental notion that probability was concerned with inferential relations between premises and conclusions expressing degrees of certainty. Consider the following illustration, only about six months after the review, from a 1932 lecture during the early development of the *GT*.

> The general upshot of this ... seems to be that the fluctuations of output and employment ... depend almost entirely on the amount of current investment – not indeed with logical necessity but with a high degree of probability in practice. ... Thus whilst we cannot deduce from observing changes of investment the exact amount of the changes in other factors, we can infer with a degree of probability approaching to certainty the direction of these other changes. (*XXIX*, p. 41)

This is the language of a logical theorist rather than that of a subjectivist. Further evidence is scattered throughout the *Collected Writings* in numerous remarks, the presuppositions and tone of which are those of an adherent of logical probability. Many of his arguments arrive at conclusions to be reasonably held on the evidence, the intervening discussion being devoted to assembling information, scrutinizing its relevance and assessing the degree of support it lends the conclusion. A second instance is provided by Keynes and Sraffa's (1938) exercise in literary detection concerning Hume's *Abstract*, an exercise based on the procedure of arguing from given evidence to a probabilistic conclusion, in this case one approaching certainty (*XXVIII*, ch. 4). Its presence may be implicit, but the model of the *TP* remained Keynes's basic method of reasoning.

A fourth consideration is that Keynes remained forever critical of the general theory of mathematical expectation upon which Ramsey's subjective approach was founded. The theory was criticized as inadequate in the *TP*, and this stream of criticism continued in his later attacks on the Benthamite calculus. In 1937, he described mathematical expectations theory as an 'extraordinary contraption of the Benthamite School' which, by multiplying numerical probabilities and advantages, generated 'a mythical system of probable knowledge' (*XIV*, p. 124). He not only declined to encourage such a calculus, but in 1938 also accused Benthamism of being 'the worm gnawing at the insides of modern civilisation and ... responsible for its present moral decay' (*X*, p. 445).[7]

Fifthly, as indicated by the passage quoted from the review, Keynes did not think Ramsey had successfully analysed what may be described as the fundamental problem of the *TP* – the distinction between rational belief and mere belief. This represents an expression of dissatisfaction with the subjectivist notion of rational belief as consistent or coherent actual belief, and its corollary that rational belief has no necessary connection with truth. Keynes's concept of rational belief in the *TP* and elsewhere is quite different, for it conceives of rational belief as ultimately grounded on truth. For Keynes, rational belief is dependent upon true propositions. Either the proposition *a* is true, or the proposition expressing the probability-relation between *a* and *h* is true. Thus Keynes was far from ready to embrace the subjective notion of rational belief, a conclusion reinforced by his remark about Ramsey not yet having got to the bottom of induction. Here the 1931 review is quite consistent with the stance of the *TP*, both suggesting that there is much more to induction that mere usefulness. Since the attempt to get to the bottom of rational argument, including induction, was a crucial object of the *TP*, Keynes had good reason for hesitating before a philosophy which failed satisfactorily to answer one of his basic questions.

The *GT* provides several highly significant illustrations of Keynes's continuity of belief in the framework of the *TP*. Two important instances will be cited, one relating to probability, the other to weight of argument. In his famous lines of 1937, Keynes explained one of the major senses in which he used the term uncertainty:

> By 'uncertain knowledge' ... I do not mean merely to distinguish what is known
> ˙ for certain from what is only probable. The game of roulette is not subject, in
> this sense, to uncertainty; nor is the prospect of a Victory bond being drawn.
> Or, again, the expectation of life is only slightly uncertain. Even the weather is
> only moderately uncertain. The sense in which I am using the term is that in
> which the prospect of a European war is uncertain, or the price of copper and
> the rate of interest twenty years hence, or the obsolescence of a new invention,
> or the position of private wealth holders in the social system in 1970. About
> these matters there is no scientific basis on which to form any calculable
> probability whatever. We simply do not know. (*XIV*, pp. 113–14)

Here is set forth the notion of *irreducible uncertainty* – a form of uncertainty not reducible to probabilities – whose similarity to Knight's distinction between risk and uncertainty has often been noted.[8] In the present context, what is striking about this passage, so often quoted yet so rarely analysed, is that it is quite incompatible with the subjectivist standpoint. On the subjective interpretation of probability, there is nothing to prevent rational agents from forming (numerical) probabilities about propositions relating to the distant future. The only restraint they face is that such probabilities be consistent with their other probabilities; otherwise they are perfectly free to assign probabilities to any proposition at all. The subjective theory is thus unable to provide a foundation to this vital sense of uncertainty in the *GT*. By contrast, Keynes's views are perfectly explicable in terms of the *unknown probabilities* of the *TP*. Rational agents are here faced with such a paucity of information in relation to their reasoning power that they are unable to detect the probability-relation a/h between a (say the rate of interest twenty years hence) and the relevant information in their possession (h) which is so scanty. It is in *this* sense that agents 'simply do not know' – they are deprived, by weakness of logical insight, of knowledge of a/h.[9]

The second instance concerns Keynes's retention of the *TP*'s novel concept of the 'weight of argument' in the theoretical background to the *GT*. This link between the two works is made clear in the *GT* (*VII*, pp. 148, 240) and his 1938 correspondence with Townshend (*XXIX*, pp. 293–4). It again supports the continuity thesis and runs counter to the conventional viewpoint. From the standpoint of subjective probability theory, the weight of argument is of little or no interest. While the accumulation of evidence is highly relevant to subjectivism in influencing revisions of probabilities, the weight of argument as an independent concept is redundant and can be dispensed with.[10] It is clear, then, in both cases, that had

Keynes really been converted to subjective probabilities he could not have written the *GT* in the way that he did, and could not have consistently held the views he advanced with so much conviction.[11]

The final argument concerns the general philosophical stances of Keynes and Ramsey. Despite their mutual respect, there were considerable philosophical antimonies between them, stemming partly from the divergent influences of Moore and Wittgenstein respectively. Whereas Keynes's philosophy was basically a form of rationalism adhering to objectivism and truth in both probability and ethics, Ramsey's was a form of pragmatism with strongly subjectivist foundations. In ethics, for example, Keynes embraced Moore's notion of goodness as an objective, intuitively knowable indefinable, while Ramsey regarded ethics as reducible to psychology.[12] Each philosophy, moreover, was a fairly strongly interconnected whole. In Keynes's case, certain fundamental themes were common to the different areas of his thought – to probability, ethics, rational belief, rational conduct, epistemology and mathematics, for example. The consequence was that a radical change to the foundations of one area (say probability) was likely to challenge the foundations of other areas and to create the need for extensive modifications throughout. Yet we find *no* upheavals in these other areas. Some changes are evident, but one is struck by the absence of fundamental departures from Keynes's underlying philosophical foundations. The absence of such departures, and the opposition between Keynes's and Ramsey's general philosophical stances, serve to cast further doubt on the conventional interpretation.

These, then, are the reasons of substance which refute the view that in 1931 Keynes underwent conversion to Ramsey's views in either probability or philosophy generally, and which support the contentions of the continuity thesis that Keynes remained an adherent of the logical theory of probability as well as of the general framework of his philosophical ideas.

The review revisited

In the light of these arguments, it is instructive to return to a closer examination of Keynes's 1931 review. Grounds for caution are revealed even within the review itself. Careful reading indicates elements of criticism of Ramsey by Keynes which make it necessary to distinguish between what Keynes accepted and what he did not. Bateman (1987) also stresses this distinction, although his treatment differs from that given below.

On Keynes's account, Ramsey showed that the probability calculus could ensure that degrees of belief, in some sense, formed a *consistent* system. *This* proposition was accepted. What he was *not* content with was Ramsey's treatment of rational belief and induction. At this point, it is judicious to refer to Ramsey's arguments concerning logic (1931, pp. 184–98), a matter usually, but wrongly, ignored by the conventional interpretation. To Ramsey, logic fell into two parts, a lesser and a larger logic. The *lesser* logic, also called formal logic or the logic of consistency, included deductive logic and probability theory. The *larger* logic, known also as human logic, inductive logic, the logic of truth and the logic of discovery, was a distinct form, independent of and sometimes incompatible with formal logic. Its concern was to discover the best general mental habits for humans to have, best being decided by how well the habits worked, this in turn being defined by success in producing opinions which were either true, or for the most part true, or more often true than those generated by alternative habits. Rationality or reasonableness was conceived in terms of the employment of these best or most useful habits. 'Induction', Ramsey argued, 'is such a useful habit, and so to adopt it is reasonable.' But beyond the fact that it worked, he thought no further justification of induction was possible. Keynes's response to Ramsey's theory may now be seen also to fall into two parts. On the one hand, he accepted, within the domain of the lesser logic, that Ramsey had demonstrated that subjective degrees of belief could be pressed into a consistent system obedient to the probability calculus. But on the other, within the realm of the larger logic, he did not accept that rationality was adequately represented by usefulness; Ramsey had not completely successfully distinguished 'rational ... belief from belief in general', nor was it explanatory of induction to say that it was merely a 'useful mental habit'. Thus Keynes did not capitulate to Ramsey's solution to the central question of the *TP*, how to theorize rational degrees of belief, including induction. In this area the *TP* had not, in Keynes's mind, been eliminated by Ramsey's theory and was therefore still standing in the field. Thus even without the external evidence supporting the argument for continuity, closer internal investigation of the review in the light of Ramsey's original essay reveals good reason for placing at least a firm qualification on the conventional interpretation.

In the light of these and previous remarks, it is instructive to consider an alternative reading of Keynes's text which makes it more consistent with the continuity thesis. The key question is just how far back the 'so far' in Keynes's text extends. On the conventional view, it goes back at least to the sentence commencing 'Ramsey argues', from which it is inferred that Keynes jettisoned his objective view of probability. The alternative reading has it extend only to 'and he succeeds', from which it merely follows that Keynes accepted subjective belief as a possible foundation for the probability calculus with no comment being passed on his basic allegiances. One cannot insist, however, that either reading is necessarily the correct one (for there can be no definitive answer here), or that Keynes was always and everywhere consistent in his writings. But his philosophical writings contain more consistency than some have allowed, and the existence of an alternative rendition which restores consistency to his overall position is certainly relevant to an analysis of why the review has, in fact, proved so misleading.

Keynes and Ramsey

But if the evidence shows that Keynes did not actually abandon the framework of his logical theory, why did he imply in 1931 that he had? Some explanation is called for. The following account relies on two propositions; first, that Keynes was enormously busy in 1930–1 with matters economic, and second, that for some years prior to this he had felt vulnerable to a challenge from Ramsey whose intellect he held in greatest respect. As a result, when the challenge finally arrived, he verbally succumbed without fully absorbing the implications of his 'surrender' and without making clear its precise nature.

What deeply preoccupied Keynes in 1931 were weighty issues in economic theory and policy. Theoretically, he was engaged in debating the *TM*, his then *magnum opus*, in commencing the reformulation of his economic thought towards the *GT*, and in lecturing in the USA on world unemployment. On the policy side, he played major roles in the deliberations of the Macmillan Committee, in the financial crisis which saw Britain's eventual departure from the gold standard, and in a controversial tariff campaign to reduce British unemployment. There were also older matters, such as the finalization of German war debts and reparations.[13]

The second element is the development of Keynes's feeling of vulnerability towards Ramsey. In 1922 it was hardly evident – he respected Ramsey as a damaging critic opposed to the logical account, but he remained confident that the *TP* analysis was along the right lines, even though further work was required. In January that year, he wrote to Broad:

> But what I really attach importance to is, of course, the general philosophical theory. I am much comforted that with that you are in general agreement. But I find that Ramsey and the other young men at Cambridge are quite obdurate, and still believe that *either* Probability is a definitely measurable entity, probably connected with Frequency, *or* is of merely psychological importance and is definitely non-logical. I recognise that they can raise some very damaging criticisms against me on these lines. But all the same I feel great confidence that they are wrong. However, we shall never have the matter properly cleared up until a big advance has been made in the treatment of Probability in relation to the theory of Epistemology as a whole.[14]

But as time passed, and with Keynes maintaining his retreat from direct engagement in fundamental philosophy, his feelings of vulnerability grew. In a 1926 letter to his German translator, he returned to the same themes, but now with more detail, different emphases and lowered confidence.

> I have not thought about the subject very deeply in recent times. But as time goes on I myself feel that there is a great deal in the book which is unsatisfactory, and, indeed, I felt this even when I was writing it.[15] It was published as it stood because it seemed to me that it would help on the subject that I should do so more effectively than if I was to try to make further refinements and revisions which might quite likely prove beyond my capacity. I believe that the ultimate theory of the subject may differ very considerably from mine. But I still think that the problems as I have posed them may be the right starting point for further research.
>
> Amongst those students in England for whose opinion I feel most respect I find a marked reluctance against finally abandoning some variant of the frequency theory. They admit my criticisms hold good on existing versions, and they are not yet ready to prepare a version which can resist them. But they maintain all the same that they have a strong instinct that some kind of frequency theory will be found in the end to be more fundamental to the whole conception of Probability than I have yet allowed. I shall not be surprised if they prove right. I suspect, however, that the first step forward will have to come through progress being made with the partly psychological subject of vague knowledge, and that further developments in a strictly logical field must wait for a clear distinction between logical probability proper and the theory of what I have called vague knowledge.[16]

Here his expressed vulnerability is towards the frequency theory, but Ramsey's shadow is still detectable, for Ramsey sought, partially at least, to harmonize his subjective account with frequencies (1931, pp. 158–9, 187–8). It also deserves remembering that on a personal level Keynes was capable of being generous, even over-generous, to those who disagreed with him, provided he considered them highly intelligent and able. That he so regarded Ramsey ('one of the brightest minds of our generation', *X*, p. 336) is plain.[17] The review was presumably intended as a tribute to a fellow Cambridge philosopher, economist and Apostle who tragically died before his full genius had flowered.

Taken as a whole then, the above factors suggest that Keynes, preoccupied with economic theory and policy, aware of an opposition containing at least one powerful mind and with virtually no motivation towards deep philosophical discussion, did not spend as much time as he would previously have done in thinking through all the implications of Ramsey's theory and its impact on his own. The consequence was that his surrender on paper was entirely misleading, and misrepresented his genuine concession to Ramsey.

What, then, was the real pull of Ramsey's thought on Keynes? I suggest three elements, of which the last is the most significant. First, a collapse of Keynes's conviction that the approach of the *TP* enjoyed unchallenged supremacy; second, a partial acceptance of some of Ramsey's strictures about the precision of ideas; and third, encouragement towards an *internal* shift within Keynes's philosophical framework – all three being compatible with his remaining committed to his basic philosophical position.

Concerning the first, Keynes was convinced by Ramsey that the probability calculus could be derived from subjectivist foundations. In the *TP* he had criticized the frequency theory for its inability to do this satisfactorily, and since the subjectivist theory had not been developed, this left the logical theory in an unchallenged position. Now it had a new rival, as a result of which he could not be so confident as to the overall dominance of the logical interpretation. On this point, he certainly had to 'yield to Ramsey' and think him 'right'. Regarding the second, Ramsey had argued that a 'chief danger' to philosophy was 'scholasticism, the essence of which is treating what is vague as if it were precise' (*X*, p. 343). There is some evidence that during the 1930s Keynes modified his views on ideas and meanings in this direction, accepting that some notions at least were 'essentially vague' (*X*, p. 440; also p. 442), but without relinquishing his background philosophy.

However, it is the third element – the internal shift – that deserves most emphasis. This may be characterized as a movement towards a more flexible view of human behaviour. It was not the subjectivization of probability theory that was really influential for Keynes in Ramsey's philosophy, but several aspects of his novel conception of 'human logic'. This is a side of Ramsey that subjectivists have not emphasized, but it is a side with obvious attractions for Keynes. He certainly saw merit in the conception as a possible way forward:

> Yet in attempting to distinguish a 'human' logic from formal logic on the one hand and descriptive psychology on the other, Ramsey may have been pointing the way to the next field of study when formal logic has been put into good order and its highly limited scope properly defined. (*X*, p. 339)

The first aspect is the idea of an expanded conception of logic that sought to theorize actual human reasoning. In the review, Keynes repeated his opposition, already evident in the *TP*, to the reduction of logic to 'dry bones' empty of human experience and content (*X*, p. 338). In this area there was a broad coincidence of viewpoint with a central objective of the *TP*. The second aspect is the notion that human logic lies somewhere between formal logic and purely descriptive psychology, that is, between a discipline that is too narrow, and one that, in embracing both the rational and non-rational, is too vast. A parallel may be drawn here between

Keynes's supportiveness regarding human logic, and the close of his 1926 letter to Urban where he thought progress in logic and probability would initially come through further analysis of the 'partly psychological subject of vague knowledge'. Vague knowledge, as the *TP* explains, arises when logical relations are *indistinctly* perceived, this feature situating it somewhere between known and unknown probabilities. It was not the same as knowledge proper, nor did it seem 'susceptible of strict logical treatment'. Keynes thought it important, however, both in the *TP* and in 1926, but being baffled by it – 'at any rate I do not know how to deal with it' (*VIII*, p. 17) – left it as one of the loose ends of his analysis. Ramsey's human logic may have appeared as a possibly fruitful avenue in relation to vague knowledge, since both shared the attributes of being reasonable in some sense without being purely logical or purely psychological. The third aspect is the suggestion that in that area of rationality which is not subservient to logic in the strict sense (regardless of whether strictness here refers to Ramsey's formal logic or Keynes's probability logic), human reasoning operates by means of rules and habits, including instinctual ones. This may be seen as additional input into Keynes's later link between reason and convention in areas of economic behaviour. Keynes began the long haul towards the *GT* a few months after the appearance of the *Treatise on Money* in October 1930, and his Ramsey review appeared in October 1931 during the early stages of this reformulation. My contention is thus that Ramsey helped nudge Keynes towards relaxing the idea that the 'strong' theory of rationality (which was the major focus of the *TP*) was completely adequate as a representation of ordinary rationality, and towards giving greater play to the various alternative strategies of 'weak rationality' (which were only implicit in the *TP*).[18] None of this, however, is intended to suggest that Keynes subscribed to Ramsey's pragmatist understanding of human logic, only that he was indirectly influenced by the idea *within* the conceptual framework of the *TP*, and that the influence emerges in the context of 'weak rationality'; that is, in some region lying between pure logic and mere psychology.

To sum up: I suggest that Keynes, at this relatively late stage of life, was too steeped in his original philosophical framework to relinquish it for another. The beliefs and mental habits formed, deepened and practised over the twenty-eight years prior to 1931 were too ingrained.[19] However, he did what he could within this framework to accommodate to new facts, ideas and criticisms, especially if they seemed to point to greater realism and understanding, or to offer hope in dealing with the unfinished business of the *TP*. What is more, no alternative philosophy was available that he regarded as equally satisfactory – Ramsey's pragmatism failed him in key areas, Marxism he saw as illogical, and empiricism never lured him.

What else might he reasonably do but remain where he was and attempt improvements? In another context, 'My Early Beliefs' reveals the same willingness to modify a philosophical position without collapsing into apostasy. My conclusion is thus that Ramsey *did* influence Keynes, but that the influence was *not* a radical conversion to subjectivism in probability or elsewhere, and was indirect rather than direct. It was in the nature of an encouragement to Keynes, within his own framework, to widen his horizons, to place greater emphasis on the modes of 'weak rationality' and to desist from theorizing predominantly in terms of 'strong rationality' as he had done in the *TP*. This expansion naturally has significant implications for the *GT*.

Bateman's argument

According to Bateman, Keynes's conception of probability underwent at least *two* changes after 1921. The first is identical with that suggested by previous commentators, the switch to subjectivism in 1931 in response to Ramsey. The second change is said to be evident in Keynes's remarks on Tinbergen's econometric work. Dating this change is more difficult, but it is claimed to have emerged by 1938. After this transition, the contention is that Keynes adopted a *dual* position on probability, accepting both the relative frequency and subjective conceptions in different spheres. On this view, once Keynes had abandoned the logical concept of the *TP*, he never returned to it.

Two features of Bateman's discussion of the first change are noteworthy. To begin with, it relies entirely on the words of Keynes's 1931 review and their usual interpretation. The correctness of this interpretation and the sufficiency of the paragraph in the review to settle the question is implicitly assumed. Secondly, Bateman rightly points out the need to distinguish those parts of Ramsey's theory that were acceptable to Keynes from those which were not. He then locates the idea that consistent subjective beliefs are rational within the *unacceptable* parts, from which it is concluded that while Keynes now accepted subjective probabilities, he also regarded them as *irrational*.

In relation to the second change, Bateman draws upon Keynes's treatment of induction, and its application to statistical inference in the final part of the *TP*. In particular, it is suggested that Keynes concluded the *TP* with a significant concession towards the frequency theory – namely, that at some time in the future the frequency theory *might* have to be admitted in the natural sciences as a replacement for the logical theory. On this view, the *TP* had already prepared the ground for the possibility of future acceptance of the frequency theory in the natural sciences. Although it took time to occur, the second change is then said to be unambiguously revealed in Keynes's review of Tinbergen and the associated correspondence (*XIV*, pp. 285–320). From 1938 onwards, Keynes is thus presented as a dualist in probability theory, accepting the frequency theory for that sphere of natural science involving stable frequencies, and the subjective theory in all other areas, including economic decision-making.

Having briefly outlined the nature of Bateman's argument, I turn now to some of the criticisms that may be levelled against it. In the first place, no test of the hypothesis against Keynes's post-1931 output is attempted. It is even claimed that Keynes's later economic writings are not important to the question of changes in his thinking about probability, and that the path of such thinking can be traced without reference to these writings. This proposition seems to me to be quite erroneous. The motivation behind it is commendable – the desire to avoid the unsatisfactory features of reading *backwards* from the *GT* into the *TP* – but it is not necessary to advance such a dubious claim to satisfy this motive. It leads to an artificial division between Keynes's later economic theorizing and his views on probability, and is capable of generating major inconsistencies between the two. As argued previously, the treatment of uncertainty in Keynes's later economic writings is simply inconsistent with the subjective theory. Keynes could not therefore have written the *GT* had he been a subjectivist in probability theory (unless the possibility is entertained of radical inconsistencies in the thought of someone highly practised in logical argument).

Another difficulty Bateman's thesis encounters in relation to the *GT* concerns his characterization of Keynes's economic agents. These are portrayed as employing consistent subjective probability sets, and at the same time as being irrational. Now this is a highly peculiar stance in several respects. In relation to Bateman's thesis, it implies that Keynes had not really digested the subjective theory fully, for on this theory rationality *means* consistency. And if Keynes had only half-accepted the subjective theory, then much of the steam is taken out of the conventional viewpoint. It returns us to the puzzle of sorting out what Keynes actually did, and did not, accept in 1931, a puzzle to which what seems to me to be the right kind of answer has been suggested above. A second peculiarity arises in relation to Keynes's economic writings. Nowhere does Keynes set forth, implicitly or explicitly, these assumptions about economic agents. Indeed, economic theory of the kind Keynes engaged in would be impossible on the assumption that agents were irrational. Keynes certainly had grave reservations about the *traditional* theory of rationality used in economics, but his solution was not to abandon rationality. It was to substitute, wherever possible, his own alternative theory, a theory descended directly from the logical framework of the *TP*. In a nutshell, this theory was that economic agents behave as rationally *as their circumstances permit*, different circumstances thus calling forth different forms of rational behaviour. By orthodox standards, some of these responses might appear irrational, but the cause of this lay in the environment in which agents were embedded, not in assumptions of irrationality. Finally what of Keynes's own use of probabilistic inference? Are we to conclude that Keynes, as an alleged subjectivist, regarded his own probability-based arguments as irrational? This too does not square with either the letter or spirit of Keynes's writings, or the portraits assembled by colleagues and commentators. None of these peculiarities arise, however, in relation to the continuity thesis, since Keynes's own reasonings and his remarks on economic agents are all compatible with the underlying framework of the *TP* and the logical concept of probability.

In relation to Keynes's second putative change, Bateman's reading of Keynes on Tinbergen begins with sound points but then makes an unsupported leap. It is very difficult to see how the conclusion drawn can in any way be inferred from the evidence presented. The two main premisses are not here disputed, namely, that Keynes thought economic material had to suggest homogeneity or uniformity over time before inductive or statistical techniques could be properly applied, and that he thought there were differences between the natural and moral sciences. But there is a gulf between these and other propositions on the one side, and the allegedly clear conclusion on the other that Keynes accepted the frequency theory as applicable in the natural sciences and the subjective theory in economics. What Bateman sees as an unambiguous connection seems to me to be non-existent. To my mind, the gulf is unbridgeable, but even if it were, the lines of connecting argument need to be set in place. On the other hand, Keynes's views on Tinbergen and on science can be explained quite adequately in terms of his earlier philosophical positions. With regard to the conclusion of the *TP*, it is also tenuous and unnecessary to postulate a possible concession by Keynes to the frequency theory at some future date. What has been overlooked here is the fact that Keynes gave relative frequencies a definite role *within* the framework of the logical theory. Frequencies entered the data *h* of argument, from which it becomes possible to conclude, in the absence of counter-indications, that probabilities may equal relative frequencies in certain situations. As well as being evident in the *TP*, the point was alluded to in Keynes's Apostles paper of 1904 in which he first set forth his logical conception of probability.

> I do not, of course, deny that the evidence, on which any statement claiming to be probable rests, may be and very frequently is of the nature of a series; my reason for supposing that *x* is probable may often be the fact that in the past, under circumstances similar in certain respects, *x* has happened more often than not; my point is this – that the evidence need not always be of this nature

and that in any case to base a statement of probability on past frequency is not the same thing as to make a certainly true statement with regard to future frequency.[20]

Using frequency *information* in this way, however, is an entirely different matter from opening the door to future acceptance of the frequency *theory* of probability. Again, Keynes's views can be explained by means of the *TP*, without the need to invoke conceptual shifts which are difficult to sustain.

Conclusion

The arguments in favour of the continuity thesis and against the conventional viewpoint appear to be as close to conclusive as it is possible to obtain in questions of this kind. Whatever Keynes's intentions were when he wrote of 'yielding' to Ramsey (a statement with at least two interpretations), it is clear from his later writings that he did not in fact abandon the logical theory of probability in favour of the subjective. If this discussion has a moral, it is that it is insufficient to advance conjectures on the basis of certain interpretations of specific passages in Keynes's writings. The only real tribunal in this area is the test of one's hypotheses against the evidence of *all* his other writings, within which his economic writings are a crucially important and certainly not irrelevant part. Whereas these other writings conflict with the subjective theory, they are fully intelligible within the framework of his logical theory.[21]

Notes

1. A paper delivered to the History of Economics Society meeting in Toronto, June 1988. I would like to thank conference participants for their comments, particularly my discussant, Henry Kyburg, whose remarks were most helpful. I am also grateful to King's College, Cambridge for permission to quote from the Keynes papers.
2. The discussion is partly based on arguments initially set out in O'Donnell (1982), a revised and expanded version of which is to be published as O'Donnell (1989). References to Keynes's writings are to the Royal Economic Society's edition of the *Collected Writings of John Maynard Keynes*, and take the form of the volume number in italics followed by page numbers. The *Treatise on Probability (TP)* is volume *VIII*, the *General Theory (GT)* volume *VII*.
3. For further discussion of philosophies of probability, see, for example, Weatherford (1982) and Kyburg (1974, ch. 1). For detailed examination of Keynes's approach, see O'Donnell (1982; 1989, chs 2–6).
4. Ramsey (1931, ch. 7, 'Truth and Probability').
5. The review, in slightly abbreviated form, is reprinted in *Essays in Biography* (*X*, pp. 336–9).
6. Hicks (1979, p. 105 n2) also doubts that Keynes modified his views in Ramsey's direction but provides very little discussion.
7. In 1929 Ramsey (1931, p. 256) himself raised some doubts about his use of mathematical expectation in 1926. On Keynes's criticisms of Bentham and Benthamism, see also *VIII*, p. 21; *IX*, Pt IV, ch. 2; *X*, p. 184 n5, pp. 445–7; *XIV*, pp. 112–13, 122, 124.

8. It can be argued, in fact, that Keynes preceded Knight by at least a decade in developing this distinction; see O'Donnell (1989, pp. 262–3).
9. Throughout Keynes's philosophy, both before and after the *TP*, there is an intimate connection between knowledge and truth. In the present context, the knowledge that is absent concerns the true probability relation, a/h.
10. For further discussion of the weight of argument, see O'Donnell (1982) and (1989, ch. 4). Kyburg (1968, p. 59) also suggests subjectivism has difficulty in entertaining a notion of rational belief with the two independent dimensions of probability and weight.
11 For further discussion of continuity between the *TP* and the *GT*, see O'Donnell (1982; and 1989 chs 8–12).
12. Ramsey (1931, pp. 289–90) also took aesthetics, contrary to Keynes, to be a matter of psychology without objective standards. In fact, Ramsey's subjectivism in several areas can be viewed as a reaction to the objectivism promulgated by Keynes.
13. On Keynes's activities in 1931, see volumes *XIII*, *XVIII* and *XX* of the *Collected Writings*.
14. Keynes to C. D. Broad, 31 January 1922 (Keynes Papers, King's College Library).
15. At the conclusion of the *TP*, desiring to withdraw from active participation in the probability debate, Keynes left doors open for further work which would extend and possibly modify his arguments and conclusions:

    I believe that the foregoing analysis is along the right lines and that it carries the inquiry a good deal further than it has been carried hitherto. But it is not conclusive, and I must leave to others its more exact elucidation. (*VIII*, p. 457)

    The inquiry ... I have pushed as far as I can. It deserves a profounder study than logicians have given it in the past. (*VIII*, p. 459)

    In writing a book of this kind the author must, if he is to put his point of view clearly, pretend *sometimes* to a little more conviction than he feels. He must give his own argument a chance, so to speak, nor be too ready to depress its vitality with a wet cloud of doubt. It is a heavy task to write on these problems; and the reader will perhaps excuse me if I have *sometimes* pressed on a little faster than the difficulties were overcome, and with decidedly more confidence than I have always felt. (*VIII*, p. 467, emphasis added)

    These remarks reflect the attitude of a non-dogmatic pioneer, however, and should not be read as indicating any deep or final scepticism on Keynes's part, or any possible future concession to the frequency theory (on which see the following discussion of Bateman's interpretation).
16. Keynes to F. M. Urban, 15 May 1926 (Keynes Papers, King's College Library). In the *TP* Keynes found himself forced, by the absence of a 'recent exposition' of the frequency theory, to advance a 'generalized' version for purposes of criticism. As a result, he was not 'absolutely certain' that 'a partial rehabilitation' of the frequency theory was ruled out (*VIII*, p. 119).
17. Earlier, after seeking Ramsey's assistance on certain points during the discussion of the *TP*, Keynes described him in a letter of 31 January 1922 to Broad as 'far and away the most brilliant undergraduate who has appeared for many years in the border-country between Philosophy and Mathematics' (Keynes Papers, King's College Library). At the time Ramsey was only eighteen. Others whose minds Keynes respected, even when opposed to his own, were Jevons, Edgeworth, Wittgenstein, Robertson, Hawtrey and, to some extent, Hayek.
18. For further discussion of the key distinction between strong and weak forms of rationality, see O'Donnell (1982; 1989, chs 4, 12).
19. There is an important element of self-reference, I submit, in the two following remarks by Keynes. The first is the opening sentence of the 1931 review, while the other occurs in the final paragraph of the *GT*.

    Logic, like lyrical poetry, is no employment for the middle-aged. (*X*, p. 336)

    ...in the field of economic and political philosophy there are not many who are

influenced by new theories after they are twenty-five or thirty years of age. (*VII*, pp. 383–4)
   In 1931, Keynes was forty-eight.
20. 'Ethics in Relation to Conduct', Keynes Papers, King's College Library.
21. Since experience shows that the continuity issue is capable of provoking a variety of viewpoints, I am moved to propose a ground-rule for subsequent debate. My plea is that participants should seek to ensure that their interpretations are consistent with all of Keynes's post-1931 writings, not only as regards the cluster of concepts surrounding probability, uncertainty, expectations and rationality, but also as regards his policy writings. Alternatively, if an inconsistency in Keynes is postulated, then additional arguments supporting the inconsistency should be advanced. The aim behind such a proposal is to encourage interpretations which are robust and well argued.

References

Bateman, B. W. 1987, 'Keynes's changing conception of probability', *Economics and Philosophy* 3 (October).

Braithwaite, R. B. 1946 'Obituary note on Keynes', *Mind* LV.

Braithwaite, R. B. 1975, 'Keynes as a philosopher', in Keynes (1975).

Good, I. J. 1965, *The Estimation of Probabilities*, Research Monograph no.30, Massachusetts Institute of Technology Press, Cambridge, Mass.

Hicks, J. 1979, *Causality in Economics* Basil Blackwell, Oxford.

Jeffreys, H. 1961, *Theory of Probability*, 3rd edn., Oxford University Press, Oxford.

Keynes, M. (ed.) 1975, *Essays on John Maynard Keynes*, Cambridge University Press, Cambridge.

Kyburg, H. E. 1968, 'Bets and beliefs', *American Philosophical Quarterly* 5(1) (January).

Kyburg, H. E. 1974, *The Logical Foundations of Statistical Inference*, D. Reidel, Dordrecht.

Lindley, D. V. 1968, 'Keynes, John Maynard II. Contributions to statistics', *International Encyclopedia of the Social Sciences*, Macmillan and the Free Press, New York.

O'Donnell, R. M. 1982, *Keynes: Philosophy and Economics, An Approach to Rationality and Uncertainty*, PhD dissertation, Cambridge, England.

O'Donnell, R. M. 1989, *Keynes: Philosophy, Economics and Politics, The Philosophical Foundations of Keynes's Thought and their Influence on his Economics and Politics*, Macmillan, London.

Ramsey, F. P. 1931, *The Foundations of Mathematics and Other Logical Essays*, ed. R. B. Braithwaite, Routledge & Kegan Paul, London.

Schumpeter, J. A. 1946, 'John Maynard Keynes 1883–1946', *American Economic Review*, 36(4) (September).

Weatherford, R. 1982, *Philosophical Foundations of Probability Theory*, Routledge & Kegan Paul, London.

5 The Elusive Logical Relation: An Essay on Change and Continuity in Keynes's Thought

B. W. Bateman

In his essay 'Continuity in Keynes's Conception of Probability', Rod O'Donnell has offered a relatively new interpretation of J. M. Keynes's thought. Whereas commentators have traditionally taken Keynes (1931) at his word that he abandoned his logical theory of probability in reaction to Frank Ramsey's 1926 critique, O'Donnell has suggested that we re-read this apparent capitulation in light of Keynes's subsequent writings. Embedded in those writings is said to be evidence that Keynes really had in mind a shift within the framework of his *Treatise on Probability* which preserved his original belief in the logical theory of probability. Sir John Hicks (1979), Tony Lawson (1985) and Robin Rowley and Omar Hamouda (1988) have previously suggested that Keynes was not really capitulating in his response to Ramsey, but O'Donnell has offered a more comprehensive argument for what he terms the 'continuity thesis'.

As against my 1987 essay, which elaborated Keynes's change of heart largely in reference to his review of Ramsey's *Foundations of Mathematics* and his exchange with Tinbergen on econometrics, O'Donnell suggests that *all* of Keynes's post-1931 writings be considered in establishing the empirical validity of the continuity thesis. Whereas I had originally used the Ramsey review and the Tinbergen exchange as inductive evidence and extrapolated from them the hypothesis that one would find individuals employing subjective epistemic probabilities in *The General Theory*, O'Donnell wants *The General Theory* to be a part of the inductive evidence. And while I still feel completely comfortable with my original intent not to encumber the examination of these other writings with a preconception of what should be there given one's interpretation of *The General Theory*, I agree that one way or another a thesis must be compatible with *all* the evidence. Thus, this essay is a consideration of four *pieces of evidence* that bear on the question of Keynes's post-1931 conception of probability: his 1938 essay 'My Early Beliefs', *The General Theory*, his correspondence with Townshend, and his exchange with Tinbergen. This would seem to cover everything.

The purpose in considering each of these cases will be to show how they manifest Keynes's abandonment of the logical theory of probability. His logical theory had rested on the supposition that there are unique, objective degrees of belief that relate a premiss and a conclusion; thus, any two people with the same information could intuit this logical relation and thereby agree on the probability of (or degree of belief in) the conclusion. Adherents of both the continuity thesis and the changing thesis agree on this much.[1] The point of disagreement is on whether Keynes continued to believe that these logical relations existed.

Unfortunately for the continuity thesis, *Keynes never once mentions the existence of these logical relations after 1931.* O'Donnell's argument thus consists of an effort to infer continued belief in their existence; using circumstantial evidence, he attempts to construct a case for believing that Keynes's statements follow from a belief in objective logical relations. In each case, however, there is direct or indirect evidence that Keynes's failure to mention the logical relations is due to the fact that he did not believe in their existence.

My early beliefs

The primary document in any consideration of the influence of Keynes's early philosophical work on his later thought must certainly be 'My Early Beliefs'. This essay, written in 1938, but published posthumously in 1949, was delivered to the Bloomsbury Memoir Club and takes as its point of departure a 1915 meeting between D. H. Lawrence and several of Keynes's circle of friends at Cambridge. The meeting was a failure in that Lawrence was repelled by what he saw at Cambridge and Keynes's memoir is a critical examination of his early beliefs to see if Lawrence might not have been justified in his revulsion. At first sight, this seems an unlikely ground for a discussion of probability, but as Keynes points out, probability lies at the heart of the story.

At first sight, the story is also somewhat ironic since he concludes that Lawrence was justified in his revulsion given that Keynes and his friends lacked a respect for the general rules of society. How, one wonders, could D. H. Lawrence be *repulsed* by anyone who lacked respect for rules? Should not Lawrence have been *attracted* to such people? And even more ironically, how is it that Keynes could have changed into a person more acceptable to Lawrence by coming to accept the importance of general social mores?

The answer, in Keynes's explanation, is that his own rejection of rules was based on the rationalist calculation of what was good. What Lawrence encountered was a closed circle of individuals who had appropriated for themselves the right to judge what was right or wrong. Although they may have agreed on the end, there was a violent clash on the appropriate means to achieving that end, Lawrence was repulsed by Keynes's rationalist beliefs, not by his attitude on rules. Similarly Keynes argues, he became more akin to Lawrence's position later in his life when he abandoned his rationalistic beliefs, even though this abandonment led him to believe in the efficacy of rules.

But what of probabilities? How do they fit into the story? Keynes mentions that they do when he says that 'The large part played by considerations of probability in his [G. E. Moore's] theory of right conduct was, indeed, an important contributory cause to my spending all the leisure of many years on that subject' (JMK, X, p. 445). And this is made clear when he says that he and the others under Moore's influence considered questions of probable outcome in their rationalistic calculations of right conduct. 'In valuing the consequences did one assess them at their actual value as it turned out eventually to be, or their probable value at the time? If at their probable value, how much evidence as to possible consequences was it one's duty to collect before applying the calculus?' (JMK, X, p. 439). But given that he was speaking to a group consisting mainly of writers and other artists, most of whom he believed had never even read Moore's *Principia Ethica*, Keynes said no more about the technical aspects of his work in probability.

One need not look far, however, to find an explanation of probability's role in Keynes's early rejection of rules.[2] Keynes's early essays (deposited in the King's College Library) and chapter 26 of *Probability* detail the story. Moore had argued in *Principia Ethica* for the need to follow general rules of conduct in conditions of uncertainty under the assumption that these rules suggested the actions with the highest frequency of good outcomes. Keynes rejected this argument by redefining probabilities; he asserted that probabilities are degrees of belief rather than relative frequencies. This meant that when one made an expected value calculation under conditions of uncertainty that one was weighting the good (or bad) of each possible outcome by the degree of belief in its occurrence rather than by the frequency of its outcome. This broke the hegemony of rules by removing the need to turn to them to identify frequencies of occurrence. In a particular situation, one need only intuit the objective good and the objective degree of belief attaching to each outcome and then base one's action on the resultant calculation. By constructing objective, logical relations as the basis for these degrees of belief Keynes was able to make probabilities situation-specific (i.e. the correct logical relation was always dependent on one's actual information) and known strictly through intuition. The argument was persuasive enough to convince Moore to drop his argument for following rules in his subsequent book *Ethics* (1912).

Unfortunately for the continuity thesis, Keynes was eventually to become disenchanted with the pursuit of objective degrees of belief and objective good. Of these early rationalistic beliefs, he reports that 'some sort of relation to neo-platonism it surely was. But we should have been very angry at the time with such a suggestion' (JMK, X, p. 438). With time, however, it became impossible to maintain a belief in these platonic essences.

> Thus we were brought up – with Plato's absorption in the good in itself, with a scholasticism which outdid St. Thomas, in calvinistic withdrawal from the pleasures and successes of Vanity Fair, and oppressed with all the sorrows of Werther. It did not prevent us from laughing most of the time and we enjoyed supreme self-confidence, superiority and contempt towards all the rest of unconverted world. But it was hardly a state of mind which a grown-up person in his senses could sustain literally. (JMK, X, p. 442)

Now one might protest that this last passage is only a rejection of the *attitude* that accompanied Keynes's early Platonic beliefs, but that interpretation is inconsistent with the rest of Keynes's story. The memoir's major conclusion is that Keynes and his friends became less repulsive by abandoning their belief in rationalistic calculation. In what amounts to one of the greatest vacillations of a man Harrod (1951, p. 302) characterized as an 'inveterate vacillator', Keynes came to accept the necessity of certain rules of conduct, and the only interpretation of Keynes's beliefs consistent with this acceptance is that he abandoned his belief in the logical relations that stand behind degrees of belief. If his original rejection of rules was based on these logical relations, then it seems obvious that he would have abandoned them when he abandoned this original position on rules. This seems inescapably the case when one considers his changed feelings about the efficacy of basing arguments on Platonic, rationalistic essences. If we are to believe the continuity thesis, we must be persuaded that Keynes could have accepted rules while still maintaining the basis for his original rejection of them, or equivalently, we must be persuaded of why his statements about his rejection of his earlier rationalistic, Platonic thinking do not apply to his early conception of probability.

All we have in favour of the continuity thesis, however, is that it is 'significant' that Ramsey is not mentioned in the memoir and that it offers a 'qualified reaffirmation' of the early Moorean influence on Keynes's later thought. But neither of these would really seem to be support for the continuity thesis. Ramsey was eleven years old in 1915 when the meeting with Lawrence took place and so would not be expected to appear. Since Keynes mentions, but does not repeat, the full story of the connection of his work in probability to his rejection of rules, he also would not have been expected to have discussed the technical side of his later change of heart about probability. Again, Ramsey's absence is not unexpected. The reaffirmation of Moorean values is no real evidence for the continuity thesis either. All Keynes says is that he gained from Moore a continuing dislike for Benthamite utilitarianism; significantly, however, this is qualified to point out that the original basis for this rejection, the objective, Platonic nature of 'true' good, no longer holds and it is only a general rejection of Benthamite utilitarianism that remains. The part of Moore's argument that he rejects is more germane than the part he keeps, and actually casts serious doubt on the continuity thesis.

The General Theory

The question of the nature of the expectations in *The General Theory* is a hoary and polemical one. It would take a *long* descriptive essay simply to catalogue the many answers that have been offered. And although one of these interpretations is discussed in the conclusion, for present purposes it is possible to stick to the argument at hand and avoid the detour of this large secondary literature.[3]

The argument at hand starts from the fact that Keynes makes extensive use of probabilities in *The General Theory*. Using them as weights in the expectations of agents, he finds use for them in the aggregate demand, aggregate supply, consumption, investment and liquidity preference functions. They are first introduced in chapter 3, 'The Principle of Effective Demand'. 'An entrepreneur, who has to reach a practical decision as to his scale of production, does not, of course, entertain a single undoubting expectation of what the sales-proceeds of a given output will be, but several hypothetical expectations held with varying degrees of probability and definiteness' (JMK, VII, p. 24). After this, they enter frequently in 'mathematical expectations' or 'certainty equivalents' when Keynes represents expectations as a sum of the values of possible outcomes each weighted by its probability of occurrence.

The first question then is whether these probabilities refer to relative frequencies or to degrees of belief. If the latter, a second question is whether they are subjective degrees of belief reflecting the rationalistic, Platonic logical relation connecting one's information to propositions asserting each of the possible outcomes.

It would seem impossible to hold that Keynes had in mind relative frequencies for these calculations. This follows from his many comments about the volatility of expectations in the face of new information and the way in which he describes speculators forming their expectations on the basis of stock and bond market swings. Concrete evidence would also seem to follow from his well-known 1937 essay 'The General Theory of Employment' when he says, 'About these matters [investment outcomes] there is no scientific basis on which to form any calculable probability whatever'. Keynes says in *Probability* that the natural sciences are on the way to providing a justification for the use of relative frequencies (p. 428); he acknowledges that they have done so in his correspondence on the debate with Tinbergen; and here he is explicitly denying that the probabilities employed by economic agents are relative frequencies akin to those generated by stable physical or biological processes.[4]

This brings us to the question of the possible existence of the logical relations upon which agents might base their degrees of belief. The existence of these logical relations is never mentioned and, in fact, Keynes explicitly denies that there is a philosophical basis for unique, objective probabilities.

> We are assuming, in effect, that the existing market valuation, however arrived at, is uniquely correct in relation to our existing knowledge of the facts which will influence the yield of the investment, and that it will only change in proportion to changes in this knowledge; though, philosophically speaking, it cannot be uniquely correct, since our existing knowledge does not provide a sufficient basis for a calculated mathematical expectation. (JMK, VII, p. 152)

This passage, which has been used as the basis for untold interpretations of Keynes's book, seems to say no more than that there is no philosophical basis for forming objective probabilities. And since the philosophical basis for Keynes's earlier probabilities was the existence of logical relations, it would seem that Keynes's economic agents are employing subjective degrees of belief which cannot be inferred from, or calculated on,the basis of said logical relations.

The absence of these logical relations is not the only problem which *The General Theory* provides for O'Donnell's defence of the continuity thesis, however. One element of his defence is that Keynes could not have really adopted Ramsey's subjective theory since it depended on the use of mathematical expectation to calculate the degrees of belief and Keynes was 'forever critical' of mathematical expectation. But if this was the case, then some argument must be made as to why Keynes uses mathematical expectation so extensively to represent agents' expectations.

The Townshend correspondence
A particularly compelling statement of Keynes's acceptance of Ramsey's schema for calculating subjective degrees of belief using mathematical expectation is found in his 1938 correspondence with his former pupil, Hugh Townshend. He and Townshend were corresponding about the nature of expectations when Keynes wrote on 27 July explaining that the

Ramsey method could be employed to determine the numerical values for the subjective probabilities implicit in agents' *arbitrary* decisions.

> The matter you are tackling is a very important and interesting one often in my mind. But the enclosed treatment seems to me still too much half-baked. I fancy one has to tackle it on the basis of 'equivalent certainties'. But, above all, one wants a few rather clear and striking examples. I doubt if your example of the St. Petersburg paradox is good in this connection, since it is too extreme. But a main point to which I would call your attention is that, on my theory of probability, the probabilities themselves, quite apart from their weight or value, are not numerical. So that, even apart from this particular point of weight, the substitution of a numerical measure needs discussion.
>
> Moreover the economic problem is, of course, only a particular department of the general principles of conduct, although particularly striking in this connection because it seems to bring in numerical estimations by some system of arranging alternative decisions in order of preference, some of which will provide a norm by being numerical. But that still leaves millions of cases over where one cannot even arrange an order of preference. When all is said and done, there is an arbitrary element in the situation. (JMK, XXIX, pp. 288–9)

O'Donnell quotes the sixth sentence of the paragraph in an effort to argue that since Keynes did not believe that probabilities are inherently numerical that he could not have accepted Ramsey's conception of probabilities in which 'they can all be expressed numerically', but this represents a misunderstanding of what Keynes and Ramsey said.

First, there is the paramount question of the existence of the logical relations. Again, there is *no* mention of them. Indeed, people are depicted as making decisions in the face of uncertainty in an *arbitrary* manner rather than on some rationalistic basis. As Ramsey suggests, it may be possible to infer implicit probabilities from these arbitrary decisions, but the decisions are not made on the basis of logical relations. Thus, to imply that 'my theory' is a reference to his earlier work seems a clear misunderstanding.

Second, it is simply wrong to premiss an argument on the assertion that Ramsey believed that *all* probabilities are numerical. Ramsey never said this and, in fact, said just the opposite in his essay. In considering his schema of inferring probabilities from betting quotients he makes several concluding, qualifying remarks. Among these is his admission that his schema will not work for cases with an infinite number of outcomes:

> Thirdly, nothing has been said about degrees of belief when the number of alternatives is infinite. About this I have nothing useful to say, except that I doubt if the mind is capable of contemplating more than a finite number of alternatives. It can consider questions to which an infinite number of answers are possible, but in order to consider the answers it must lump them into a finite number of groups. (Ramsey, 1931, p. 183)

But even beyond the mistaken notion that Ramsey believed all probabilities are numerical is a mistaken notion of the nature of his measurement schema. Ramsey never says that degrees of belief are inherently numerical, only that he has a method for making rough first approximations of them in some limited cases. Likewise, Keynes believed that while degrees of belief are not necessarily numerical, they are susceptible to a pragmatic first approximation in some cases (Ramsey, 1931, p. 2).

To the extent, then, that O'Donnell has placed his defence of the continuity thesis on the numerical nature of Ramsey's probabilities, he has greatly weakened the plausibility of his argument. There is nothing incompatible between what Keynes and Ramsey said in this regard.

And, of course, for the third time, we have failed to find any direct evidence of Keynes's belief in the objective logical relations that had previously undergirded his theory of probability.

The Tinbergen debate

As in the case of *The General Theory*, the Keynes–Tinbergen debate raises hoary and polemical questions. For that reason, it is best to stick to the purpose at hand and examine the evidence for information concerning Keynes's conception of probability at the time of the debate (1939–40).

There is not much direct to say, however, for the debate involves an argument over the nature of statistical induction. Keynes talks extensively about the importance of careful inductive work, but he never couches the discussion in terms of the probability of the hypothesis which is being examined. This might be taken as a toss-up since Keynes argues about induction (a carry-over from *Probability*) but also never mentions the elusive logical relations.

But because O'Donnell takes the presence of inductive arguments in Keynes's writings as evidence of a belief in the continued existence of logical relations, it is worthwhile pointing out that there is not a necessary relationship between the two. Certainly, when Keynes spoke of inductive arguments in *Probability*, he was speaking of the way in which information was used to ascertain the true logical relationship, but he admits himself (JMK, VIII, pp. 293–4) that he can offer no ultimate justification for believing that the inductive process actually does lend credence to an hypothesis. Thus, his admission at the end of the book that carefully induction in the natural sciences might eventually justify belief in a frequency theory. And Bertrand Russell was quick to point out in his review (1922) of *Probability* that it was possible to separate Keynes's argument about the process of induction from his definition of probabilities as logical relations. It is, therefore, not surprising to find no mention of logical relations in Keynes's critique of Tinbergen; it is perfectly reasonable to speak of the inductive process regardless of whether one believes in the existence of logical relations. In a similar vein, it was perfectly reasonable for Keynes, in his review of Ramsey, to accept Ramsey's conception of probability while rejecting his justification of induction.

Conclusion

The *raison d'être* of this essay is the search for the elusive post-1931 logical relation. In each of the four cases studied, however, there is no mention of their existence and a clear implication that Keynes no longer believed in them. And given Ramsey's direct and withering attack on their existence, one would surely have expected some rejoinder from Keynes in his review if he had thought Ramsey unfair or incorrect. After all, Keynes took Ramsey on very directly in saying that his theory of induction was implausible:

> But let us now return to a more fundamental criticism of Mr. Keynes' views, which is the obvious one that there really do not seem to be any such things as the probability relations he describes. He supposes that, at any rate in certain cases, they can be perceived; but speaking for myself I feel confident that this is not true. I do not perceive them, and if I am to be persuaded that they exist it must be by argument; moreover I shrewdly suspect that others do not perceive them either, because they are able to come to so very little agreement as to which of them relates any two given propositions. (Ramsey, 1931, p. 161)

Could Ramsey have been more blunt? Could Keynes have had a clearer statement to refute?

In fact, it is appropriate to conclude by going back to consider what Keynes did say in the review, both to clear up the question of his attitude towards the logical relations and to clear up a possible misunderstanding of my own position. The key consideration is whether or not Keynes believed that his agents were in some sense rational:

> But while Keynes was willing to accept Ramsey's subjective epistemic theory of probability, as well as his suggestion that the probability calculus had a useful role to play in determining the consistency of subjective probabilities, he was not willing to accept Ramsey's contention that consistent subjective degrees of belief were in any way rational.

> ...in attempting to distinguish "rational" degrees of belief from belief in general he was not yet, I think, quite successful. It is not getting to the bottom of the principle of induction merely to say that it is a useful mental habit. (Keynes, 1972, p. 339)

> In *A Treatise on Probability*, Keynes's argument that probabilities were rational was based on his idea that they had been inferred correctly from the available information; in Ramsey's argument the rationality of probabilities is

strictly a function of their consistency. Keynes was willing to accept that people form subjective probabilities in the course of their everyday decision making, but he was not willing to accept that such probabilities were rational. That is, he was willing to give up the idea that probabilities as he conceived them were objective, but since the rationality of probabilities was synonymous with their objectivity he insisted that these subjective probabilities were not rational. (Bateman, 1987, pp. 107–8)

O'Donnell objects to this interpretation for two reasons. First, it is said that in accepting Ramsey's subjective probabilities, but not their rationality, one undercuts the idea that Keynes accepted Ramsey's position at all. Second, it is said that *The General Theory* could not have been written on an assumption of irrationality.

The first of these positions is very odd and ignores much of my argument. There is no logical reason to suppose that Keynes would have accepted *everything* that Ramsey suggested simply because he accepted the core idea of subjective probabilities. Does anyone ever take anything whole cloth when they adapt a new position? One of the oldest jokes among statisticians involves the idea that Bayesian ideas are not predominant because no two Bayesians have exactly the same concept of probability. But while I have made a very careful argument in my 1987 essay as to why Keynes's ideas on induction led to these expected differences between Keynes and Ramsey, O'Donnell overlooks this completely when he says, 'In relation to Bateman's thesis, it implies that Keynes had not really digested the subjective theory fully, for on this theory, rationality *means* consistency'. There is no *implication* on my part, but rather a fully worked-out explanation of Keynes's position.

As the passage I have quoted above indicates, the abandonment of rationality on Keynes's part implies nothing more than an abandonment of Keynes's belief that people's actions are based on some true, objective concepts. It is, of course, quite easy to turn the word irrational to many purposes. I argue, for instance, in my essay that while G.L.S. Shackle and his followers have taken this phrase as implying that Keynes was an 'analytical nihilist' who believed that economic theorizing is an impossible enterprise, nothing could be further from the truth. Keynes says in his review that Ramsey's theorizing is brilliant, even though he acknowledges that it is based on non-rational beliefs.

And in the literature which O'Donnell is so anxious to examine, Keynes is quite explicit about this irrationality.[5] In 'My Early Beliefs', he says that his early thinking was shallow given his belief in man's pursuit of the Platonic, rationalistic truths:

> The attribution of rationality to human nature, instead of enriching it, now seems to me to have impoverished it. It ignored certain powerful and valuable

springs of feeling. Some of the spontaneous, irrational outbursts of human nature can have a sort of value from which our schematism was cut off. (JMK, X, pp. 448–9)

Likewise, in the correspondence with Townshend he is very explicit about irrationality in reference to the idea of the probabilities employed in decision-making, and even repudiates the idea that rationality is tied to the existence of logical relations.

> I think it important to emphasise the point that all this is not particularly an *economic* problem, but affects every rational choice concerning conduct where consequences enter into the rational calculation. Generally speaking, in making a decision we have before us a large number of alternatives, none of which is demonstrably more 'rational' than the others, in the sense that we can arrange in order of merit the sum aggregate of the benefits obtainable from the complete consequences of each. To avoid being in the position of Buridan's ass, we fall back, therefore, and necessarily do so, on motives of another kind, which are not 'rational' in the sense of being concerned with the evaluation of consequences, but are decided by habit, instinct, preference, desire, will, etc. All this is just as true of the non-economic as of the economic man. But it may well be, as you suggest, that when we remember all this, we have to abate somewhat from the traditional picture of the latter. (JMK, XXIX, p. 294)

There is a very direct statement here that ration*ality is* possible, but not in relation to objective, logical relations. The key concept determining rationality is now the *actual consequence* of an outcome; if people are 'irrational' it is because they act without reference to the *true outcomes* of their actions. Logical relations are no longer the basis of rationality.

O'Donnell has argued for an interpretation of Keynes which has him continuing to adhere to his logical theory of probability while desiring to expand on his original idea of 'unknown probabilities' in the context of Ramsey's 'lesser logic'. Such machinations seem unwarranted on the evidence. What seems most probable on the evidence is that Keynes abandoned his logical theory of probability and his earlier concept of rationality for a new concept of rationality. Otherwise we might have some concrete evidence regarding the elusive logical relations.

Notes

1. There is a completely different version of the continuity thesis than the one to which O'Donnell refers. Anna Carabelli (1988) would *not* agree with this depiction of Keynes's early thought although she too has a continuity thesis. There is not space in this essay to deal with both versions of the continuity thesis, so only the Hicks–O'Donnell–Lawson–Hamouda–Rowley version is treated here.
2. For a fuller account of the story told in this paragraph, see Bateman (1988).
3. For treatment of a sizeable portion of this literature see Bateman (1987).
4. I must protest O'Donnell's assertion that my account of this part of Keynes's changed

conception of probability is 'an unsupported leap'. My entire essay revolves around a discussion of Keynes's concept of induction in relation to his ideas of probability. One may disagree with this interpretation, but that hardly justifies an assertion that it does not exist.

5. O'Donnell does not address Braithwaite's (1975) argument concerning Keynes's abandonment of rationality.

References

Bateman, B. W. 1987, 'Keynes's changing conception of Probability', *Economics and Philosophy* 3(2) (October), pp. 97–120.

Bateman, B. W. 1988, 'G. E. Moore and J. M. Keynes', *American Economic Review* 78(5) (December), pp. 1098–106.

Braithwaite, R. B. 1975, 'Keynes as a philosopher', in M. Keynes (ed.), *Essays on J. M. Keynes*, Cambridge University Press, Cambridge.

Carabelli, A. 1988, *On Keynes's Method*, Macmillan, London.

Harrod, R. F. 1951, *The Life of J. M. Keynes*, Macmillan, London.

Hicks, J. R. 1979, *Causality in Economics*, Basic Books, New York.

Keynes, J. M. 1921, *A Treatise on Probability*, Macmillan, London.

Keynes, J. M. 1931, 'Ramsey as a philosopher', *The New Statesman and Nation* (3 October).

Keynes, J. M. 1936, *The General Theory of Employment, Interest and Money*, Macmillan, London.

Keynes, J. M. 1972, *Essays in Biography*, Vol. X: *The Collected Writings of John Maynard Keynes*, D. E. Moggridge (ed.), St Martin's, New York.

Keynes, J. M. 1973, *The General Theory and After. Part II: Defense and Development*, Vol. XIV: *The Collected Writings of John Maynard Keynes*, D. E. Moggridge (ed.), St Martins, New York.

Keynes, J. M. 1979, *The General Theory and After: A Supplement*, Vol. XXIX: *The Collected Writings of John Maynard Keynes*, D. E. Moggridge (ed.), Macmillan, London.

Lawson, T. 1985, 'Uncertainty and economic analysis', *Economic Journal* 95(380), pp. 909–27.

Moore, G. E. 1903, *Principia Ethica*, Cambridge University Press, Cambridge.

Moore, G. E. 1912, *Ethics*, Henry Holt, New York.

O'Donnell, R. M. 1990, 'Continuity in Keynes's conception of probability', in D. E. Moggridge (ed.), *Perspectives on the History of Economic Thought*, Edward Elgar, London.

Ramsey, F. P. 1931, *The Foundation of Mathematics*, Routledge & Kegan Paul, London.

Rowley, R. and Hamouda, O. 1988, 'Troublesome probability and economics', *Journal of Post Keynesian Economics* 10(1) (Fall), pp. 44–64.

Russell, B. 1922, 'Review of *A Treatise on Probability*', *Mathematical Gazette* XI, pp. 119–25.

Tinbergen, J. 1940, 'On a method of statistical business-cycle research: a reply', *Economic Journal* (March), pp. 141–54.

6 The Rise and Fall of the 'Entrepreneur Economy': Some Remarks on Keynes's Taxonomy of Economies

Ingo Barens

Er muß sozusagen die Leiter wegerfen, nachdem er auf ihr hinaufgestiegen ist.
Ludwig Wittgenstein

I

Several authors have stressed the importance of the fact that Keynes aimed at developing a 'monetary theory of production' for a proper understanding of the 'revolutionary' essence of the contribution the *General Theory* made to economics. According to these authors, Keynes based his new theory of output and employment on the concept of a 'monetary economy', fundamentally different from a barter economy, the domain of orthodox neoclassical theory.[2]

Unfortunately, until the publication of volume XXIX of the *Collected Writings of John Maynard Keynes* only very scant textual evidence existed of Keynes's preoccupation with a 'monetary theory of production'. It was only in his contribution to the 1933 *Spiethoff-Festschrift* that he did enlarge on the necessity and nature of such an approach.[3] But his line of reasoning is very hard to follow, with Keynes – though being very out-spoken about the existence of fundamental differences between the *'real exchange economy'* of orthodox theory and the *'monetary economy'* he is aiming at (i.e. one that would be capable of capturing the essential features of real world economies) – only giving bits and pieces of his ideas and only hinting at the arguments behind his conclusions.[4]

But the material of volume XXIX (the contents of the famous 'Tilton Laundry Basket') has made abundantly clear that, in 1932–4, Keynes indeed was engaged in a comparative analysis of an entire spectrum of such diverse economies as a *barter economy*, a *cooperative economy*, an *entrepreneur economy* and a *neutral economy*. For some time Keynes did devote the introductory chapters of the planned *General Theory*, (at the time with the working title 'The Monetary Theory of Employment' (XXIX, p. 62–3), to a thorough presentation of this taxonomy, though eventually deciding to discard these draft chapters.

Despite its alleged crucial importance for understanding Keynes's criti-que of his predecessors, there have been amazingly few efforts towards a comprehensive reconstruction of Keynes's taxonomy.[5] Furthermore, no attempt has been undertaken to throw light upon the reasons that might have led Keynes eventually to abandon this elaborate taxonomy, even though it is sometimes held that there still is something to be learnt from Keynes's comparative analysis.[6]

In this paper an attempt will be made to unearth the reasons that may have led Keynes to discard the introductory chapters dealing with his comparative analysis.

The paper is organized as follows: after reconstructing Keynes's taxonomy in section II, section III shows how Keynes derived some tentative conclusions concerning the 'tacit assumptions' of 'Classical Theory' from it. Section IV critically discusses the spectrum of different economies, pointing out a fundamental deficiency in its construction making it impossible to isolate the 'truly decisive' assumption, i.e. the one responsible for the full employment outcome. Section V traces the origin of this deficiency back to the notion that Say's Law will have different implications regarding the level of employment the economy is gravitating to, depending on the assumption made about the 'law of production' characterizing different economies; section VI shows how this idea becomes obsolete as soon as Keynes has to abandon the notion of 'normal profits' carried over from the *Treatise on Money* in favour of an analysis in terms of an aggregate supply curve, i.e. an analysis explicitly proceeding in terms of profit-maximization. In the penultimate section (VII) it is shown how this shift in turn makes obsolete the taxonomy of economies. The final section adds some thoughts about the possible origin of Keynes's attempt to work on the basis of this taxonomy, some possible additional reasons why he abandoned it so easily, and the relation of the analysed development to the so-called Cambridge Didactic Style.

II

While working on his new theory of output and employment Keynes always tried to locate the crucial difference(s) between his own approach and the full employment analysis of 'Classical Theory'.[7] As he made clear in his contribution to the *Spiethoff-Festschrift*, this turned into a search for the 'tacit assumptions of orthodox theory' (XXIX, p. 410).[8]

In order to isolate these 'tacit assumptions', in an early stage of his transition from the *Treatise on Money* to the *General Theory* Keynes 'constructed' a variety of different economies.[9] By way of comparing, on the one hand, the equilibrium (or normal) level of employment prevailing in each of these economies and, on the other hand, the different assumptions defining these economies, he hoped to pin down the crucial assumption marking the dividing line between the full employment world of 'Classical Theory' and the underemployment world of his own approach in terms of effective demand.

In this comparative analysis, Keynes constructed four different economies with the help of three sets of assumptions (the following reconstruction is based on the material in XXIX, pp. 52–7, 66–102).

The *first set of assumptions* was about the use of money; the relevant question being whether money was used or not (money being a thing – but not necessarily the *only* thing – that can be stored but not be privately produced).

The *second set of assumptions* was about the relation between aggregate demand and aggregate supply; the relevant question being whether aggregate demand would be equal to aggregate supply at all levels of output, i.e. whether Say's Law – in the sense as it was understood by Keynes (VII, p. 18; XXIX, pp. 80, 256) – is valid or not.

The *third set of assumptions* was about the motivation of productive activity, about the 'law of production' (XXIX, p. 78); the relevant question being whether production was motivated by the expectation of (more) product (or more profit reckoned in terms of output) or by the expectation of (more) *money* profits. Obviously, the distinction Keynes was driving at was one between a law of production in *real* terms concerned with the factors of production comparing the marginal disutility of effort and the marginal utility to be derived from its marginal product (*à la* Marshall's example of a boy picking blackberries, maybe; Marshall 1920, p. 331) and a law of production in *monetary* terms concerned with entrepreneurs comparing (expected) sums of money (money costs *vs.* money proceeds; XIV, p. 385).

The *first* economy then would be one without the use of money and (of course) without production being motivated by money profits and (of course again) without 'aggregate demand' being capable of diverging from 'aggregate supply'. Keynes called this economy a *barter economy* (XXIX, p. 66).[10]

In the *second* economy money was used, but only as a convenience, i.e. all current money incomes would be spent on purchasing current output either directly or indirectly and production was motivated by the amount of product to be gained. Keynes called this economy a *cooperative economy* (or a *real-wage economy*) (XIII, p. 410; XXIX, pp. 54, 67, 77–8). Keynes states that in a *barter economy* as well as in a *cooperative economy* the existence of underemployment equilibrium would be impossible; or, to be somewhat more precise, that unemployment would only exist because of 'stupid obstinacy about terms on the part... of the factors of production' or some other form of 'those aberrations of a temporary or otherwise

Table 6.1   Keynes's taxonomy of economies

	Barter economy	Cooperative economy	Entrepreneur economy	Neutral economy
Money is used	no	yes	yes	yes
Say's Law is valid	yes	yes	no	yes[a]
Production motivated by money profits	no	no	yes	yes
Equilibrium at less than full employment	no	no	yes	no[b]

a. Invalidity of Say's Law prevented by economic policy.
b. Underemployment prevented by economic policy.

nonfundamental character such as the classical theory has always envisaged as a possibility' (XXIX, 97).[11]

In a *third* economy money is used and the productive activity is organized by entrepreneurs renting capital goods and hiring labour. These entrepreneurs are motivated by money profits.[12] Current incomes are *not* spent entirely on current output. Keynes called this economy an *entrepreneur economy* (or a *money-wage economy* or (*generalized monetary economy*) (X, p. 97, XXIX, pp. 67, 78, 87).

In an *entrepreneur economy*, according to Keynes, underemployment not only would be possible, but would be the normal state of the economy (XIII, 407; XXIX, 79).

In addition Keynes introduced a variant of the *entrepreneur economy*. In this *fourth* economy, as in the third, money is used and production is motivated by money profits. But in contrast to the *entrepreneur economy* due to appropriate measures of economic policy (a) aggregate demand is made to always keep step with aggregate supply, and (b) aggregate demand always is kept at the full employment level (XXIX, p. 91; on these two 'conditions of neutrality' more will be said below). Keynes called this a *neutral entrepreneur economy* (or a *neutral monetary economy*, or a *neutral money economy*) or simply *neutral economy* (X, p. 97, XXIX, pp. 67–8, 78). In this *neutral economy* full employment would prevail as the result of suitable economic policy.

Table 6.1. gives the results of the reconstruction of Keynes's taxonomy of economies, [13,14]

III

With the help of this taxonomy Keynes tried to trace the 'tacit assumptions' of orthodox theory.

One set of assumptions he can discard out of hand. As Table 6.1 shows, the use of money by itself is not a sufficient condition for equilibrium at less than full employment (XXIX, pp. 66–7, 76–7, 85). This left Keynes with three economies and two sets of assumptions. By comparing the equilibrium levels of employment prevailing in these three economies he came to the conclusion that 'the classical theory is, in effect, assuming either a co-operative or a neutral economy' (XXIX, p. 101). That is, 'Classical Theory' either assumes the two different 'laws of production' to be equivalent (XXIX, pp. 78–9) or it assumes 'a *particular*...policy on the part of the monetary authority' (XXIX, p. 55), i.e. one always keeping the rate of interest at a level compatible with full employment (XXIX pp. 118–19); (see, in addition, VII, pp. 242–4; for further possible ways to secure 'neutrality', see, for instance, XXIX, pp. 95–6).

But this result leaves a central problem unsolved: *which* of the two sets of assumptions *really* is the decisive one, i.e. what must be considered the truly decisive difference between the *cooperative economy* (full employment) and the *entrepreneur economy* (underemployment) As Table 6.1 shows, the change from the *cooperative economy* to the *entrepreneur economy* does not entail a twofold change in the underlying assumptions. On the one hand, there is the shift from the validity of Say's Law to its invalidity and, on the other hand, there is the shift from the 'law of production' in real terms to the 'law of production' in monetary terms. Because of this twofold change in the assumptions, comparing the two economies must fail to throw light upon the question which one of these assumptions is the decisive one.

IV

Before tackling the problem of the relative importance of the assumptions about Say's Law *vis-à-vis* the assumptions about the 'law of production', it may be helpful to have a closer look into the 'logic' of the remaining three economies with the help of a time-honoured diagram.

Figure 6.1. shows the working of the *cooperative economy*: Say's Law implies the coincidence of both aggregate supply curve and aggregate demand curve; because of the 'law of production' in terms of product there is an inherent tendency for the economy to settle in point F, the level of incomes (or *earnings*) compatible with full employment (E_0). The precise position of F is, of course, determined in the labour market (leaving aside other factors of production).

Figure 6.2 shows the working of the *entrepreneur economy*: the invalidity of Say's Law implies the existence of only *one* intersection of aggregate supply curve and aggregate demand curve; there is an inherent tendency for the economy to settle at G, i.e. at a level of incomes (e_1) incompatible with full employment. Pushing production and employment beyond point G will have two contrasting effects: it will entail an increase

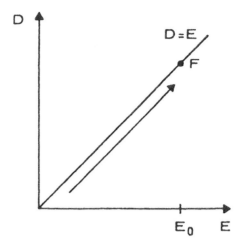

Figure 6.1   A cooperative economy

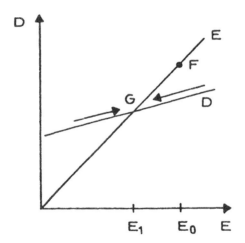

Figure 6.2   An entrepreneur economy

in terms of product and at the same time it will entail a decrease in money profits because for levels of output beyond G the money proceeds would be insufficient to cover the money costs incurred.

In this situation the decision rule of entrepreneurs must clash with the decision rule of workers:

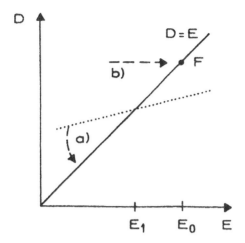

Figure 6.3 A neutral economy

> The amount of employment offered by each individual firm will be arrived at by comparing two sums of money – the expected sale proceeds and the expected costs corresponding to different levels of employment; whilst the maximum employment agreeable to the workers will be arrived at by a psychological comparison of the advantage ... of the wages of additional labour with the disadvantage...of such labour. (XIV, p. 385)

Because the *entrepreneur economy* is subject to the 'law of production' in monetary terms the amount of employment entrepreneurs are willing to offer is lower than the amount of labour the workers are willing to supply, i.e. at point G there is *involuntary* unemployment.[15]

Figure 6.3 shows the working of the *neutral economy*: by way of appropriate measures (a) the aggregate demand curve is made to merge with the aggregate supply curve, and (b) aggregate demand is pushed to the full employment level at F.[16]

A closer inspection of the *neutral economy* will help to answer the question of the relative importance of the two sets of assumptions. According to Keynes, the *neutral economy* is 'simply the peculiar and limiting case of the ways in which an entrepreneur economy can behave', it is 'an entrepreneur economy ... made to behave in the same manner as a co-operative economy' (XXIX, p. 79).

According to Keynes, two conditions have to be fulfilled in order to transform an *entrepreneur economy* into a *neutral entrepreneur economy*:

> If ... some mechanism is introduced into an entrepreneur economy so as to insure

(1) that aggregate expenditure and aggregate costs always keep step and change by equal amounts and
(2) that chance causes operating to keep employment below full employment are counteracted,

then our entrepreneur economy...will satisfy the conditions laid down by our definition for a neutral economy. (XXIX, p. 91)

Keynes is explicit about the reason why *two* 'conditions of neutrality', as they may be called, have to be fulfilled;

The second of the above conditions is required because the effect of the first condition by itself is...to establish a state of neutral equilibrium so that the system is in equilibrium for *any* level of employment. Hence a touch may be required to insure that the actual level will be one of full employment as it would be in a co-operative economy. (XXIX, p. 91)

On the basis of these remarks it will be possible to find an answer to the problem under discussion. To do so, it will be convenient to construct still another economy, this time a variant of Keynes's *neutral economy*.

Imagine an *entrepreneur economy* in which the only first 'condition of neutrality' is fulfilled; in want of a better name it may be called a *semi-neutral economy*. In this *semi-neutral economy* Say's Law will be valid as it would be in a *cooperative economy* (even if this has to be accomplished by way of suitable measures on the part of political authorities) and there will be money profits as the motive force of production as in the *entrepreneur economy*. What will be the resulting equilibrium level of employment?

According to Keynes, the first 'condition of neutrality' does not suffice to establish a full employment equilibrium but only 'neutral' equilibrium. Thus leaving aside the *barter economy* as well as the *neutral economy* there will be the following three economies:

• the *cooperative economy* with stable equilibrium at the full employment level;
• the *semi-neutral economy* with 'neutral' equilibrium at any level of employment.

And:

• the *entrepreneur economy* with stable equilibrium at a level of employment depending on the state of effective demand (see Table 6.2).

Figure 6.4 shows the working of this *semi-neutral economy*: economic policy only makes sure that aggregate demand curve and aggregate supply curve coincide; there will be no inherent tendency for the economy to

Table 6.2   Keynes's adjusted taxonomy of economies

	Cooperative economy	Semi-neutral economy	Entrepreneur economy
Money is used	yes	yes	yes
Say's Law is valid	yes	yes	no
Production motivated by money profits	no	yes	yes
Equilibrium at less than full employment	no	yes	yes

settle at any specific level of employment – any position that has been reached will be maintained.

Cooperative economy and *semi-neutral economy* are sharing two characteristics (use of money, validity of Say's Law) but are yielding different equilibrium levels of employment. The reason for this difference must lie in the one remaining difference between the *cooperative economy* and the *semi-neutral economy*: the fact that production in the one is motivated by *product*, while in the other it is motivated by *money profits*.

The conclusion to be drawn from these considerations is that apparently the 'law of production' is of utmost importance concerning the equilibrium level of employment the economic system is gravitating towards. Thus the truly decisive assumption seems to be the one about the motivation of production. This in turn would be the reason why Keynes at that stage of his transition towards the *General Theory* did put such

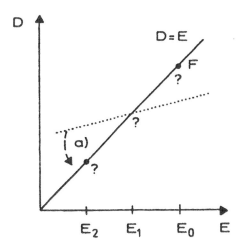

Figure 6.4   A semi-neutral economy

extreme emphasis on the fact that it is the pursuit of *money profits* what motivates production in the real world of productive processes organized by *entrepreneurs*:

> The classical theory supposes that the readiness of the entrepreneur to start up a productive process depends on the amount of value in terms of product which he expects to fall to his share; i.e. that only the expectation of more *product* for himself will induce him to offer more employment. But in an entrepreneur economy this is a wrong analysis of the nature of business calculation. An entrepreneur is interested, not in the amount of product, but in the amount of *money* which will fall to his share. He will increase his output if by doing so he expects to increase his money profit, even though this profit represents a smaller quantity of product than before (XXIX, p. 82).[17,18]

V

The results derived so far can be summarized as follows: in different economies Say's Law yields different equilibrium levels of employment. Whether its validity translates into full employment depends on the behavioural assumption about the motivation for taking up productive activities. In an economy governed by a 'law of production' in terms of product Say's Law is equivalent to full employment, whereas in an economy governed by a 'law of production' in terms of money it is not.

This result in turn throws up two further questions, questions that, as the further discussion will show, prove to address just two aspects of the same problem.

The first question aims at the underlying reason for this dependence of the employment implication of Say's Law on the 'law of production'. The second question is concerned with the relation of this view of Say's Law to the view expressed in the *General Theory*, where Say's Law is seen as the *sufficient* condition for the establishment of full employment equilibrium 'Say's Law ... is equivalent to the proposition that there is no obstacle to full employment' (VII, p. 26). The answer to these questions will at the same time reveal the reason why in the end Keynes abandoned his comparative analysis of economies.

VI

In order to understand how Keynes in this comparative analysis may have arrived at the conclusion that Say's Law will yield different equilibrium levels of output and employment in different economies (depending on the prevalent 'law of production') one has to go back to the *Treatise* and its central behavioural assumption.

In the *Treatise* Keynes held the view that in their production decisions entrepreneurs are guided by 'normal profits' in terms of money, or a 'normal remuneration', as he called it (V, p. 112; Keynes does not address the problem of determining 'normal profits'). If actual (or expected) profits are equal to normal profits, entrepreneurs will have no incentive to change the prevailing level of production. If, on the other hand, actual (or expected) profits diverge from normal profits, entrepreneurs will either cut back production and employment – if profits are below their 'normal remuneration – or will expand production and employment – if profits are above their 'normal remuneration'. Furthermore, according to the argument of the *Treatise*, actual profits will equal normal profits if, and only if, savings (in the *Treatise* sense) are equal to investment, i.e. if aggregate demand (or 'aggregate disbursement' as it is sometimes called by Keynes) is equal to aggregate supply (aggregate costs of production). Thus with aggregate demand equal to aggregate supply, entrepreneurs will receive their 'normal remuneration', the level of production and employment will be constant and the economy will be in equilibrium.[19]

Apparently, this behavioural assumption of the *Treatise*, together with its notion of 'normal profits', was carried over by Keynes into his comparative analysis of different economies. Against the background of this assumption and with Say's Law being understood as equality of aggregate demand and aggregate supply at all levels of output, the following conclusion must have suggested itself most forcefully to Keynes: under Say's Law savings always will equal investment and therefore aggregate demand always will equal aggregate supply; this in turn does imply that entrepreneurs will receive normal profits at every level of production and employment. Therefore entrepreneurs will be content with any level of production and employment they have happened to decide upon and therefore any level that has been realized will be maintained, i.e. will be a 'neutral' equilibrium (XXIX, p. 92). 'If over any period the aggregate expenditure is ... equal to the costs which have been incurred ... there will be no tendency ... for the aggregate of employment to change' (XXIX, p. 90).[20] The consequence is obvious: 'What the level of output is, is a matter of indifference to entrepreneurs as a whole' (XXIX, p. 159).

This carrying-over of the behavioural assumption of the *Treatise* into his comparative analysis of different economies seems to be the rationale behind Keynes's view that in an *entrepreneur economy* with entrepreneurs motivated by *money profits*, i.e. governed by a comparison of two sums of money, Say's Law will *not* be a sufficient condition for the establishment of full employment whereas in an economy such as the *cooperative economy* governed by a 'law of production' in terms of product, i.e. governed by a comparison of utility vs. disutility, full employment will be the normal result. This result, of course, stands in striking contrast to the position Keynes eventually came to adopt in the *General Theory*, where he states that under Say's Law, 'competition between entrepreneurs would always lead to an expansion of employment up to ... full employment' (VII, p. 26).[21]

The reason for this drastic change of view seems to be straightforward. In the *Treatise* the notion of normal profits was linked to the existence of an *unique* equilibrium level of output and employment, i.e. the full employment level. But the main finding of Keynes's new theory of output and employment is that the economy may settle at any level of employment depending on aggregate demand. But with equilibrium output and employment variable, the notion of normal profits linked to an unique level of output and employment must lose its plausibility. It has to be generalized into the notion of an *entire range of different equilibrium levels of profits* (with equilibrium profits being a function of the level of output), that is, it has to be generalized into the notion of an aggregate supply curve.[22] Finally, in a marginalist setting, the level and share of profits will rise together with the level of output. Thus it is no longer plausible to assume that entrepreneurs are indifferent to the level of output and employment. If Say's Law is valid, entrepreneurs, even as they are interested only in money profits, will push the economy to the full employment level, as stated in the *General Theory*.

VII

This change in Keynes's position concerning the implication of Say's Law has dramatic consequences for the analytical usefulness of his taxonomy of economies.

If the implications of profit-maximization are taken into account explicitly, then even a *semi-neutral economy* will show an inherent tendency towards full employment. In this case, the distinction into two 'laws of production', one based on real terms (sacrifice, effort, utility, etc.), the other based on monetary terms (money profits) loses all analytical relevance. Regardless of the 'law of production', Say's Law always will suffice to procure full employment. This in turn makes the distinction into a *cooperative economy* and an *entrepreneur economy* obsolete. The only meaningful distinction that remains is one between an economy in which Say's Law does hold and an economy in which it does not and that is precisely the distinction made in the *General Theory*.[22] This seems to be the reason why eventually Keynes discarded the introductory draft chapters dealing extensively with his comparative analysis of different economies.[24]

This conclusion is even strengthened by the 'background noise' these preliminary manuscripts have left in the final version of chapter 2 of the *General Theory*. Thus when Keynes refers to the 'real-exchange economy' of Pigou and J. S. Mill or to a 'non-exchange Robinson Crusoe Economy'

(VII, pp. 19–20) he no longer stresses any 'law of production', but simply refers to these economies as examples of Say's Law being necessarily valid. And at one place in the *General Theory*, Keynes even comes extremely close to explicitly endorsing precisely that 'law of production' he in the draft manuscripts had denounced as misleading and irrelevant for the analysis of real world economies: 'rising prices may delude entrepreneurs into increasing employment beyond the level which maximises their individual profits measured in terms of product' (VII, p. 290).

VIII

In the light of these results the conclusion to be drawn seems to be that there is nothing (or, at least, *nothing new*)[25] to be learned from the discarded taxonomy of economies. Everything of analytical value in Keynes's comparative analysis already has found its way into the final version of the *General Theory*. Keynes's preoccupation with this taxonomy and his strong emphasis on the fact that entrepreneurs in their decision to produce and to employ are motivated by the pursuit of money profits turn out to have been only a passing stage in Keynes's intellectual development towards the *General Theory* – the more he perfected his new theory of output and employment, the clearer it became that these notions were losing their analytical relevance. And as a passing stage these notions have to be considered as victims of the 'Cambridge Didactic Style'.[26]

Apparently, what Keynes did write in the preface to his *Treatise on Money* does apply to his *General Theory* as well:

> I feel like someone who has been forcing his way through a confused jungle. Now that I have emerged from it, I see that I might have taken a more direct route and that many problems and perplexities which beset me during the journey had not precisely the significance which I supposed at that time. (V, pp. xvii–xviii)

But in writing the *General Theory*, Keynes seems to have been kept from thinking those 'foolish things one can temporarily believe if one thinks too long alone' (V, p. xxiii) by a host of discussions over various drafts before the publication of the book.

In the context of this paper, special mention may be made of Kahn's possible contribution. As Joan Robinson is reported to recall, it was Kahn who 'reminded him of the fundamentals of the science... and induced him to advance more acceptable propositions' (Lambert, 1969). Furthermore, in his fellowship thesis Kahn had dealt with Marshallian short-period analysis.[27] So he would have been excellently equipped to lend Keynes a helping hand in his attempts to root the Principle of Effective Demand firmly in the Marshallian short period. As the surviving draft tables of contents for the *General Theory* suggest, the discarding of the draft chapters dealing with the taxonomy of economies took place sometime between December 1933 and well before October 1934 during a time of intensive discussions with Kahn (see, XIII, pp. 421–4). Keynes himself links the discarding of these chapters to 'a stiff week's supervision' from Kahn (XIII, p. 422).[38]

Finally, attention should be drawn to a development that may have made it easier for Keynes to abandon his attempt to trace the 'tacit assumptions' of 'Classical Theory' by comparing different economies. In 1933 Pigou's *Theory of Unemployment* was published, at last supplying Keynes with the reference model he for so long had been searching for.

Notes

1. This paper has greatly benefited from discussions with Helmut Baisch and Otto Roloff as well as from comments by Edward J. Amadeo, Axel Leijonhufvud and Thomas K. Rymes. The usual disclaimer applies.
2. See for instance Davidson (1978) and Minsky (1975).
3. *Der Stand und die nächste Zukunft der Konjunkturforschung. Festschrift für Arthur Spiethoff*. (München, 1933). Keynes's contribution was untitled. It has been reprinted under the title 'A Monetary Theory of Production' in (XIII, p. 408–11).
4. For decades D. Dillard has been the only author to pay any attention to the analytical content of Keynes's contribution to the *Spiethoff-Festschrift*; see, for instance, Dillard (1955; 1983). In addition he kept it from oblivion by arranging its re-publication under the title 'On the Theory of a Monetary Economy' in 1963; see Dillard (1963).
5. Rotheim (1981) attempts a reconstruction, but as the present paper will show, arrives at an incorrect specification of the economies discussed by Keynes. Dow and Earl (1982) appear to be more inspired by Hahn's (1977) ideas about the problem of wage payments in kind than by Keynes's notion of effective demand being too low to provide for full employment. Kregel (1980) deals with Keynes's taxonomy, but his analysis does not draw on the material of vol. XXIX, but on notes of Keynes's lecture of 1932 and 1933 made by R. B. Bryce; these notes are now available in *Keynes's Lectures* (see note 13 below). Hession (1984) refers to Keynes's taxonomy and Leijonhufvud (1983) discusses the role of money in these economies from the perspective of Clower's dual decision hypothesis. For a comparison between Keynes's *entrepreneur economy* and Marx's critique of Say's Law, see Sardoni (1987, ch. 6).
6. See for instance Rotheim (1981) and Harcourt and O'Shaughnessy (1985).
7. As defined by Keynes himself; see (VII, p. 3). As the question whether full employment will be the normal result of market processes is the main concern of Keynes's analysis, the focus will be on Marginalist Theory.
8. During the examination of Pigou's testimony before the Macmillan Committee Keynes strongly emphasized the implicit assumptions of Pigou's arguments; see Committee (qq. 6435–79). This interest in the assumptions underlying the 'Classical Theory' may even be traced back to the early 1920s; see Robinson (1947, p. 60).
9. The following is based on parts of Barens (1987).
10. This *barter economy* was not restricted to the exchange of given stocks of goods but focused on the production of goods.
11. In both economies it is possible for the factors of production to be rewarded in *agreed shares* either of the actual output (this would be the case in the *barter economy*) or of the sale proceeds of the output (this would be the case in the *cooperative economy*): 'The essential point is that by whatever roundabout methods every factor of production

ultimately accepts as its reward *a predetermined share* of the expected output either in kind or in terms of something which has an exchange value equal to that of *the predetermined share*' (XXIX, p. 77; emphasis added).

Although in the *cooperative economy* wages are paid in money, as long as Say's Law is valid, it is possible for the factors of production to predetermine a share of the sale proceeds that is equal to their share of the actual output as it would result in the *barter economy*. If Say's Law is not valid, the money paid out to the factors of production does not necessarily flow back to the entrepreneurs through the sale of products; in this case, because the wage bill in terms of money has been fixed before taking up production, the actual shares of the factors of production will diverge from the expected shares that induced the level of production and employment.

Looked at from this perspective, the 'best idea since Keynes's, Weitzman's 'share economy' (see Weitzman, 1984), can be traced back to Keynes himself (for a comparison of Weitzman's 'share economy' with Keynes's ideas, see Asimakopulos (1988) and Davidson, (1988)).

12. The explanation of this motivation in terms of money profit 'is evident. The employment of factors of production... involves the entrepreneur in the disbursement, not of product, but of money' (XXIX, p. 82).

13. Student notes of Keynes's lectures in the Michaelmas terms of 1932 and 1933 give a slightly different picture (notes were taken by Bryce, Cairncross, Douglas, Fallgatter, Salant, Tarshis and Thring respectively; see Keynes's Lectures). In his 1932 lectures, Keynes draws a distinction between a 'barter economy' without any use of money, a 'money economy', in which money is only used 'as a "neutral" and convenient means of affecting an exchange' (therefore Keynes alternatively calls this economy a 'neutral' or 'neutral money economy' or a 'real-exchange' or 'real wage economy') and a 'monetary economy', in which money *plays a part of its own* and is *an operative factor*' (Keynes's Lectures, p. 11; see in additon pp. A1 and D2). This distinction is very similar to the one made in his contribution to the *Spiethoff-Festschrift*.

   In his 1933 lectures, Keynes makes use of the *cooperative economy*, the *neutral economy* and the *entrepreneur economy*, but not of the *barter economy*. Apparently the latter is subsumed under the *cooperative economy*, as is hinted at in the draft manuscripts (XXIX, p. 67).

14. Anyadike-Danes (1979; 1985) has shown, D. H. Robertson in his monetary analysis made use of an approach that is quite similar to Keynes's taxonomy. According to Anyadike-Danes, Robertson constructed four economies in order to isolate those economic fluctuations, if any, that would occur even in the absence of any monetary disturbance. These economies may be called the 'non-monetary cooperative economy', the 'non-monetary non-cooperative economy', the 'monetary cooperative economy' and the 'monetary non-cooperative economy'. If these concepts are translated into Keynes's own taxonomy the 'non-monetary cooperative economy' would equal the *barter economy*, the 'monetary cooperative economy' would equal the *cooperative economy* and the 'monetary non-cooperative economy' would equal the *entrepreneur economy*. Thus while Keynes did not consider an economy that would equal Robertson's 'non-monetary non-cooperative economy', his *neutral economy* does not fit into Robertson's classification.

   Considering Keynes's close cooperation with Robertson on the latter's *Banking Policy and the Price Level*, it may be here that the original of Keynes's approach can be found. This conjecture is somewhat strengthened by the fact that Keynes sometimes indeed is led to discuss fluctuations in effective demand (XXIX, p. 801), although his central concern was the determination of the equilibrium level of (under)employment.

15. '[I]n an entrepreneur economy...the volume of employment, the marginal disutility of which is equal to the utility of its marginal product, may be 'unprofitable' in terms of money' (XXIX, p. 79).

16. Passing mention can be made of an apparent inconsistency in this set of 'conditions of neutrality': condition (a) seems to be irrelevant, because it surely would suffice to 'shift' the aggregate demand curve to point F to establish full employment.

17. According to the lecture notes taken by Salant, Keynes seems to have added in his lecture of 23 October, 1933 the following statement concerning the position of the entrepreneur: 'He would be better off by sitting on that money' (Patinkin and Leith, 1977, p. 63). For a transcript of Salant's lecture notes, see Keynes; Lectures; for the quote itself see p. M4.
18. For a comparison of Ricardo's and J. S. Mill's notion of the economic system to Keynes's notion of an *entrepreneur economy*, see Barens (1987, pp. 114–23).
19. See Amadeo (1989) and Dimand (1988) for an analysis of the theoretical framework of the *Treatise*.
20. Keynes himself links the necessity of both 'conditions of neutrality' to the *Treatise*: 'In my *Treatise on Money* the equality of savings and investment…was a condition equivalent to the equality of aggregate expenditure and aggregate costs, but I failed to point out that this by itself provided only for neutral equilibrium and not for, what one might call, optimum equilibrium' (XXIX, pp. 91–2).
21. Thus in the *General Theory* Say's Law is a sufficient, but not – as closer inspection of Keynes's theory soon was to reveal – a necessary condition for the existence of full employment.
22. For Keynes's various attempts to tackle the problem created by the confrontation of his behavioural assumption based on the notion of normal profits with the results of his new analytical approach in terms of Effective Demand see for instance (XXIX, pp. 71–3). That Keynes never abandoned this idea of equilibrium profits is testified by his preface to the French edition to the *General Theory* (VII, p. xxxiii).
23. In the *General Theory* Keynes in addition puts forth even another distinction, one between a 'non-monetary economy' and a 'monetary economy', depending on the behaviour of the money rate of interest (see, VII, pp. 239–40). This classification of economies is left aside in the present paper.
24. The fact that Keynes discarded his taxonomy of economies does not mean that money as well loses its analytical relevance. Quite to the contrary, money still is most important to Keynes's Theory of Effective Demand because its 'essential properties', on the one hand, make it possible for leakages from the flow of incomes to occur, thus invalidating Say's Law, and, on the other hand, govern the level of injections to the flow of incomes (investment demand); for a discussion of the changes money's role as a barrier to full employment underwent in the course of Keynes's transition to the *General Theory* see Barens (1988).
25. According to Leijonhufvud (1983; 1986, pp. 414–15; 1988) what can be learned from the material of volume XXIX is that it at last gives direct textual proof to central aspects of his interpretation of the *General Theory*. But it seems to be rather doubtful whether this material, as far as this specific reading of the *General Theory* is concerned, really proves more than just the fact that Keynes did compare one economy without money to economies with money. To begin with, contrary to Leijonhufvud's (1983, p. 198n) contention that the '"Cooperative economy" … was one in which labour is bartered for goods', Keynes explicitly states that money *is* used in such an economy: 'Since this economy does not exclude the use of money for purposes of transitory convenience, it might perhaps be better to call it a *real-wage economy*, or a *cooperative economy*' (XXIX, p. 67; see XXIX, pp. 76–8 and especially XXIX, p. 85 as well; a similar mis-specification can be found in Kregel (1980) and Rotheim (1981). In addition (and consequently, see section II above), he places more emphasis on certain properties of the money in use (i.e. being storable but not producible) than on the use of money as such (i.e. its being the only good traded in all markets); thus, according to Keynes, even with money in use, this would give rise only to problems of relative demand, but not of *'aggregate* effective demand' (XXIX, 80; see XXIX, pp. 52–3 as well), as long as money can be privately produced (XXIX, pp. 85–6). Furthermore, this material makes it clear beyond doubt that Keynes intended his Principle of Effective Demand to be a new *theory of equilibrium*, even of long-period equilibrium (XXIX, pp. 54–7). Accordingly, the notion of a *deviation-amplifying multiplier* (Leijonhufvud, 1988, p. 213n) never held a place in Keynes's thinking; by way of contrast, on the basis of this material, the

multiplier should be understood as the result of stability analysis and thus as the reflection of *stable macroeconomic equilibrium*. Finally (and again consequently), this (and related) material contains no evidence that Keynes based his notion of a propensity to consume on considerations bearing resemblance to Clower's dual decision hypothesis; this notion simply seems to have been Keynes's attempt to lend plausibility to a macroeconomic stability condition; see Barens (1989).

26. See Fouraker (1958) and Moggridge (1980, p. 37).
27. See Kahn (1930).
28. On 13 April 1934, Keynes wrote to Kahn: 'I have been making rather extensive changes in the early chapters of my book, to a considerable extent consequential on a simple and obvious, but beautiful and important...precise definition of what is meant by effective demand' (XIII, p. 422). The fact that even this new definition of effect demand, resting on the notion of a representative entrepreneur, in turn seems to have been discarded (see Asimakopulos, 1984) has no bearing upon the conclusions advanced in this paper.

References

Amadeo, E. J. 1989, *The Development of Keynes's Principle of Effective Demand*, Edward Elgar, Upleadon, Gloucestershire.

Anyadike-Danes, M. K. 1979, *Dennis Robertson and the Construction of Aggregative Theory*, unpublished University of London Doctoral Dissertation.

Anyadike-Danes, M. K. 1985, 'Dennis Robertson and Keynes's *General Theory*, in G. C. Harcourt (ed.), *Keynes and His Contemporaries*, Macmillan, London.

Asimakopulos, A. 1984, 'The *General Theory* and its Marshallian microfoundations', mimeo, Montreal.

Asimakopulos, A. 1988, 'The aggregate supply function and the share economy: some early drafts of the *General Theory*', in O. F. Hamouda, and J. N. Smithin (eds), *Keynes and Public Policy After Fifty Years*, Volume 2: *Theories and Method*, Edward Elgar, Upleadon, Gloucestershire.

Barens, I. 1987, *Geld und Unterbeschäftigung. John Maynard Keynes's Kritik der Selbstregulierungsvorstellung*, Duncker & Humblot, Berlin.

Barens, I. 1988, 'Die (doppelte) Rolle des Geldes bei Keynes', in H. Hagemann and O. Steiger (eds), *Keynes' General Theory nach fünfzig Jahren*, Duncker & Humblot, Berlin.

Barens, I. 1989, 'From the "Banana Parable" to the principle of effective demand. On origin, development and structure of Keynes' *General Theory*', in D. A. Walker, (ed.), *Perspectives on the History of Economic Thought. Selected Papers from the History of Economics Society Conference 1987*, Edward Elgar, Aldershot.

Committee on Finance and Industry 1931, *Minutes of Evidence*, HMSO, London.

Davidson, P. 1978, *Money and the Real World*, 2nd edition, Macmillan, London.

Davidson, P. 1988, 'Weitzman's share economy and the aggregate supply function', in O. F. Hamouda and J. N. Smithin (eds), *Keynes and Public Policy After Fifty Years*, Volume 2: *Theories and Method*, Edward Elgar, Upleadon, Gloucestershire.

Dillard, D. 1955, 'The theory of a monetary economy', in K. Kurihara (ed.), *Post-Keynesian Economics*, Macmillan, London, pp. 3–30.

Dillard, D. 1963, 'Introduction to J. M. Keynes, On the theory of a monetary economy', *Nebraska Journal of Economics and Business*, 2, pp. 1–6.

Dillard, D. 1983, 'Effective demand and the monetary theory of employment', Paper prepared for the conference: Keynes Today: Theories and Policies, September 1983, Paris.

Dimand, R. W. 1988, *The Origins of the Keynesian Revolution. The Development of Keynes' Theory of Employment and Output*, Edward Elgar, Upleadon, Gloucestershire.

Dow, S. and Earl, P. 1982, *Money Matters. A Keynesian Approach to Monetary Economics*, Martin Robertson, Oxford.

Fouraker, L. E. 1958, 'The Cambridge Didactic Style', *Journal of Political Economy* 66, pp. 65–73.

Hahn, F. 1977, 'Keynesian economics and general equilibrium theory: reflections on some current debates, in G. C. Harcourt (ed.), *The Microfoundations of Macroeconomics*, Macmillan, London.

Hamouda, O. F. and Smithin, J. N. (eds) 1988, *Keynes and Public Policy After Fifty Years*, Volume 2: *Theories and Method*, Edward Elgar, Upleadon, Gloucestershire.

Harcourt, G. C. and O'Shaughnessy. T. J. 1985, 'Keynes's unemployment equilibrium: some insights from Joan Robinson, Piero Sraffa and Richard Kahn', in G. C. Harcourt (ed.), *Keynes and His Contemporaries*, Macmillan, London.

Hession, C. 1984, *John Maynard Keynes*, Macmillan, New York.

Kahn, R. F. 1930, *The Economics of the Short Period*, unpublished Fellowship Dissertation, King's College Library, Cambridge.

Keynes's Lectures, 1932–35: Notes of Students, compiled and edited by T. K. Rymes, Carleton Economic Papers, Carleton University, Ottawa.

Keynes, J. M. 1971–, *The Collected Writings of John Maynard Keynes*, Macmillan, London.

Kregel, J. A. 1980, 'Markets and institutions as features of a capitalist production system', *Journal of Post Keynesian Economics* III (Fall), pp. 32–48.

Lambert, P. 1969, 'The evolution of Keynes's thought from the *Treatise on Money* to the *General Theory*', *Annals of Public and Cooperative Economy*, 40, pp. 243–63.

Leijonhufvud, A. 1983, 'What would Keynes have thought of rational expectations?', in D. Worswick and J. Trevithick (eds), *Keynes and the Modern World*, Cambridge University Press, Cambridge.

Leijonhufvud, A. 1986, 'Real and monetary factors in business fluctuations', *Cato Journal* 6 (Fall), pp. 409–20.

Leijonhufvud, A. 1988, 'Did Keynes mean anything? Rejoinder to Yeager', *Cato Journal* 8 (Spring/Summer), pp. 209–17.

Lekachmann, R. (ed.) 1964, *Keynes' General Theory. Reports of Three Decades*, St. Martin's Press, New York.

Marshall, A. 1879/1930, *The Pure Theory of Domestic Values*, Series of reprints of scarce tracts of economic and political science, The London School of Economics and Political Science, London.

Marshall, A. 1920, *Principles of Economics*, 8th edition, Macmillan, London.

Minsky, H. P. 1975, *John Maynard Keynes*, Columbia University Press, New York.

Moggridge, D. E. 1980, *Keynes*, 2nd edition, Macmillan, London.

Patinkin, D. and Leith, H. C. (eds) 1977, *Keynes, Cambridge and the General Theory*, Macmillan, London.

Pigou, A. C. 1933, *The Theory of Unemployment*, Macmillan, London.

Robertson, D. H. 1926, *Banking Policy and the Price Level*, P. S. King, London.

Robinson, E. A. G. 1947, 'John Maynard Keynes 1883–1946', *Economic Journal* 57, pp. 1–68.

Rotheim, R. J. 1981, 'Keynes's monetary theory of value (1933)', *Journal of Post Keynesian Economics* III (4) (Summer), pp. 568–85.

Sardoni, C. 1987, *Marx and Keynes on Economic Recession. The Theory of Unemployment and Effective Demand*, Wheatsheaf Boosk, Brighton.

Weitzman, M. L. 1984, *The Share Economy. Conquering Stagflation*, Harvard University Press, Cambridge, Mass.

7 Keynes's Dichotomy and Wage-Rigidity Keynesianism: a Puzzle in Keynesian Thought

Amitava Krishna Dutt and Edward J. Amadeo

I. Introduction

Keynesian macroeconomics is usually distinguished – by mainstream supporters and detractors of Keynes alike – from the alternative new classical approach in having rigid prices.[1] Yet Keynes (JMK, VII) emphatically denied that his theory had anything to do with wage–price stickiness. While he did assume the money wage to be fixed, this was for him a simplifying assumption to be dispensed later (JMK, VII, p. 27). Moreover, Keynes's 'classical' economists – for example, Marshall (1920) and Pigou (1927; 1933) – as indeed Keynes well knew (JMK, VII, p. 257) were well aware of the fact that wage rigidity causes unemployment. If this was all that he was saying he was clearly saying nothing new.

It is an interesting puzzle in the history of Keynesian thought as to why, despite Keynes's emphatic statements to the contrary, the crucial feature of his work has been considered to be price rigidities in general, and specifically, wage rigidity. Given that this view – henceforth called the wage–rigidity view – is still widely entertained, a definitive answer to this puzzle (based on a thorough *post-mortem*) seems premature; we shall here be content with the discussion of some relevant facts and some speculations as to why this state of affairs has come about.

We shall proceed by first (in section II), as background, providing an interpretation of Keynes's method in the *General Theory*. This will be followed, in section III, with a discussion of the wage-rigidity view. The next three sections will discuss and evaluate three possible answers to the puzzle.

II. Keynes's dichotomy

Keynes can be interpreted as using a dichotomy in the *General Theory*, which divides his analysis into two parts. The first, developed in chapters 3 – 18, which we call the static or equilibrium part, takes the money wage to be given (some tangential remarks excepted), and examines the determination of short-run equilibrium: its main implication is that for this given wage,[2] the level of employment in the economy can settle at a position which is below the full-employment level.[3] In the second, which we can call the dynamic or historical part, presented in chapter 19, he dispenses with the fixed money-wage assumption and argues, contradicting classical theory, that a reduction in the money wage may quite possibly depress employment. He provides a non-exhaustive list (see JMK, VII, p. 266) of effects, which he thought to be important, which were relevant for this.

1. The reduction will redistribute income away from wage-earners, and from entrepreneurs to rentiers: the effect on employment depends on the marginal propensities to consume of the different groups, a negative effect being likely.
2. It will increase investment spending if the reduction is expected to be reversed in the future, but will reduce it if further reductions are expected.
3. It will result in a decline in the price level, which will reduce the need for cash balances, reduce the interest and therefore tend to stimulate investment; however, if this decline is expected to be reversed in the future, or if the price and wage changes increase uncertainty, the demand for money may not fall.
4. It may improve the confidence of entrepreneurs and break through their pessimism and encourage investment; but it may cause worker unrest and discontent, which may have exactly the opposite effect.
5. The resulting fall in price will increase the burden of debt of the entrepreneurs and indeed lead some of them to insolvency with a consequent adverse effect on investment.[4]

He also adds that a flexible-wage economy is not desirable, since it would result in price instability which would increase uncertainty in business decision-making (JMK, VII, p. 268).

This division into two parts can be thought of as an analytical dichotomy,[5] the use of which involves taking certain things as given (in Keynes's case the money wage) – or of ignoring them altogether – in the analysis of certain other things. Some of these factors can, and usually are, later brought into the analysis, but in a less formal manner than the analysis which ignored them or their variability. Economic theorizing necessitates the use of such dichotomies, since the interdependence of all possible things cannot be taken into account in every analysis. However, the validity of a particular dichotomy depends on whether the structure of the theory using the dichotomy is not fundamentally altered by the incorporation (in an appropriate way) of some of the factors left out or held constant.[6] It is important to understand why Keynes may have used his dichotomy.

First, if the money wage is relatively stable in the short run, then assuming it to be given for a short-run model seems justified. Keynes seems to suggest that the money wage was rigid (JMK, VII, pp. 251, 303), and provides at least one reason for this in terms of workers' concern with their *relative* rewards (JMK, VII, p. 14). Although he does not explicitly provide this rationale, his discussion on dependent and independent variables (JMK, VII, p. 247) seems to suggest that he would approve of it. The relative rigidity of the money wage, however, does not absolve Keynes of the responsibility of showing how changes in it would affect the structure of his theory, since the money wage did in fact change, even if slowly.

Second, unlike the relationships discussed in the 'core' of his work (in which the money wage is taken as given) which are to him predictable and systematic, the effects of changes in the money wage are complicated and uncertain, the actual outcome depending on a large variety of forces, many difficult to formalize. Thus, when Keynes finally does discuss them, he does so relatively informally, almost by the way of providing some examples.

Finally, Keynes postpones the discussion of the effects of changes in money wages for a tactical reason. He writes:

> It was not possible ... to discuss this matter fully until our own theory had been developed ... My difference from ... [classical] theory is primarily a difference of analysis; so that it could not be set forth clearly until the reader was acquainted with my own method. (JMK, VII, p. 257)

His discussion suggests that this difference had to do with stressing effective demand and uncertainty and expectations, which he discussed in earlier chapters on consumption, investment and liquidity: the effects on changes in the money wage on employment depended on these, rather than on the effect on production costs as in the classical analysis.

III. The development of the wage-rigidity view

The wage-rigidity view of Keynes's *General Theory* appeared soon after the book appeared. Early formalizations of Keynes's model by Hicks (1937), Meade (1937) and Lange (1938) assumed that the money wage is fixed. Subsequently, Modigliani (1944) analysed a Keynesian model in which the money wage was rigid below full employment and showed that the crucially distinctive feature of Keynes's work was the assumption of the fixed money wage, and this was the assumption that allowed Keynes to have unemployment equilibrium. Only if the liquidity trap existed, so that the interest rate became rigid, could unemployment exist without a rigid money wage;[7] otherwise a reduction in the money wage would reduce the price, raise the real supply of money, reduce the interest rate and raise investment spending and employment.

Pigou (1943), Haberler (1946) and Patinkin (1956) pointed out that money-wage rigidity was essential for Keynes's conclusion of unemployment equilibrium – even if the interest-elasticity of investment was zero and the liquidity trap existed – because as the price level fell, the real balance effect would increase aggregate spending. More recently, Kohn (1981) has made the claim in a stronger form, removing the qualifications made by them: even without the real balance effect, money wage rigidity is argued to be a necessary and sufficient condition for unemployment equilibrium. As stated above, most macroeconomists now seem to identify Keynesianism with the fixed money wage assumption. Indeed, the research agenda of mainstream Keynesians has been to analyze models which assume (and sometimes endogenously explain) wage-price stickiness.

IV. Was Keynes wrong?

One possible answer to our puzzle is that the dynamic part of his analysis has been found wanting, and the 'Keynesians' have decided to make the assumption of wage rigidity to rescue Keynes's analysis from logical error. This view claims that if unemployment results in a reduction in the money wage, aggregate demand increases by the interest rate mechanism or the real balance effect. It claims that Keynes does discuss the first effect (and it has been dubbed as the 'Keynes effect' in the literature) but, according to this argument, he does not give it its due, despite the fact that the cases in which it disappears – the liquidity trap and the absolute interest-inelasticity of investment – are very special ones. He is criticized for completely overlooking the real balance effect.

Keynes, as mentioned above, pointed out that there were several reasons why the 'Keynes effect' could be subverted. A reduction in the price level could increase the real supply of money, but if such changes resulted in greater uncertainty, there could be an increase in the demand for money; it was not obvious that a reduction in the interest rate would follow. Moreover, even if the interest rate did fall, the greater uncertainty and lower aggregate demand due to the redistribution of income could reduce investment.

Regarding the real balance effect, although Keynes did not mention it in his chapter 19 discussion, there is every evidence that this is not simply an oversight on his part since, as Presley (1986) argues, Keynes was closely involved in Robertson's examination of the working of this effect; it would seem to follow that Keynes *chose* to leave it out of consideration. The effect, in any case, as Kalecki (1944) pointed out, provides an incomplete picture of changes in the position of asset-holders in the economy. Since nominal assets held by them are not just liabilities of monetary authorities (outside money), but more importantly, those of other individuals, firms and banks, a fall in the price level redistributes real wealth from debtors to creditors: if debtors have higher marginal propensities to spend (with respect to changes in real wealth) than creditors, a net reduction in real spending can follow.

Also, as mentioned above, Keynes mentioned several other reasons why a wage-cut need not expand employment, which seem to have been completely ignored by the proponents of the wage-rigidity view (Kohn, 1981, for example).

Keynesians other than the believers of the wage-rigidity view have buttressed Keynes's arguments (especially the one relating to income distribution) and provided some additional reasons why a fall in the money wage may not increase the level of employment.[8] For example, the arguments made by the wage-rigidity theorists assume an exogenously-given nominal supply of money: when the price level falls, *given* the nominal supply of money, there will be a real excess supply of money. This need not happen, however, if the supply of money is endogenous due to the behaviour of banks and central banks, as is argued to be the case by many post-Keynesians. The neo-Ricardians have added yet another argument: if capital goods are interpreted as heterogeneous produced goods, and the prices taken for the valuation of capital are Sraffian prices of production, it may turn out that the value of capital may not be a declining function of the rate of profit (or interest). In this case, the investment schedule may be upward-rising, and there may be no (stable) intersection with the full employment saving schedule. With the rate of interest failing to bring saving and investment to equality at full employment, output must be the equilibrating variable; it may therefore fall to a level less than full employment. Without investment having the required interest-elasticity, wage flexibility will not result in full employment.

V. Was Keynes misleading?

A second argument may be made that even though Keynes was not wrong, he misled his followers by not focusing enough on the dynamic part of his theory. Several arguments may be made.

First, rather than spending much time on the dynamic model which examined the consequences of wage movements, he concentrated on the development of the static model with a fixed wage; it is thus natural for the reader to be misled by this lopsidedness. This, however, overlooks the fact, as already noted, that early in the book Keynes points out his assumption regarding the fixed wage and its role, and although he devotes only one chapter to effects of changes in the money wage, he examines the issues relevant for his method in previous chapters.

A second argument is that Keynes made some statements in the *General Theory* which reveal the importance of the assumption of wage rigidity. In his discussion on price changes in chapter 21, for example, he writes:

> If...money-wages were to fall without limit whenever there was a tendency of less than full employment ... there would be no resting place below full employment until either the rate of interest was incapable of falling further or wages were zero. In fact we must have *some* factor, the value of which in money terms is. if not fixed, at least sticky, to give us *any* stability of values in a monetary system. (JMK. VII, pp. 303–4)

This does show that for the constancy of the price level (and the wage rate) the money wage must not fall, but does not imply that Keynes is saying that this money-wage rigidity is required for unemployment to exist. Since it is not generally true that a fall in the money wage (or its downward flexibility) will remove unemployment, the blame for it cannot necessarily be laid on wage rigidity. Indeed, it is possible that wage changes have *no* impact on unemployment, so that the unemployment rate would be an equilibrium one, although money values would not be stable.

A third argument is that Keynes, after the publication of the *General Theory* endorsed the static equilibrium interpretation of his work by writing of Hicks's (1937) formalization: 'I found it very interesting, and really have next to nothing to say by way of criticism' (JMK, XIV, p. 79). It should be remembered, however, that Hicks – unlike Modigliani and the others – did not argue that wage rigidity explains unemployment; he simply provided a formalization of the static aspects of Keynes's theory. The post-Keynesians have been too critical of the IS–LM model for ignoring expectations, uncertainty and historical time, and these criticisms give Keynes's endorsement of the model more significance than it deserves. The model – as even Hicks (1982, p. 100) states – should be properly thought of as formalizing only a part of Keynes's analysis: the determination of short-run equilibrium. However, it should not be used for purposes for which it was not intended, in particular, for determining the crucial feature of the Keynesian revolution. It is this illegitimate use of the model that led – at least in part – to the development of wage-rigidity view. Recognition of the dynamic arguments, with appropriate attention to uncertainty and a variety of other influences, is essential for understanding the complete Keynesian system, influences which are hidden and lost in the functional forms of the equations of the IS–LM model. Also, this focus on this single piece of evidence is unwarranted. Keynes's 1937 paper (JMK, XIV) in response to his critics (where he spends more time on the discussion of uncertainty and expectations, central to his dynamic or historical analysis which is relevant for his wage flexibility discussions, than on the static model) tells a different story. Indeed, Young (1987) has gone so far as to argue that this paper may well have been in part Keynes's answer to the formulations by Hicks (and others).

While we have argued this interpretation, we cannot help but notice that Keynes could have been perhaps a little more explicit, a little more forceful, in differentiating his theoretical contributions from those of the classics. If he did not, can there be a reason for it? Perhaps a part of him did believe in the wage-rigidity argument to some extent? An examination of his work prior to the *General Theory* to trace the development of his views on the role of wage rigidity in generating unemployment,[9] could suggest this. In the *Treatise* (JMK, V, pp. 171, 183–6), in discussing the effects of a reduction in the quantity of money or a rise in the bank rate, Keynes argues that there may be a temporary fall in the level of output causing unemployment to occur if the wage rate was sticky; but unemployment will, over time, reduce the money-wage, and raise employment both by reducing the cost of employing workers and by raising investment demand (due to a lower interest rate caused by the deflation), so that full employment is restored. In his lectures of 1932 and 1933 Keynes argued that if wages were as flexible as the supply price of machines, labour would always be fully employed (JMK, XXIX, pp. 50–2). Thus it seems that Keynes did entertain this wage-rigidity view not too long before the publication of the *General Theory*, and this may serve to show that he had not yet truly broken the umbilical cord from this approach. But he certainly was on his way to doing so since even before these lectures, Keynes was beginning to reveal his doubts about the efficacy of wage-cuts in removing unemployment. As early as June 1931, in a discussion on the question 'Are Wage Cuts a Remedy for Unemployment?' (JMK, XIII, pp. 367–72), Keynes discusses the adverse (from the point of view of reducing unemployment) income distributional consequences of wage cuts on aggregate saving and investment; similar doubts – again based on income distributional consideration – are raised in the early drafts of the *General Theory* (JMK, XIII, pp. 390–4), where Keynes argues that the overall effect of a wage cut on output may well be unfavourable. A full analysis of when and why Keynes definitely changed his mind on the matter remains to be conducted.

VI. Is the wage-rigidity view wrong?

If Keynes cannot be dismissed to be wrong, and if he is not entirely to blame for the misinterpretation, it follows that the wage-rigidity view may be in error and for it, its proponents are to blame.

This raises two questions. First, why have Keynes's 'followers' followed him and fought so strongly in his name although they have not followed his interpretation for the causes of unemployment? Second, why have they erred?

Regarding first question it would seem that there is much, aside from the fundamental cause of unemployment, to fight for. There is the existence of unemployment and its policy implications: it turns out that policy implications of whether one believes or does not believe in the wage-rigidity view are similar (except on the question of the desirability of wage flexibility). Moreover, there was a theoretical advance compared to 'classics', even if Keynes's unemployment, was caused by wage rigidity: he discussed spill-over effects into goods market through his use of aggregate demand and aggregate supply schedules, he advanced the discussion of elements of demand, and his work lent itself easily to empirical investigations.

Regarding the second question several tentative answers may be given. First, its method was more familiar and its results could be readily absorbed into mainstream theory and be understood in its terms; indeed, as we have already seen, unemployment had already been explained in terms of wage rigidity. In contrast, the method of the dynamic part was unfamiliar: this is the truly revolutionary character of Keynes' method, the full implications of which are yet to be grasped.[10] Second, and because of this, wage-rigidity could be more easily introduced into formal models. The initial contributions of Hicks and Lange did that, as also did later contributions. But not so for other arguments. Only a start has been made, by introducing these factors as basically exogenous elements into standard static equilibrium models (Dutt, 1986-7), or by endogenizing some of the arguments into standard macro-models (Howitt, 1986), or even by models with optimizing micro-foundations, limiting attention to a few factors (Hahn and Solow, 1986). The difficulties involved in formalizing these issues, coupled with the methodological morality of neoclassical economics (see Dow, 1980) which puts a premium on modelling as opposed to verbal analysis, shifts attention away from the other, dynamic, issues: the focus on wage-rigidity is the result. Third, the tendency in academia not to read originals, but to read the 'latest' literature. Thus, if there is a misinterpretation somewhere, especially by some influential interpreter, it tends to persist, since many others – who do not read Keynes – are influenced by it. Now very few people read the *General Theory* (perhaps due to a love for fashionable issues and pressures of publishing mathematically elegant models), and even fewer reach chapter 19. Finally, there could be political and ideological reasons. A strong belief in the benefits of free markets, and the observation that unemployment exists, naturally leads to the conclusion that the latter is explained by (temporary and perhaps removable) distortions and imperfections. An even more obvious ideological position is revealed if the blame for these rigidities is placed on the labour unions. While not all theories of wage rigidity seem to take this position, workers seem to have a major role in creating this 'mischief'.[11]

VII. Conclusion

We conclude that the identification of Keynesian economics with wage rigidity is not warranted, and can be explained mainly in terms of the theoretical structure and methodological morality of mainstream economic theory, by academic pressures and fashions, and perhaps by ideology.

Once this is more widely recognized, the debates between the new classicals and mainstream Keynesians regarding whether rigidities are important will become largely irrelevant. Keynes's revolution will be seen as having much more to do with the introduction of dynamic factors than with money wage rigidity, and more effort will be expended on understanding them.

Acknowledgement

An earlier version of this paper was presented at the History of Economics Society meetings, Toronto, 19 June 1988. We are grateful to Victoria Chick and Sandy Darity for useful comments and discussions. When this paper was initially written and presented in Toronto, the first author was at the Department of Economics, Florida International University.

Notes

1. See Modigliani (1986) and McCallum (1987, p. 126), for recent examples.
2. See also Chick (1985) for an interpretation of how Keynes abstracted from dynamics and history by fixing the wage in the static model.
3. By which we mean a position of excess supply of labour at the going wage. An alternative definition, used by Darity and Horn (1983) based on one of Keynes's definitions, allows the labour market to clear, and therefore robs the wage-rigidity view of any significance.
4. He also discusses some open-economy issues which are omitted here.
5. See Coddington (1983).
6. See Dutt (1990) for a more precise discussion.
7. Modigliani overlooked the case of zero interest inelasticity of investment.
8. See Dutt and Amadeo (1990) for more details and references.
9. See Amadeo (1989) for a fuller discussion of some of these points.
10. See, however, Kohn (1986) for a view that Keynes was shunting macroeconomics from the path of sequential (dynamic) analysis to equilibrium (static) analysis. While this interpretation is correct for the relatively formal aspect of Keynes's work, it does injustice to the many dynamic issues that he analyses using the equilibrium approach as a point of departure with which to analyse them.
11. Even the efficiency-wage theory, which explains wage rigidity in terms of the profit-maximizing behaviour of the firm usually assumes an efficiency-wage relationship which can be interpreted to be resulting from worker 'mischief'.

References

Amadeo, E. J. 1989, *The Development of Keynes's Principle of Effective Demand*, Edward Elgar, Aldershot.

Chick, V. 1985, 'Time and the wage-unit in the method of *The General Theory*: history and equilibrium', in T. Lawson and H. Pesaran, (eds), *Keynes' Economics. Methodological Issues*, M E. Sharpe, Armonk, New York.

Coddington, A. 1983, *Keynesian Economics: The Search for First Principles*, Allen and Unwin, London.

Darity, W., Jr and Horn, B. L. 1983, 'Involuntary unemployment reconsidered', *Southern Economic Journal* 49(3), pp. 717-33.

Dow, S. 1980, 'Methodological morality in the Cambridge controversies', *Journal of Post Keynesian Economics* 2(3) (Spring).

Dutt, A. K. 1986-7, 'Wage rigidity and unemployment: the simple diagrammatics of two views', *Journal of Post Keynesian Economics* (Winter).

Dutt, A. K. 1990, *Growth, Distribution and Uneven Development*, Cambridge University Press, Cambrige.

Dutt, A. K. and Amadeo, E. J. 1990, *Keynes's Third Alternative?* Edward Elgar, Aldershot..

Haberler, G. 1946, 'The place of *The General Theory of Employment, Interest and Money* in the history of economic thought', *Review of Economics and Statistics*, 28 (November), pp. 187-94.

Hahn, F. and Solow, R. 1986, 'Is wage flexibility a good thing?', in W. Beckerman (ed.), *Wage Rigidity and Unemployment*, Johns Hopkins University Press, Baltimore, MD.

Hicks, J. R. 1937, 'Mr. Keynes and the Classics: a suggested interpretation', *Econometrica* 5 (April), pp. 147-59.

Hicks, J. R. 1982, *Money, Interest & Wages*, Harvard University Press, Cambridge, Mass.

Howitt, P. 1986, 'Wage flexibility and unemployment', *Eastern Economic Journal* 12(3) (July-September).

Kalecki, M. 1944, 'Professor Pigou on 'The Classical Stationary State': a comment', *Economic Journal* 54.

Keynes, J. M. 1971-82, *The Collected Writings of J. M. Keynes*, ed. D. Moggridge, Macmillan, London, Vols V, VII, XIII, XIV and XXIX.

Kohn, M. 1981, 'A loanable funds theory of unemployment and monetary disequilibrium', *American Economic Review* 71(5) (December), pp. 859-79.

Kohn, M. 1986, 'Monetary analysis, the equilibrium method, and Keynes's "General Theory"', *Journal of Political Economy* 94(6), pp. 1191-224.

Lange, O. 1938, 'The rate of interest and the optimum propensity to consume', *Economica* 5 (February), pp. 12-32.

McCallum, B. 1987, 'The development of Keynesian macroeconomics', *American Economic Review* 72(2) (May).

Marshall, A. 1920, *Industry and Trade*, 3rd edition, Macmillan, London.

Meade, J. A. 1937, 'A simplified model of Mr. Keynes' system', *Review of Economic Studies* 4 (February).

Modigliani, F. 1944, 'Liquidity preference and the theory of interest and money', *Econometrica* 12 (January), pp. 45-88.

Modigliani, F. 1986, *The Debate Over Stabilization Policy*, Cambridge University Press, Cambridge.

Patinkin, D. 1956, *Money, Interest and Prices*, Harper & Row, New York.

Pigou, A. C. 1927, *Industrial Fluctuations*, Macmillan, London.

Pigou, A. C. 1933, *Theory of Unemployment*, Macmillan, London.

Pigou, A. C. 1943, 'The classical stationary state', *Economic Journal* 53 (December), pp. 343-51.

Presley, J. R. 1986, 'J. M. Keynes and the real balance effect', *The Manchester School* (March).

Young, W. 1987, *Interpreting Mr. Keynes. The IS-LM Enigma*, Polity Press, Cambridge.

8 Some Methodological Issues in the Theory of Speculation

Victoria Chick

The speculative demand for money and securities, which formed such an important part of Keynes's *General Theory* (1936), has not featured in recent summaries of monetary theory, even those by post-Keynesians (Moore, 1978; Rousseas, 1986; Arestis, 1988). Yet who could doubt the importance of speculation in foreign exchange or the significance of speculation in the 1986–7 stock market boom and its subsequent, October 1987, crash?

Defining speculation has never been straightfoward, even if, like art, one prides oneself on recognizing it when one sees it. According to both Keynes and Friedman, speculators are buyers and sellers of securities who act on expectations; but Keynes's hypothesis of the way speculators form their expectations is remarkably simple, even primitive. Each speculator has his/her own notion of what constitutes a 'normal' rate of interest. If the actual rate is higher than this normal rate, that person expects the rate to fall; if it is lower, he/she expects it to rise. Therefore the higher (lower) the actual rate of interest the greater the (probable) weight of opinion that the rate will fall (rise) and the larger the demand for securities (money) on speculative account. This theory has the advantage that the current rate of interest, which is observable, stands as a proxy for a concatenation of personal expectations which are not observable, either individually or collectively.

The theory has been disliked – not only for the *ad hoc* character of its hypothesis of speculators' behaviour but also for its subjectivity, its assertion of individuality[1] (Tobin, 1958; Leijonhufvud, 1978), and perhaps most of all for its threat both to the concept of 'rational markets' and to belief in the market's stability.

Milton Friedman, in a famous article (1953), attacked the prediction of instability. He purported to show that if speculators were to make a profit it could be shown that they reduced the amplitude of the 'underlying' fluctuations in exchange rates. His result was disputed (Baumol, 1957; Telser, 1959) without challenging the underlying methodology.

Tobin (1958), as everyone knows, claimed to 'improve' on Keynes's theory by getting the same inverse relation between idle money and the rate of interest from investors' attempts to balance risk and return, with no need for individual differences in expectations. Even if all agree on the characteristics of each security, a market for securities (and money) can be created between those with different preferences between return and risk.

There is in Tobin no specification of the process by which the distribution of interest rates (or security prices) is generated from time-series data. In his answer to Friedman, Baumol modelled the 'underlying' path of exchange rates by a sine wave, without discussion. In the context of fluctuations of security prices, the sine wave represents a stylized fact: movement over the business cycle, as governed by productivity and thrift.

By contrast, specifying the generating function is at the core of rational expectations: the essence of rational expectations is to find the expectations mechanism which is consistent with the 'theory', i.e. the assumed generating function, so that expectations are fulfilled except for random variation.

In this paper, the approaches to speculation of Keynes, Friedman–Baumol–Telser (FBT), and rational expectations (with Tobin's model coming in occasionally) are compared in three respects: (i) the motives of speculators, (ii) the relationship of speculators to other market participants, and (iii) the nature of the market within which speculators operate. A comparison is then made between the methodology of each approach and methodological changes in physics. FBT's approach reflects the methodology of classical physics, rational expectations has affinities with early interpretations of the Heisenberg principle, and Keynes's methodology, it turns out, is the most modern.

I. The motives of speculators

There are those who would argue that any asset-holding involves speculation, as future prices, absolute and relative, are uncertain. This approach strips speculation of any specific meaning. It is possible, however, to distinguish speculators from other market participants by differences in motivation and source of profit. Speculators are those who buy and sell securities and/or foreign exchange with the aim and intention of capturing short-term capital gains and avoiding capital losses. Their time horizon is rather too short to pay much attention to interest rates on particular assets, as differences in these are dominated in the short run by changes in capital values.

Their behaviour stands in contrast to 'long-term investors', who place funds in securities markets (at home or across the exchanges) with the aim of accumulating wealth by earning interest and if possible, long-term capital gains. Thus a central question is whether a particular approach admits of *differences* in motive between speculators and other market participants, where both groups are in the market to make money but do so by different means.

Keynes's stance was perfectly clear: *speculation* he defined as 'the activity of forecasting the psychology of the market', in contrast to *enterprise*, 'the activity of forecasting the prospective yield of assets over their whole life' (Keynes, 1936, p. 158). Speculators have a short time-horizon and are motivated therefore by capital gains rather than interest: speculators engage in a 'battle of wits to anticipate the basis of conventional valuation a few months hence, rather than the prospective yield of an investment over a long term of years' (p. 155). In this description speculators are tied to the market. Their problem is how to deal with what Pesaran (1984) has called 'behavioural uncertainty': the need to forecast the behaviour of other market participants (which would not be a problem if everyone behaved alike).

Elsewhere in *The General Theory* Keynes speaks of speculators 'knowing better than the market what the future will bring forth', suggesting either superior 'insider knowledge' or the use of a different and superior information set than that used by other market participants. Diverse (or divergent) expectations may exist both within the group identified as speculators and also between them and other market participants – indeed the stability of the market depends on diverse opinion.

The coexistence of two types of agents – speculators and 'others' – is also implicit in FBT. These authors took as their starting point regular fluctuations in exchange rates, comparable in the present context to fluctuations in interest rates which vary over business cycles, rising in booms and falling in slumps in accordance with 'fundamentals' – the forces of productivity and thrift, Keynes's 'enterprise'. Baumol's contribution to this debate represented these fluctuations by a sine wave. No generating function was specified.

While to Keynes the game of speculation involves forecasting the opinion of other market participants, FBT's speculators operate by forecasting these 'fundamental' fluctuations. Friedman's demonstration of the stabilizing effect of speculation rests on the assumption that successful speculators are those who foresee the turning points of this function and sell just before the peaks and buy just before the troughs. By acting against the 'fundamental' market pressure they thus dampen the fluctuations: thus profitable speculation is stabilizing.

Baumol's contribution was to point out that speculators could make just as much profit by selling and buying just *after* the peaks and troughs, which would tend to accelerate the upswings and downswings and might even increase the overall amplitude of the series. His difference with Friedman derives from his assumption of extrapolative expectations in contrast to the regressive expectations of Friedman. The basic premiss of an independent, objective time-series of interest rates, on which speculators play but which is not permanently affected by speculative activity, is common to both. This raises the problem of identifying those at whose expense the successful speculator makes profits. The Government Broker is not active. Who is left but the unsuccessful speculator? Speculation, in the FBT model, is thus seen as a zero-sum game requiring a steady supply of new 'gulls' to replace those who had learned their lesson.

A further problem arises from the definition of speculators as 'those who forecast': how is speculation to be distinguished from arbitrage? This problem was raised at the time of the Friedman debate by Eastman and Stykolt (1956). It has not been resolved.

Tobin found the proposition of diverse expectations among speculators, and implicitly also the existence of different strategies in securities marekts, uncongenial: if there is one best way to make profit, why does not everyone adopt it? He resolved this problem by appealing to a trade-off between return and risk, towards which people had different *preferences*.

The agents in Tobin's model are distinguished not by *motives* but by *preferences*. Depending on one's 'taste' for risk or safety one is a risk-averter, a risk-lover or a 'plunger'. The latter is so attracted to risk that he/she carries undiversified portfolios, 'plunging' from securities to money as circumstances change. The tone of the article leaves little doubt that this 'taste' is to be regarded as slightly mad, the only 'normal' behaviour being risk-aversion. Plunging is, of course, exactly what Keynesian or FBT speculators do![2] I have argued elsewhere (Chick, 1983, p. 204) that plunging is not mad at all, but is rational behaviour for speculators, as far as their speculative assets are concerned.[3]

In distinguishing between motives and preferences I have in mind that motives vary from person to person for *economic* reasons: an agent may have a long time-horizon (associated with the 'enterprise' motive) if he/she is, say, saving for retirement; a desire for capital gains may be motivated by, say, favourable tax treatment of capital gains; one speculates only if one has both the taste for it and also the time to devote to it; others may prefer to let their paper gains and losses cancel out; and so on.

Suppose that someone wanted to speculate in the context of Tobin's model, where interest rate behaviour is represented by a stable and symmetrical probability distribution, a normal distribution. If auto-correlation is not a feature of its generation, then clearly, everyone's rational expectation of the future rate of interest, whatever its date, is the mean of that distribution. And if the date is far enough away, even auto-correlation has no importance. Both speculators and long-term investors will agree on this. Therefore, there will be no trading generated by the speculative motive: when everyone's expectations are the same, everyone will wish either to buy or to sell; transactions languish for lack of anyone to trade with[4] (Chick, 1983, pp. 213–17).

Despite attempts by rational expectations theorists to incorporate 'behavioural uncertainty' (see, e.g., Frydman, 1982; Townsend, 1982), or differences in knowledge (Grossman and Stiglitz, 1980) and to distinguish market participants by the extent or accuracy of their knowledge, individual differences of behaviour have been judged (Tirole, 1982; Runde and Torr, 1985) inconsistent with the notion of rationality embodied in the rational expectations approach: the only 'motive' which has met with universal approval by other practitioners of the school is to discover the 'true model' and form one's expectations in conformity with it. (See the summary of this issue in Torr, 1984; 1988.) While this is presumed to be everyone's motive, thus leaving no room for divergent roles – let alone diverse expectations – among agents in a particular market, bringing expectations into line with 'the truth' presents one of the thorny problems in the rational expectations literature: convergence.[5]

On the matter of whether a separate class of economic agents called speculators can coexist with others pursuing different aims, rational expectations has so far[6] given a negative answer: there is only one form of rational behaviour, namely conformity with the true model. Tobin, while superficially differing from this position in allowing for different behaviours, does not actually address the sort of expectations which speculators must form. We have seen that speculation is out of keeping with Tobin's parameterized risk. The expectation required to be formed by the Keynesian or Friedmanian speculator concerns not the overall behaviour of a time-series as captured by statistics (the mean and standard deviation) describing a stable distribution of its outcomes, but rather a specific expectation of the value of the variable for a specific day or range of days in the future. Rational expectations theory allies in this respect with Tobin: the problem is to form correct expectations of the variable's probability distribution conditioned on the information available to the present date (Lucas and Prescott, 1971).

The above investigation has produced strange alignments: Keynes with Friedman against Tobin and rational expectations. In the next section, which explores the relationship of speculators to other market participants, we find different affinities. (A dualist will find this paper most uncongenial.)

II. Speculators and other market participants

In the FBT model, speculators enter the market sporadically, near peaks and troughs, and have only a transitory effect on the underlying sine wave.

When they cease to be active the determination of the rate of interest reverts to whatever deeper model gives rise to that wave.

By contrast, in rational expectations, all actors are included as part of the system whose behaviour constitutes the true model. Mainstream economics before rational expectations tended to treat certain difficult parts of the economic system as exogenous: the government, for example, was seen as impinging on 'the economy' – that is, the private sector – from outside. Rational expectations theory reminds us that such a dichotomy is mistaken: the government, by acting, *changes* the expectations and hence the behaviour of the private sector, and changes thereby the world it is trying to affect. If rational expectations were able to countenance two different sorts of behaviour, and diverse expectations within the class called speculators, the influence of speculation would have to be included in the model of interest rate determination which all rational agents are trying to discover.

Keynes, while not treating this matter formally, is in agreement with rational expectations on this crucial issue: by contrast to the treatment in FBT, speculators' actions affect the future course of interest rates, and their actions have real effects, since the rate of interest affects investment. How *much* effect speculators have is a matter of *degree*, not of principle: 'Speculation may do no harm as bubbles on a steady stream of enterprise. But the position is serious when enterprise becomes the bubble on a whirlpool of speculation' (Keynes, 1936, p. 159).

Shackle has been the most percipient and radical interpreter of Keynes's theory of interest. He altogether doubts the possibility of a stable equilibrium for that variable: he describes it as 'inherently restless'. This restlessness derives from the behaviour of speculators as follows:

> If we consider the influence of speculation in isolation, there is no one expectation about the immanent behaviour of the interest rate ...which if held by everyone would cause the rate to remain constant for more than a short time....[U]ncertainty about the future...is itself an autonomous cause of change....[I]f the same opinion as to the immediately future behaviour spreads to everybody, the rate of interest will change at the moment when this belief takes hold, unless, indeed, the belief is that it will rise just fast enough for the corresponding price-fall of securities to cancel the accruing interest; but in this case it will remain constant, and falsify the belief that is holding it constant, whereupon it will fall. (Shackle, 1968, pp. 51–3; italics in the original suppressed.)

(Note that Shackle does not suggest that *trades* will take place, only that *prices* – or interest rates – will change, which they may do even in the absence of trading. See also Keynes, 1936, p. 199.)

Not even the tension of opposites, between bulls and bears, can be counted on to maintain a steady rate of interest:

> [If the rate of interest] is held constant by the existence of two camps holding opposite opinions as to its immediate future movements, one or other of these opinions must be wrong. The action of those who find their opinion falsified will cause the rate of interest to change. (ibid., p. 53)

Keynes noted that 'In a static society or in a society in which for any other reason no one feels any uncertainty about the future rates of interest, the Liquidity Function L2 ... will always be zero in equilibrium' (1936, pp. 208–9).

Shackle's examples suggest that this equilibrium is like those – made such fun of by Joan Robinson (e.g. 1978) – which were impossible to get into unless one was already there: when speculators disappear, the rate of interest will be stable and if the rate of interest were stable they would disappear, but until they stop trading, the rate of interest is 'restless' and there is always something for them to speculate about.

Shackle's exploration of the dynamic effects of speculation illustrates by sharp contrast just why Tobin's static model cannot cope with speculation: speculation is inherently a dynamic phenomenon, involving the forecasting of interest rates on specific future dates, not the expected value of their overall behaviour. Note also the fundamental difference with FBT, where the 'fundamentals' reassert themselves and speculation has no lasting effect.

III. The nature of the market
Neither Keynes nor Friedman et al. specify the source of the underlying fluctuations in terms of any rigorous model; as noted earlier, the ups and downs of security prices or exchange rates were taken as stylized facts. If their cause can be reduced to supply and demand for the securities or currencies themselves, then one has little scope for speculation unless speculators have superior knowledge, for arbitrage, based on knowledge of this 'true model' will ensure that only random fluctuations remain (Samuelson, 1972). This is not a proposition which originated with rational expectations, though it is entirely congenial to it: once participants know the determinants of supply and demand, there remain only random errors, about which no (further) expectations can rationally be formed.

The question for rational expectations in the present context would seem to be the meaning and content of the 'true model'. In FBT the 'truth' is (non-speculative) 'fundamentals'. The idea that there are determinants of the rate of interest which are, in the end, quite unaffected by speculators' behaviour might seem a suitable candidate for treatment by rational expectations. The economist's 'model' to which agents in a rational expectations theorist's world must adjust appear to have a status similar to the 'laws of nature', which man ignores to his/her peril but which are completely independent of his/her actions. Torr (1984) uses the example of fishermen and the tide tables; the tables are useful to the fishermen, but whether fishermen pull their boats sufficiently up the beach to be safe from the tides is of no interest to the sea.

A model of interest rate determination which is unaffected by the actions of speculators is like a theory of the tides. It places speculators at one remove from the 'real action', denying Shackle's description of the continual reassessment and alteration of expectations which results as much from speculators' actions as from changes in the 'fundamentals'. To the extent that speculators' expectations feed off the market itself rather than being based on a different information set, a rational expectations approach would have to build in not only the expectations of the speculators but the effect of those expectations on the subsequent behaviour of the market, which in turn alters speculators' expectations.

Such a world would not only be non-ergodic (see Davidson, 1982–3, for the importance of this property to rational expectations): this is a world in which anything can happen, depending on the *sequence of actions* as well as the formation of expectations. Whether supply and demand 'fundamentals' could even be fitted into such a scheme, let alone serve as its base, is doubtful, for supply and demand are based on the presumption of stationarity (see the discussion in Torr, 1988).

The sort of market that Shackle describes is now the subject of literature on multiple equilibria and 'bubbles'. At least one attempt to incorporate bubbles into a rational expectations model was defeated by the mathematical difficulty of the enterprise (Blanchard and Watson, 1982). The conceptual status of these features within rational expectations is a matter of unsettled controversy (Kindleberger, 1988; Calvo, 1988), even where the notion of multiple equilibria is limited to those generated by different initial conditions, whereas what is at issue here is path dependency.[7]

IV. Different world-views: a comparison with physics

It seems to me that there is a striking analogy, in terms of world-view, between the three conceptions of the relation between speculators and the rest of the market as outlined in this paper and the evolution of thinking in physics about the relation between the observer and the thing observed, with the speculators playing the role of the observer and 'the [rest of the] market' the thing to be observed. The Friedman–Tobin model works within the world-view of classical physics. The rational expectations model is reminiscent of the early understanding of the Heisenberg Principle, when the difficulty of pinning down electrons was perceived as something which in principle could be overcome by more refined methods of measurement. The Keynes story, in which the behaviour of speculators influences the subsequent path of the decision variable, conforms to the modern understanding of the Heisenberg principle, in which the observer (here, the speculator) influences the outcome of the experiment.

In classical physics, the observer faces an objective world which can, in principle, be understood if one can discover the 'laws' by which it is governed. The observer seeks to discover these laws by asking questions about aspects of this 'world', taking measurements, and formulating theories. These activities are believed to leave the 'world' unaffected, apart from minor damage which might be caused by an observer's measurement procedures. The Friedman–Tobin speculator, like the observer in classical physics, observes 'fundamental' fluctuations and even makes use of them, without altering their course materially. Such difference as they make has its parallel in the damage inflicted by measurement procedures.

In contrast to the classical assumption that – if only we could observe them accurately – particles were discrete entities moving along determinate paths, modern physics accepts a probabilistic description of the position and/or velocity of particles. This is Heisenberg's uncertainty principle. This principle has passed through two distinct stages of interpretation. (For an account aimed at a general audience, see Bohm, 1984.) In the first stage, it was still believed that there was an objective universe, but that the observer's inability to describe the position or momentum of particles except in probabilistic terms was attributable only to the irreducible element of unpredictability in every measurement procedure.

This early interpretation was held, most notably, by Einstein. The conclusion drawn from it was that there was no reason *in principle* why deterministic laws of the universe (comparable to the 'true' model of the economy) did not exist; the only reason that they were not discoverable was the crudeness of human measuring procedures compared to the object of measurement.

It would therefore be a mistake to believe that because rational expectations presupposes stochastic processes it has affinities with modern physics. (Drakopoulos, 1987, also makes this point.) It is rather to this early interpretation of the Heisenberg principle that the rational expectations story has affinity. In rational expectations a certain amount of irreducible randomness is accepted, and discovering the true model is impeded by this 'noise', but in principle the true model is discoverable.

It is – surprisingly or not, depending on your priors – the methodological stance of Keynes and Shackle which is closest in spirit to the methodology of modern science, which accepts a more radical interpretation of the Heisenberg principle. In this version of the principle, it is accepted that the observer influences experimental outcomes and the answer one gets depends on the questions asked. (For a description of the crucial experiment, see Stoppard, 1988.) The analogy to this proposition, applied to the present problem, implies the full interaction of speculators and others in the market.

The result of accepting their interaction is that one's view of the operation of the market is fundamentally altered from what it would be if speculators were not there: the observer and the thing observed are one. There is an irreducible quality of uncertainty about the nature of the thing 'observed' (in the present case, securities or foreign exchange markets) which is not captured merely by including an error term.

That economists in the nineteenth century modelled their work by analogy to physics is well known and in some quarters deplored. To raise the question of a similarity between three stages of methodological development in physics and the methodological basis of the three models at the core of our present discussion is not to suggest that modelling economics after physics is necessarily a good idea. I would, however, tentatively suggest that modelling economics on a physics that has been superseded for over 60 years (Heisenberg published his paper in 1927) is particularly foolish. It might be helpful to take on board the now-established ideas of 'modern' physics before Chaos overtakes us.

Acknowledgements

The author wishes to thank an undergraduate student for provoking the thoughts which led to this paper; Edward Amadeo for encouraging their development; William Darity Jr, Xeni Dassiou, John Driffill, Gabriele Galati, Christopher Torr and Richard Vaughan for useful bibliographical suggestions, comments and stimulating discussion. I have a general, and very large, debt to Christopher Torr's work on the issues at hand.

Notes

1. To Keynes's little xenophobic jibe that monetary control is 'more precarious in the United States where everyone holds the same opinion at the same time' (1936, p. 172), Leijonhufvud (1978, p. 190) replied, perhaps defending the conformism of his adopted country, that 'In England...everyone thinks for himself and most people, therefore, arrive at the wrong conclusion'.
2. Plunging does *not* imply, as so many people have said (see, e.g. Dennis, 1981, p. 106) that the plunger, when he/she is in bonds, holds no money; money is still held for transactions purposes. Nor does it imply that plungers (or speculators) are *certain*. They must, however, be *decisive* in the face of uncertainty; thus they act *as if* they are certain.
3. It is not, of course, rational to 'plunge' with all one's assets. Since Tobin writes as if the whole portfolio is involved, (see the previous footnote for one aspect of this point) his antipathy to plunging is understandable.
4. Prices may change, however, perhaps a great deal, in the hope of finding someone willing to trade. This may invalidate Tobin's distribution, but that is neither here nor there, as the theory was never suited to the speculation problem, which is my point. It is now

accepted in some quarters at least that Tobin's theory is about precautionary and investment portfolios, not speculation. (See, e.g., Harris, 1981.)
5. The problem of convergence is that even when everyone knows the true model this knowledge is not sufficient for a rational expectations equilibrium – the transition to rational expectations cannot be made unless each actor knows that others also know the model and have rational expectations about it. This is a modern version of Joan Robinson's dictum that it was impossible to *get into* equilibrium: one has to have *been* in it from the time of the Fall of Man (Robinson, 1978). It also repeats what we know from Walras: that for equilibrium each actor – or an 'auctioneer' – must know the response of everyone else to the proposed vector of prices.
6. An approach which seems to be consistent with this possibility, however, is that of Shiller (1978), who shows that the Sargent/Wallace model (1973) can have multiple solutions. Shiller's alternative solution, which Sargent and Wallace did not mention, includes a variable j which cannot be forecast.

> This means that *any* unforecastable economic variable or the innovation in any variable may enter the solution! If all individuals conclude that the change in the Dow Jones average should be used in [the forecasting function] as j, then they will be rational in assuming so. If they have 'hunches' which can be translated into the variable j, then if they forecast via [the forecasting function], their hunches will yield rational forecasts. (Shiller, 1978, p. 33)

(It is the general price level next period which is being forecast.)
7. It is perhaps better to look elsewhere for formal models of speculation. Path-dependent multiple equilibria are at the core of catastrophe theory, for example. There is at least one catastrophe-theoretic model based on interaction between speculators who 'follow the charts' and 'fundamentalists' (Zeeman, 1977).

References

Arestis, P. 1988, 'Post-Keynesian theory of money, credit and finance', *Thames Papers in Political Economy*, reprinted in *Post-Keynesian Monetary Economics*, ed. P. Arestis, Edward Elgar, Aldershot.
Baumol, W. J. 1957, 'Speculation, profitability and stability', *Review of Economics and Statistics*, pp. 263–71.
Blanchard, O. and Watson, M. W. 1982, 'Bubbles, rational expectations and financial markets', in *Crises in the Economic and Financial Structure*, ed. P. Wachtel, Heath, Lexington, Mass.
Bohm, D. 1984, *Causality and Chance in Modern Physics*, 2nd edition, Routledge & Kegan Paul, London.
Calvo, G. A. 1988, 'Tulipmania', in *The New Palgrave: A Dictionary of Economics*, eds. J. Eatwell, M. Milgate and P. Newman, Macmillan, London.
Chick, V. 1983, *Macroeconomics After Keynes*, Philip Allan, Deddington, and MIT Press, Cambridge, Mass.
Davidson, P. 1982–3, 'A fallacious foundation for studying crucial decision making', *Journal of Post Keynesian Economics 5*, pp. 182–98.
Dennis, G. E. J. 1981, *Monetary Economics*, Longmans, London.
Drakopoulos, S. 1987, 'Modern physics and mainstream economic methodology', mimeo., Stirling University.
Eastman, H.C. and Stykolt, S. 1956, 'Exchange stabilisation in Canada, 1950–54', *Canadian Journal of Economics*, pp. 221–33.
Friedman, M. 1953, 'The case for flexible exchange rates', in *Essays in Positive Economics*, ed. M. Friedman, University of Chicago Press, Chicago.
Frydman, R. 1982, 'Towards an understanding of market processes: Individual expectations, learning, and convergence to rational expectations equilibrium', *American Economic Review 72*, pp. 652–68.

Grossman, S. J. and Stiglitz, J. 1980, 'On the impossibility of informationally efficient markets', *American Economic Review* 70, pp. 393–408.

Harris, L. 1981, *Monetary Theory*, McGraw-Hill, New York.

Keynes, J. M. 1936, *The General Theory of Employment, Interest and Money*, Macmillan, London.

Kindleberger, C. P. 1988, 'Bubbles', in *The New Palgrave: A Dictionary of Economics*, eds J. Eatwell, M. Milgate and P. Newman, Macmillan, London.

Leijonhufvud, A. 1978, 'The Wicksell connection: variations on a theme' in *Information and Coordination*, ed. A. Leijonhufvud, Oxford University Press, London.

Lucas, R. E. and Prescott, E. G. 1971, 'Investment under uncertainty', *Econometrica* 39, pp. 659–82.

Moore, B. J. 1978, 'Monetary factors', in *A Guide to Post Keynesian Economics*, ed. A. S. Eichner, M. E. Sharpe, Armonk, N.Y.

Pesaran, M. H. 1984, 'Expectations formation and macroeconomic modelling', in *Contemporary Macroeconomic Modelling*, eds P. Malgrange and P.-A. Muet, Basil Blackwell, Oxford.

Robinson, J. 1978, 'A lecture delivered at Oxford by a Cambridge economist', in *Contributions to Modern Economics*, ed. J. Robinson, Basil Blackwell, Oxford.

Rousseas, S. 1986, *Post Keynesian Monetary Economics*, M. E. Sharpe, Armonk, N Y.

Runde, J. and Torr, C. 1985, 'Divergent expectations and rational expectations', *South African Journal of Economics* 53, pp. 217–25.

Samuelson, P. A. 1972, 'Proof that properly anticipated prices fluctuate randomly', in *Collected Scientific Papers of P. A. Samuelson*, ed. R. C. Merton, vol. 2, pp. 782–90.

Sargent, T. J., and Wallace, N. 1973, 'Rational expectations and the dynamics of hyperinflation', *International Economic Review* 14, pp. 328–50.

Shackle, G. L. S. 1968, *Expectations, Investment and Income*, 2nd edn, Clarendon Press, Oxford.

Shiller, R. J. 1978, 'Rational expectations and the dynamic structure of macroeconomic models: a critical review', *Journal of Monetary Economics* 4, pp. 1–44.

Stoppard, T. 1988, *Hapgood*, Faber & Faber, London.

Telser, L. G. 1959, 'A theory of speculation relating profitability and stability', *Review of Economics and Statistics*, pp. 295–302.

Tirole, J. 1982, 'On the possibility of speculation under rational expectations', *Econometrica* 50.

Tobin, J. 1958, 'Liquidity preference as behaviour towards risk', *Review of Economic Studies*.

Torr, C. S. W. 1984, 'Expectations and the new classical economics', *Australian Economic Papers*, pp. 197–205.

Torr, C. S. W. 1988, *Equilibrium, Expectations and Information: A Study of the General Theory and Modern Classical Economics*, Polity Press, Cambridge.

Townsend, R. M. 1982, 'Forecasting the forecasts of others', *Journal of Political Economy* 91, pp. 546–88.

Zeeman, E. C. 1977, 'On the unstable behaviour of stock exchanges', in *Catastrophe Theory*, ed. E. C. Zeeman, Addison-Wesley, Lexington.

9 Hayek's Ailing Research Programme: The Case of Hicks's Marginal Revolution in Monetary Theory

Ivo Maes

Introduction

The 1930s are well known as 'The Years of High Theory' (Shackle, 1967). Economic theory went through a period of fermentation wherein the foundations for postwar developments were laid. But certain theories, for example those of Hayek, were abandoned. As Lachman notes: 'For Austrian economics, however, this was a tragic decade... Professor Hayek, having made a triumphal entry into the University of London in 1931 ... had become a rather lonely figure by 1939' (Lachman, 1986, p. 225).

In the early 1930s Hayek was setting up an Austrian-oriented research programme in monetary theory at the London School of Economics. One of his fundamental heuristic ideas was to develop monetary theory in line with capital theory. The focus of monetary theory should then be on the intertemporal exchange relations and the effects of monetary disturbances on the structure of production.

Hayek's theories aroused some important controversies. One of the main elements which was criticized was Hayek's use of Böhm-Bawerk's theory of capital. Hawtrey, in his *Economica* review of *Prices and Production*, called it an 'intolerably cumbersome theory of capital ... singularly ill-adapted for use in monetary theory, or indeed in any practical treatment of the capital market' (Hawtrey, 1932, p. 125).

The fundamental strategical option, whether one should advance by integrating monetary theory and capital theory, was also one of the main points of disagreement between Hayek and Keynes, Keynes rejecting this strategy: 'Dr. Hayek complains that I do not myself propound any satisfactory theory of capital and interest and that I do not build on any existing theory ... But there is no such theory at present, and, as Dr. Hayek would agree, a thorough treatment of it might lead one rather a long way from monetary theory' (Keynes, 1931, p. 394).

Hayek, to a certain extent, agrees with Keynes that there is no satisfactory theory of capital. But he maintains his research strategy: 'even if we have no satisfactory theory we do at least possess a far better one than that on which he (= Keynes) is content to rely, namely that of Böhm-Bawerk and Wicksell' (Hayek, 1931b, p. 401).[1]

These criticisms drove Hayek to a further elaboration of capital theory, a path which lead him to *The Pure Theory of Capital* (Hayek, 1941). But, even at the London School of Economics, his research strategy was not convincing to everybody. Here the case of J. R. Hicks, one of the brilliant people at the London School of Economics in the early 1930s, will be examined.[2]

At the London School of Economics (LSE)

In the autumn of 1929, after studying mathematics and economics at Oxford, John Hicks was appointed as a junior lecturer at the London School of Economics. He would stay until 1935. His first years there were mainly of preparation. Hugh Dalton gave him the advice of reading Pareto, who would have a deep influence on Hicks. 'So it was reading in the *Manuale* which started me off on economic theory, I was deep in Pareto, before I got much out of Marshall' (Hicks, 1979a, p. 196).

Also in the autumn of 1929, Lionel Robbins was appointed as professor and head of the Economics Department at the London School of Economics. He would have a profound and lasting influence.

It is remarkable how many economists, who would become famous in later years, were with Robbins at the London School of Economics in the 1930s. Besides J. R. Hicks, there were F. A. Hayek, Arnold Plant, Roy Allen, Richard Sayers, Nicholas Kaldor, Abba Lerner and Ursula Webb (Ursula Hicks after 1935). Cooperation between these economists was intense. This was institutionalized in the weekly meetings for the seminar.

There are two aspects of the 'Robbins Circle' which are quite interesting. The Circle was, broadly speaking, characterized by a belief in the working of a free market economy and it was very internationally-oriented.

Initially at least, participants of the LSE seminar shared a common *Weltantschauung*,

> a common faith... The faith in question was a belief in the free market, or 'price-mechanism' – that a competitive system, free of all 'interferences' by government or monopolistic combinations, of capital or of labour, would easily find an 'equilibrium'....Hayek, when he joined us was to introduce into this doctrine an important qualification – that money (somehow) must be kept 'neutral', in order that the mechanism should work smoothly'. (Hicks, 1982, p. 3)

Moreover, there was another difference. Cambridge was dominated by the heritage of Alfred Marshall and was rather inner-directed and insular.

The same cannot be said of the London School of Economics: 'At London, on the other hand, there was no such strong local heritage... It was natural therefore for us to seek wider affiliations, both in time and in space' (Robbins, 1971, p. 133). One can discern these influences in several ways. The Austrian Hayek was a professor. Several other foreigners were students or lecturers at the LSE. There were frequent contacts with many foreign economists who visited the LSE giving special lectures – 'Haberler and Machlup from Vienna, Bresciani Turoni from Rome, Lindahl, Ohlin and Frisch from Scandinavia, Marget, Knight and Viner from the United States' (Robbins, 1971, p. 132). These and other foreign economists were also on the reading list at the LSE. It is not surprising then that Hicks could write: 'We were such "good Europeans" in London that it was Cambridge that seemed "foreign"' (Hicks, 1963, p. 306).

Hicks's classical period[3]
During most of this time at the London School of Economics Hicks was working in the 'classical' tradition. His position is mainly exposed in two publications: *Theory of Wages* (Hicks, 1932) and in an article 'Gleichgewicht und Konjunktur' ('Equilibrium and the Trade Cycle', Hicks, 1933).

In this *Theory of Wages*, Hicks basically adhered to the classical dichotomy, i.e. the separation of monetary economics and general economic theory. He was concerned with the determination of wages and employment in a system of free competition (first part) and with the consequences of the regulation of wages, especially the influence of trade unions (second part).

But when he discusses the monetary system, one can clearly discern the influence of Hayek's *Prices and Production*, as Hicks characterizes the focus of monetary theory as 'the effect of monetary policy on the structure of production' (Hicks, 1932, p. 212).

In these days Hayek was still an adherent of General Equilibrium Theory.[4] He can even be considered as a major contributor to the evolution of the modern concept with his article 'Das Intertemporale Gleichgewichtssystem der Preise und die Bewegungen des Geldwertes' (Hayek, 1928).[5] Hayek would typically set up an intertemporal equilibrium, an equilibrium of an economy with different time-periods. Hayek's focus of attention was on the time structure of production, i.e. the relative proportion of consumption goods and investment goods.[6] This structure of production is determined by the relative prices of capital goods and consumption goods.

Hayek then investigates the influence of monetary disturbances. When analysing an increase or decrease of the supply of money, one should not consider, in his view, the general price level. Instead one should focus on the relative price of capital goods and consumption goods and the distortion of the time-structure of production.

> This view of the probable future of the theory of money becomes less startling if we consider that the concept of relative prices includes the prices of goods of the same kind at different moments, and that here, as in the case of interspatial price relationships, only one relation between the two prices can correspond to a condition of 'intertemporal' equilibrium, and that this need not, *a priori*, be a relation of identity or the one which would exist under a stable price level. (This has a particular bearing on the problem of money as a standard of deferred payments, because in this function money is to be conceived simply as the medium which effects an intertemporal exchange.) If this view is correct, the question which in my opinion will take the place of the question whether the value of money has increased or decreased will be the question whether the state of equilibrium of the rates of intertemporal exchange is disturbed by monetary influences in favour of future or in favour of present goods. (Hayek, 1931a, p. 29)

A transitory phase

Hicks turned to cycle theory after a request from Robbins to translate Hayek's *Prices and Production* model into mathematics. The first problem that Hicks encountered was the question about the exact meaning of 'equilibrium' in Hayek's model (cf. Hicks, 1982, p. 6). He also consulted Hayek's article 'Das Intertemporale Gleichgewichtssystem der Preise und die Bewegungen des Geldwertes' (Hayek, 1928), where the conditions for an intertemporal equilibrium were laid out. But Hicks's paper 'Equilibrium and the Trade Cycle' constitutes a harsh, but covert, attack on the opinions of Hayek.[7]

It is Hicks's purpose in 'Equilibrium and the Trade Cycle' to extend the paretian system, which is also the basis of Hayek's theory, to incorporate the analysis of production in time. In that case present prices are not sufficient any more to determine the behaviour of the economic agents, 'we ought to take account of the influence of future (expected) as well as current prices on their behaviour; for it is with an eye to the future prices of their products that people will embark upon "indirect" or "roundabout" methods of production' (Hicks, 1933, p. 525). In this case, just as in Hayek's model, present and future prices are no longer equal by necessity.

Hicks's approach to this problem of price determination is to divide the whole period in subperiods, which are so short that price changes in these subperiods can be ignored.[8] Taking $n + 1$ present prices and m subperiods we shall have $m(n + 1)$ prices to be determined, and $m(n + 1)$ demand and supply equations to determine these prices. But such a system can only be in equilibrium if there is perfect foresight.

> ... however, the economic data vary, there will always be a set of prices which,

if it is foreseen, can be carried through without supplies and demands ever becoming unequal to one another and so without expectations ever being mistaken. The condition for equilibrium, in this widest sense, is Perfect Foresight. Disequilibrium is the Disappointment of Expectations. (Hicks, 1933, p. 526).

Up to this point, Hicks is in line with Hayek. But where Hayek now starts with monetary disturbances and their influence on the structure of production, Hicks asks a preliminary question about the nature of money in this construction. He notes that

> Money as a medium of indirect exchange plays no part in the Lausanne equilibrium. ... the tacit assumption of perfect foresight deprives the *numéraire* of any monetary function. ... It is only for future payments that one needs to hold a stock of money. But it must be noticed that it is only to meet uncertain future payments that a stock of money is necessary. ... thus we cannot escape the conclusion that if the future course of economic data (and the corresponding future course of prices) were exactly foreseen, there would be no demand to hold money as money. People would lend out all their money holdings. (Hicks, 1933, p. 527)

It is clear, then, that as in Keynes's *General Theory*, the holding of money becomes intimately connected with uncertainty and the possibility of disappointment of expectations.[9] This implies that a monetary economy has some inherent tendencies to fluctuate. 'Even a system of pure *laissez-faire* would be subject to monetary disturbances' (Hicks, 1933, p. 529).

Hicks also identifies the liquidity spectrum: he offers a classification of assets, from low to high risk and return. He identifies expected returns and risks as the determinants of the distribution of assets.

> In advanced communities, a representative individual may be considered to hold his assets in innumerable different forms which may, however, be broadly classified: Cash, Call loans, Short-term loans, Long-term loans, Material property (incl. shares). Broadly speaking, there is an increasing risk-element as we go from left to right ; and again, broadly speaking, there is a higher promise of return in the same direction to compensate for increased risk. The distribution of assets among these forms is governed by relative prospects of return and by relative risk factors. (Hicks, 1933, p. 529)

Hicks continues to discuss the effects of changes in the expected rate of return and the anticipation of risk. So, a shock of confidence will cause a general leftward shift, towards more liquid and less risky assets. The general fall in prices which this induces, will cause a drop in profits and a depression.[10]

But here Hicks's story takes a very classical turn, as he argues that the natural way out of a recession is through a reduction in costs.

> When Depression has taken root, and expressed itself in a sequence of business losses, the natural way out is by a reduction in costs. I do not mean to imply that every Depression must end that way; a favourable change in data may make it unnecessary. But a reduction in costs is the only step that arises naturally out of the process and that is favourable to recovery. Under free competition, such a reduction will occur – in the end ; but if the labour market is not freely competitive – wage-reductions being resisted by Trade Unions – the position is doubly difficult. The period of adaptation is lengthened while risk is increased by labour unrest. (Hicks, 1933, p. 530)

This illustrates how 'Equilibrium and the Trade Cycle' constitutes an important transitory phase in Hicks's thinking. On the one hand, he emphasizes the inherent instability of a (monetary) free market economy. But, on the other hand, he still believes that a reduction in wages is necessary to restore equilibrium.

It is important to note also that Hicks's problem is of a theoretical nature, as it originates in a criticism of Hayek's treatment of money. Moreover, Hicks's criticism goes even further than Sraffa's critique of *Prices and Production*. Sraffa argues that the kind of money in the Hayek model is of a very limited character: 'The money which he [Hayek] contemplates is in effect used purely and simply as a medium of exchange' (Sraffa, 1932, p. 44).[11] Hicks even disputes this role of money as a medium of indirect exchange, as with perfect foresight people would lend out all their money holdings.

Both Hicks and Sraffa then raise the question of the nature of money in Hayek's (general equilibrium) model, a question which rather was left out of focus in later developments of general equilibrium theory. It has been taken up again in the 1960s and 1970s, but it remains an arduous task. As Desai notes: 'grafting money into a general equilibrium model proves to be as difficult a task today as the controversy in the Hayek–Sraffa debate indicated. A full fledged Walrasian economy where prices are flexible does not need money in any essential way' (Desai, 1977, p. 23, see also Clower, 1967, 1977; Hahn, 1973).

For Hicks, this critique of the nature of money in the Hayek model indicated another research strategy: 'Since the use of money is closely connected with imperfect foresight, it needs to be analysed in association with the theory of Risk' (Hicks, 1933, p. 528). An idea which he would take up in his simplifying paper.

Simplifying
In his Introduction to 'A Suggestion for Simplifying the Theory of Money' Hicks clearly indicates his loss of faith in the Austrian research programme in monetary theory and the new direction he would like to explore.

One understands that most economists have now read Böhm-Bawerk; yet whatever that union has bred, it has not been concord. I should prefer to seek illumination from another point of view – from a branch of economics which is more elementary, but. I think, in consequence better developed – the theory of value. (Hicks, 1935, p. 61)

Hicks, influenced by his work on value theory, now favours the introduction of choice-analysis in monetary theory. He has found such an approach in Keynes's *Treatise on Money*: when Keynes analyses the price-level of investment goods he shows that it depends on the relative preference of the investor, whether he prefers to hold bank deposits or securities: 'Here at last we have something which to a value theorist looks sensible and interesting ! Here at last we have a choice at the margin ! ... But in saying this, I am being more Keynesian than Keynes' (Hicks, 1935, p. 64).

It is obvious that in this approach the decision to hold money is part of a decision concerning a portfolio. Hicks uses a sort of generalized balance-sheet, where he lists all the assets and liabilities.[12] This was already quite common for banking theory. What Hicks proposes is to build up monetary theory as a generalization of banking theory.

The questions which then have to be resolved are: how will people allocate their wealth? And. what are the determinants of this allocation? For most assets it is obvious why people like to have them: they give a certain return. But money yields no return or profit: it is barren.

So long as rates of interest are positive the decision to hold money rather than lend it, or use it to pay off old debts, is apparently an unprofitable one. This, as I see it, is really the central issue in the pure theory of money. (Hicks, 1935, p. 66)[13]

Usually economists, when confronted with this question, start talking about 'frictions'. Hicks then proposes 'to look the frictions in the face, and see if they are really so refractory after all' (Hicks, 1935, p. 67).

Hicks notes that the costs of transferring assets from one form to another are the most obvious sort of friction. These transaction costs comprise both objective elements, i.e. brokerage charges, as more subjective elements. When calculating the net advantage from an investment, these costs should be subtracted from the yield of the investments. This yield of an investment will become larger for larger amounts of money invested and also for longer time-periods:

Thus. so far as we can see at present, the amount of money a person will desire to hold depends upon three factors: the dates at which he expects to make payments in the future ; the cost of investment, and the expected rate of return on investment. The further ahead the future payments, the lower the cost of investment, and the higher the expected rate of return on invested capital – the lower will be the demand for money. (Hicks, 1935, p. 68)[14]

But Hicks is not yet satisfied with his analysis. Until now he has been assuming that people had precise expectations. But, as Hicks had already pointed out in 'Equilibrium and the Trade Cycle', this cannot be true in a monetary economy. So, he introduces the risk factor.

This risk factor influences two variables in the situation: the expected period of investment and the expected net yield of the investment. An increase in one of these risks will make people less willing to undertake the investment. If so, this will increase the demand for money.[15]

Considering the treatment of risk, Hicks proposes to represent the expected yield by the mean and the risk factor by a measure of dispersion of a probability distribution.

> Where risk is present, the *particular* expectation of a riskless situation is replaced by a band of possibilities, each of which is considered more or less probable. It is convenient to represent these probabilities to oneself, in a statistical fashion, by a mean value, and some appropriate measure of dispersion. (No single measure will be wholly satisfactory, but here this difficulty may be overlooked.) Roughly speaking, we may assume that a change in the mean value with constant dispersion has much the same sort of effect as a change in the particular expectations we have been discussing before. The peculiar problem of risk therefore reduces to an examination of the consequences of a change in dispersion. Increased dispersion means increased uncertainty. (Hicks, 1935, p. 69)[16]

Hicks also notes that there is a difference between the risk of one particular investment and the risk incurred by undertaking a number of separate risky investments, due to the law of large numbers. 'These persons who have command of large quantities of capital, and are able to spread their risks, are not only able to reduce the risk on their own capital fairly low – they are also able to offer very good security for the investment of an extra unit along with the rest' (Hicks, 1935, p. 72). This has given rise to the development of institutions as banks, insurance companies and investment trusts, who create several kind of money substitutes. They make the monetary system more elastic.

Hicks has identified risk and transaction cost as elements in the determination of the allocation of wealth as being similar to price stimuli in value theory. He then observes that one should also investigate how the demand for money would change under the influence of a change in total wealth. This question also has a counterpart in value theory. 'Total wealth, in our present problem, plays just the same part as total expenditure in the theory of value' (Hicks, 1935, p. 77). In a footnote he identifies expected income as the relevant variable.

So in 1935, Hicks had left the Hayekian research programme. Instead his simplifying paper foreshadows many of the main elements of Tobin's analysis: portfolio theory applied to the balance sheet of the community; risk as a choice among probability distributions (represented by a mean value and a measure of dispersion); financial intermediation by banks and other intermediaries; a general equilibrium framework with attention to the wealth constraint, multi-market interactions and substitution effects.[17]

Conclusion

The story of the evolution of Hicks's monetary theory is a beautiful illustration of the regressive character of Hayek's research programme in the 1930s. First, Hicks discovered a theoretical flaw in Hayek's model, namely that the tacit assumption of perfect foresight deprives the *numéraire* of any monetary function. So he turned to the question why people hold money, which led him to risk and uncertainty. He re-oriented his thinking and abandoned the Hayekian idea to elaborate monetary theory in line with capital theory. Instead, by introducing marginal analysis into monetary theory, he laid the foundations for modern portfolio theory, as exemplified in the work of James Tobin.

These developments also show the importance of internal and theoretical arguments in the growth of economic knowledge. Although Hicks himself also gives a quite internalist account of this period (cf. Hicks, 1982), it may be interesting to note that this is rather in contrast with his view that monetary economics is more topical, more closely related to the circumstances of time. A view he already held in his younger days (cf. Hicks, 1943, p. 111 and also 1976, p. 216).

Acknowledgement
I would like to thank K. Bosmans, E. Buyst, M. M. G. Fase and V. Van Rompuy for comments and suggestions. The usual restrictions apply.

Notes
1. A fundamental problem of Hayek's capital theory was its focus on working capital. Fixed capital did not fit so easily into his model. (cf. Hicks, 1973b, p. 193).
2. In this paper we are only concerned with the development of Hicks's monetary thought during the early 1930s. On many points Hicks was and is very much influenced by the Austrians (cf. Hicks, 1973b).
3. The word 'classical' is here used in the same way as Keynes did in the *General Theory*. Keynes classified all his forerunners as classical economists. (cf. Keynes, 1936, p. 3). Classical economists is then a very heterogeneous notion. D. H. Robertson called Keynes's label a 'composite Aunt Sally of uncertain age' (Robertson, 1937, p. 436).
4. The modern Austrian school is well known for its criticism of equilibrium conceptions with its emphasis on the market process as a discovery process and the price mechanism as an information-signalling device. Hayek contributed to this view, starting with his paper on 'Economics and Knowledge' (Hayek, 1937). But before that date Hayek was an adherent of General Equilibrium Theory (cf. McCloughry, 1984, p. VIII).
5. See Milgate (1979).

6. Whereby investment goods or capital goods are more time-intensive than consumption goods, i.e. they require more capital-intensive or roundabout processes of production.
7. The essential ideas of Hicks's (1933) paper had appeared in a draft which circulated in 1932. The first part of it appears in Hicks's (1973, pp. 137–40). In this draft there is no reference to Keynes.
8. A method which he would also use in *Value and Capital* (cf. Hicks, 1939, p. 122).
9. The link between money and uncertainty was also known in Austrian economics (see, for example, Menger, 1909, p. 109).
10. Jan Kregel identifies Hicks's (1933) article with its leftward shift as the more fundamental contribution of Hicks to monetary theory (see Kregel, 1982). I have doubts about this, as I consider 'Equilibrium and the Trade Cycle' as a transitory article. I also doubt whether this leftward shift idea is so original. I have rather the impression that most of these ideas were already worked out by H. Thornton. Hicks also credits Thornton with several of these ideas (cf. Hicks, 1967, especially p. 177).
11. In his reply, Hayek does not answer Sraffa's attack. He refers readers to his *Monetary Theory and the Trade Cycle* (Hayek, 1929; cf. Hayek, 1932, p. 327).
12. Among his assets Hicks also lists consumption goods. In his analysis Hicks allows for the effect of changes in yields on the decision to consume. Other writers (e.g. Keynes) make a strategic distinction between two decisions: the decision to consume or save and decisions about wealth allocation (cf. Keynes, 1936, p. 115). Also Tobin followed this procedure (cf. Tobin, 1961, p. 110; 1969, p. 322). In his Nobel Lecture he returns on his earlier decision and integrates saving and portfolio decisions (cf. Tobin, 1982, p. 987).
13. Keynes too identified this as the crucial issue in monetary theory (cf. Keynes, 1937, p. 115).
14. Elements that are of crucial importance in the inventory theoretic approach to the demand for money, as developed by Baumol (1952), and as he later acknowledges (cf. Baumol, 1972, p. 150. See also Tobin , 1956.)
15. Hicks clearly assumes that people are normally risk-averse.
16. In the 1930s Hicks was an adherent of an objective approach to probability (cf. Hicks, 1931, p. 171). This contrasts sharply with Keynes who, with his *Treatise on Probability* (Keynes, 1921) was known as 'the principal exponent of the logico-subjective theory of probability' (Popper, 1934, p. 149). Later, Hicks has revised his opinion and thinks that an objective approach to probability is 'not wide enough for economics' (Hicks, 1979b, p. 105).
17. For a documentation of this view, see Maes (1986).

References

Baumol, W. J. 1952, 'The transactions demand for cash: an inventory theoretic approach', Thorn, R. S. (ed.) *Monetary Theory and Policy*, Praeger, 1976, pp. 93–105.
Baumol, W. J. 1972, 'John R. Hicks' contribution to economics', *Swedish Journal of Economics* 4, pp. 503–27.
Clower, R. W. 1967, 'Foundations of monetary theory', in Clower, R. W. (ed.), *Monetary Theory*, Penguin, Harmondsworth, pp. 202–12.
Clower, R. W. 1977, 'The anatomy of monetary theory', *American Economic Review* 67(1) (February) pp. 206–12.
Desai, M. 1977, *The Task of Monetary Theory: The Hayek-Sraffa Debate in a Modern Perspective*, Working Paper, Institut des Sciences Economiques, Université Catholique de Louvain, 1977, 25 pp.
Hahn, F. H. 1973, 'On the foundations of monetary theory', in Parkin, M. (ed.), *Essays on Modern Economics*, Longman, London, pp. 230–42.
Hawtrey, R. G. 1932, 'Review of *Prices and Production*', *Economica* 12(35) (February), pp. 119–25.
Hayek, F. A. 1928, 'Das Intertemporale Gleichgewichtssystem der Preise und die Bewegungen des Geldwertes', *Weltwirtschaftliches Archiv* XXVIII, pp. 3–76.

Hayek, F. A. 1929, *Monetary Theory and the Trade Cycle*, Routledge, London, 1933.
Hayek, F. A. 1931a, *Prices and Production*, Routledge, London.
Hayek, F. A. 1931b, 'A rejoinder to Mr. Keynes', *Economica*, 34 (November), pp. 398–403.
Hayek, F. A. 1932, 'Money and capital: a reply', *Economic Journal* (June), pp. 237–49.
Hayek, F. A. 1937, 'Economics and knowledge', *Economica* 13, (February) pp. 33–54.
Hayek, F. A. 1941, *The Pure Theory of Capital*, Routledge, London.
Hicks, J. R. 1931, 'The theory of uncertainty and profit', *Economica* 32 (May) pp. 170–89.
Hicks, J. R. 1932, *The Theory of Wages*, Macmillan, London, 1963.
Hicks, J. R. 1933, 'Equilibrium and the trade cycle', *Economic Inquiry* 18(4) (October), pp. 523–34.
Hicks, J. R. 1935, 'A suggestion for simplifying the theory of money', *Critical Essays in Monetary Theory*, Clarendon Press, Oxford, 1967, pp. 61–82.
Hicks, J. R. 1939, *Value and Capital*, Oxford University Press, London, 1946.
Hicks, J. R. 1943, 'History of economic doctrine', *Economic History Review* 13 (1–2) pp. 111–15.
Hicks, J. R. 1963, 'Commentary', *The Theory of Wages*, Macmillan, London, pp. 305–84.
Hicks, J. R. 1967, 'Thornton's paper credit', *Critical Essays in Monetary Theory*, Clarendon Press, Oxford, pp. 174–88.
Hicks, J. R. 1973, 'Recollections and documents', *Economic Perspectives*, Clarendon Press, Oxford, 1977, pp. 134–48.
Hicks, J. R. 1973b, 'The Austrian theory of capital and its rebirth in modern economics', in Hicks, J. R. and Weber, W. (eds), *Carl Menger and the Austrian School of Economics*, Clarendon Press, Oxford, pp. 190–206.
Hicks, J. R. 1976, '"Revolutions" in economics', in Latsis, S. J. (ed.), *Method and Appraisal in Economics*, Cambridge University Press, Cambridge, pp. 204–18.
Hicks, J. R. 1979a, 'The formation of an economist', *Banco Nazionale Del Lavoro Quarterly Review* 130 (September), pp. 195–204.
Hicks, J. R. 1979b, *Causality in Economics*, Basil Blackwell, Oxford.
Hicks, J. R. 1982, 'LSE and the Robbins circle', *Money, Interest and Wages*, Basil Blackwell, Oxford, pp. 3–10.
Keynes, J. M. 1921, *A Treastise on Probability*, London, Macmillan.
Keynes, J. M. 1931, 'The pure theory of money. A reply to Dr. Hayek', *Economica* 34 (November), pp. 387–97.
Keynes, J. M. 1936, *The General Theory of Employment, Interest and Money*, Macmillan, London, 1976.
Keynes, J. M. 1937, 'The General Theory of Employment', *The General Theory and After, Part II Defence and Development*, Macmillan, London, 1973, pp. 109–23.
Kregel, J. A. 1982, 'Microfoundations and Hicksian monetary theory', *De Economist* 130(4), pp. 465–92.
Lachman, L. M. 1986 'Austrian economics under fire: the Hayek–Sraffa duel in retrospect', in Grassl, W. and Smith, B. (eds), *Austrian Economics: Historical and Philosophical Background*, Croom Helm, London, pp. 225–42.
Maes, I. 1986. 'Did the Keynesian revolution retard the development of portfolio theory?' *Banca Nazionale Del Lavoro Quarterly Review*, 159 (December), pp. 407–21.
Menger, C. 1909, 'Geld', *Handwörterbuch der Staatswissenschaften, Collected Works*, Vol. IV, London, 1936, pp. 1–116.
Milgate, M. 1979, 'On the origin of the notion of "intertemporal equilibrium"', *Economica* 181 (February), pp. 1–10.
McCloughry, R. 1984, 'Editor's Introduction', F. A. Hayek, *Money, Capital and Fluctuations*, Routledge, London, pp. vii–xi.
Popper, K. R. 1934, *The Logic of Scientific Discovery*, Hutchinson, London, 1977.
Robbins, L. 1971, *Autobiography of an Economist*, Macmillan, London.
Robertson, D. H. 1937, 'Alternative theories of the rate of interest', *Economic Journal* (September), pp. 428–36.
Shackle, G. L. S. 1967, *The Years of High Theory: Invention and Tradition in Economic Thought: 1926–1939*, Cambridge University Press, Cambridge.

Sraffa, P. 1932, 'Dr. Hayek on money and capital', *Economic Journal* 165 (March), pp. 42–53.

Tobin, J. 1956, 'The interest-elasticity of transactions demand for cash', *Essays in Economics*, Vol. 1, North-Holland, Amsterdam, 1971, pp. 229–41.

Tobin, J. 1961, 'Money, capital and other stores of value', in Dean, E. (ed.), *The Controversy Over the Quantity Theory of Money*, Heath & Co., Lexington, pp. 107–19.

Tobin, J. 1969, 'A general equilibrium approach to monetary theory', *Essays in Economics*, Vol. 1, North-Holland, Amsterdam, 1971, pp. 332–9.

Tobin, J. 1982, 'Money and finance in the macroeconomic process', *Journal of Money, Credit and Banking* 14(2) (May), pp. 171–204.

10 The Two Faces of Neo-Wicksellianism during the 1930s: the Austrians and the Swedes

Mario Seccareccia

> Wicksell's work was like a mountain from whose flanks divergent streams run down and bring fertility to widely separated fields, only to merge again into a single broad river. (G. L. S. Shackle, Foreword, in Wicksell, 1954, p.7)

Professor G. L. S. Shackle's original simile of a mountain used to characterize Knut Wicksell's immensely important and durable analytical frame of reference is particularly appropriate and points to his legacy in contemporary thought. However, Professor Shackle's optimistic assumption – that the streams emerging from Wicksell's work would re-unite in a 'single broad river' – could not materialize. Moreover, in spite of his hope that postwar Keynesian thinking might help to bring together these divergent streams, it has clearly failed to do so. The purpose of this paper is to describe the common substantive elements of these competing neo-Wicksellian models that appeared during the 1930s and to discuss how and why they led to radically different policy conclusions. As described below, this was because each model stressed some different aspect of the central theory initially developed by Wicksell.

Wicksell's model of the cumulative process and its legacy

Having been influenced by the nineteenth-century debates between the Currency and the Banking Schools, in his *Interest and Prices* Wicksell argued that orthodox quantity theory was cast in a model of an economy which resembled that of a medieval village fair in which money, defined as a stock of 'pure cash', is used exclusively to facilitate exchange. In his vision of the historical evolution of the monetary system, modern economies had moved away from this more primitive Humian 'manna' exchange world and were slowly tending towards a stage, dubbed a 'pure credit' system, in which the supply of money is infinitely elastic and can accommodate 'to any position that the demand for money may assume' (Wicksell, 1936, p.135).

If money as understood within the confines of the quantity theory can no longer play the determining role in price formation, how then do

137

money prices fluctuate? In the Wicksellian world, the determination of money prices is not done independently of relative price formation, since both the vector of relative prices and the level of money prices are affected by how the endogenous flow of credit-money enters the productive system.

In an Austrian-type system of production where productive inputs are tied up for a definite length of time, credit is advanced to firms so as to finance the flow of production. The regulator of the actual time-profile of production and thus of the endogenous flow of credit-money in Wicksell's system is the structure of the rates of return, and, in particular, the relation of the 'money' rate (r) to the 'natural' rate of interest (ρ). Any discrepancy in that relation will set a process in motion that leads to a general restructuring of this time-composition of output and, with it, the pattern of money prices.

More specifically, with every rise in the perceived natural rate, ρ, unaccompanied by an increase in the money rate, r, the potential for a pure profit will emerge which induces firms to expand their productive capacity. To finance this expansion, firms must borrow money independently of the constraints set by household saving. Such a general restructuring of the time-profile of production in favour of more roundabout activities, financed by the creation of bank credit, and unaccompanied by a rise in the saving propensities of households, must by its very nature result in a state of disequilibrium in what Wicksell defined as the market for 'all commodities' (Wicksell, 1935, p.159). Wicksell, however, reasoned that such a condition of disequilibrium can be temporarily resolved only by means of what he described as an 'enforced general reduction of consumption' (Wicksell, 1935, p.14) brought about through the mechanism of inflation. This inflation will be cumulative as long as this discrepancy between the two rates exists or, more precisely, as long as the monetary flow of investment continues to exceed the amount withdrawn from the system in the form of household saving.

During the late 1920s and early 1930s, the neo-Wicksellian writers extended his analysis into four critical areas which Wicksell had already previously pioneered:

1.   the explicit two-sector division of production into activities giving rise to consumption goods and those more time-intensive activities giving rise to investment goods;
2.   the critical importance of credit in a monetary production economy;
3.   the emphasis on expectations as an analytical device in economic analysis; and

4. the widespread use of process or sequence analysis.

Following Wicksell, one common trait of this school was the rejection of the quantity theory as advocated by Fisher and others. Indeed, the most comprehensive criticism of the quantity theory ever put forward within this tradition is found in Myrdal's *Monetary Equilibrium*. This is not to suggest that other writers, such as Lindahl and Hayek, did not provide similar criticism. Yet is was Myrdal who was to systemize many of the frontal attacks launched by the neo-Wicksellians against monetary orthodoxy.

The criticism voiced by these various writers against the quantity theory was threefold in nature. First, they criticized this theory for a complete lack of integration between the monetary and real analyses. Money could affect the 'scale' of prices in the system, but not their structure. Writers such as Myrdal questioned this dichotomy: 'the expression "price level" in the quantity theory cannot be defined in such a way as to give the multiplicative factor which the theory of relative prices needs in order to be determinate' (Myrdal, 1939, p.14). Indeed, the quantity theory rested on an aggregative concept of the price level which could neither be found in the actual world nor could it serve any purpose in explaining the behaviour of specific real-world processes.

Secondly, these critics of the quantity theory pointed to the problem of causality. Working within the Wicksellian tradition, these writers believed that the origin of changes in the prices of commodities was in the real sector or, as Myrdal put it, 'dependent upon factors which lie outside the mechanism of payment proper' (Myrdal, 1939, p.15). To these writers, the only causal force determining both the price relations and the flow of credit-money was the prior change in the structure of interest rates (with its proximate impact on the flow of investment relative to saving). This belief thus prompted these writers to disaggregate price and output so as to work out the full causal sequence in price formation.

Thirdly, following Wicksell, these authors attacked the quantity theorists for not being sufficiently concerned with the existence of a *flow* of credit in a monetary production economy. Within the traditional quantity theory *cum* general-equilibrium framework, money is viewed purely as a stock offering its services at a point in time. However, as soon as production as a process occurring over a period of time is analysed, credit must be advanced to firms so as to permit them to undertake financial commitments that involve the future. In opposition to the traditional theorists, emphasis was thus placed on 'the *existence of credit* which, within reasonable limits, is always at the entrepreneur's disposal' (Hayek, 1933, p.87; emphasis in original).

The workings of the neo-Wicksellian credit cycle

From this common criticism of the quantity theory, these writers would thus undertake to set up an alternative monetary model of price formation along Wicksellian lines. Pursuing Wicksell's suggestion that 'it lies in the power of the credit institutions, acting in co-operation only with entrepreneurs, to determine the direction of production and consequently the period of investment' (Wicksell, 1936, p.155), these economists would group economic activities according to the lengths of time required in completing the final products. As in Böhm-Bawerk and Wicksell, production has a time-structure which is highly flexible in the aggregate. For instance, suppose we have in an economic system a given number of production processes which can be classified by their time-intensiveness such that as we go from the 'lower' to the 'higher' time-intensive activities we shall be moving from the more direct production of consumers' goods to the more roundabout production of producers' goods. When the structure of aggregate demand changes, so will the time-structure of production. However, at any moment in time an ideal equilibrium structure of production exists which is determined by the actions of the entrepreneurs and by the availability of credit.

While Hayek did attempt at times to carry out his analysis in this slightly more disaggregative fashion, most of the work undertaken by these neo-Wicksellian theorists was done strictly within a two-sector framework. In a two-sector economy, two sets of commodities are produced. The first group includes the consumption goods, which require less time to be produced and consumed. These consumption goods would not normally constitute a large portion of the value of the existing stock of commodities, except to the extent that individuals or firms would hold inventories mostly for speculative purposes. The second group, on the other hand, consists of the more time-intensive and durable producers' or investment goods. This latter group would form the bulk of the economy's capital stock. The gross additions to this existing stock of commodities would, on the other hand, define the flow of investment during the period.

To understand the complete workings of the neo-Wicksellian trade-cycle models, let us begin by defining a point of reference – a hypothetical state of 'monetary equilibrium'. According to Myrdal, the condition of monetary equilibrium is fulfilled at a point in time when the prospective or *ex ante* values are equal to the *ex post* or retrospective values. Such a state, however, is not necessarily static or stationary as Wicksell had assumed. On the contrary, it would be consistent with any state in which forces affecting both sectors of economic activity are in balance. It is thus a situation in which there are no tendencies for either shares of output in the system to contract or expand progressively. At the same time, Myrdal shows that this condition is general enough to cover the specific conditions for monetary equilibrium discussed by Wicksell.

The three conditions indentified by Wicksell were that a monetary equilibrium exists when:

1. the money rate equals the natural rate,
2. the flows of savings and investment are equal, and
3. the 'price level' is stable.

Defining $I(\rho)$ as the monetary flow of investment being a function of the natural rate (ρ) and $S(r)$ the flow of saving as a function of the money rate (r), then 'monetary equilibrium', as a position of rest in the sense that there exists no tendency for the flow of credit-money, M, to change, would exist when:

$$I(\rho) - S(r) = \Delta M = 0 \qquad (1)$$

Since $S(r) = Y^* - C(r)$, where Y^* is full-employment income and C is consumption demand, then it follows:

$$I(\rho) + C(r) - Y^* = \Delta M = 0 \qquad (2)$$

and there are no tendencies for prices to change when $\rho = r$.

Taking this simple Wicksellian equation as the starting-point and separating demand and output between the consumtpion- and investment-goods sectors, we obtain:

$$(P_I^d Q_I^d - P_I^s Q_I^s) + (P_C^d Q_C^d - P_C^s Q_C^s) = \Delta M \qquad (3)$$

where the subscripts I and C define the investment- and consumption-goods sectors, while the superscripts give the planned (d) and the expected (s) purchases, respectively. For instance, $P_I^d Q_I^d$ is the planned purchases (Q_I^d) (or proposed additions to the stock of existing investment goods) at the price P_I^d, while $P_I^s Q_I^s$ is the planned output (Q_I^s) (or supply) of investment goods at the expected price P_I^s as viewed by the entrepreneurs in the industry. The value $P_I^s Q_I^s$ can thus be considered as the expected proceeds by firms in the investment-goods sector. The same would apply to the planned purchases $(P_C^d Q_C^d)$ and the expected proceeds $(P_C^s Q_C^s)$ in the consumption-goods sector. If during the initial period $t = 0$ we now assume the Myrdalian condition of monetary equilibrium, one obtains:

$$(P_I^d Q_I^d - P_I^s Q_I^s) + (P_C^d Q_C^d - P_C^s Q_C^s) = 0 \qquad (4)$$

such that *ex ante* these two sets of values are both equal to zero. Hence, in a state of monetary equilibrium, the expected values are fully realized by entrepreneurs in their respective sectors.

In order to understand the causal sequence in the neo-Wicksellian trade-cycle models, let us begin with an initial state of monetary equilibrium in period $t = 0$ (depicted in equation 4 above), and suppose that, at the end of the period, the perceived yield of the new investments rises exogenously. This expectation of increased revenue pushes entrepreneurs to bid up the values of the existing stock of capital assets and, consequently, the demand price for new investments. As investors bid up the price of investment goods, the original state of equilibrium is disturbed in such a way that, at the beginning of period $t = 1$, the value $P_i^d Q_i^d$ will come to exceed $P_i^s Q_i^s$. From equation 4, we can infer that:

$$P_i^d Q_i^d > P_i^s Q_i^s \tag{5a}$$

and

$$P_c^d Q_c^d = P_c^s Q_c^s \tag{5b}$$

whereby there will emerge a flow of credit, ΔM, to permit investors to raise effectively their demand price for investment goods. Assuming an elastic monetary system, individual investors will be able to secure the liquid funds necessary to pay for the higher demand price of investment goods.

At the end of the unit-period $t = 1$, one finds that, as a group, firms producing investment goods could sell their given output at a higher price than was anticipated. To use Wicksellian terminology, firms in this sector will be making a 'surplus profit' *ex post*. This unforeseen increase in price will induce firms in the investment-goods sector to expand production and employment, as they react to their windfall profits by expanding further their productive capacity. Assuming, furthermore, that, except for the inter-sectoral exchange of investment and consumption goods, firms in each sector are vertically integrated in the sense that they own their sources of raw materials, then at the beginning of unit-period $t = 2$, we have

$$\Delta M = w\Delta N_1 + N_1 \Delta w \tag{6}$$

where w is the wage rate and N_1 is employment in the investment-goods sector. However, as Lindahl was to show, a problem now arises as to whether or not one assumes full employment of the labour force.

In a situation of full employment, it would be inconceivable that entrepreneurs would be able to attract workers from other sectors without offering higher wages (so that the second term of equation 6 above would be highly positive). Hayek, Myrdal and others allude to this possibility. However, in order to simplify this analysis, one may sacrifice this obvious degree of realism and assume, instead, that unit wage costs are given. As a result of this simplifying assumption, (in period $t = 2$) one obtains under the condition of full employment,

$$\Delta M = w\Delta N_1 = -w\Delta N_c \tag{7}$$

where N_c is the level of employment in the consumption-goods sector, and where w, the wage rate, is identical in each sector. By the end of period t = 2, one will thus account for a change in the structure of total employment in favour of the investment-goods sector.

Since the rise in the wage bill in the investment-goods sector fully compensates for the fall in the consumption-goods sector, then total demand for consumption goods during the following period (t = 3) will remain unchanged. However, the shift in resources will affect their supply. Assuming that the unit-period adopted is equal to or slightly greater than the expenditure lag as well as equal to or slightly lengthier than the period of production of the consumption goods, one will observe that *initially* the market supply of consumption goods will remain unaffected, as Hayek (1931, pp. 87–8) points out, owing to the goods in process started during the previous period (t = 2). But at the beginning of period t = 4, we may assume that the output of consumption goods will decline in some proportion to the withdrawal of resources from the consumption-goods sector that took place during period t = 2. The mechanism of adjustment will be a general rise in the price of consumption goods, so that now firms in this sector will also experience a windfall gain.

This simplistic four-period cycle is the first phase of the economic expansion. The rise in prices of consumption goods will begin a new cycle of expansion. To the extent that firms in this latter sector view it as a more or less-permanent increase in prices, then entrepreneurs will attempt to expand further their productive capacity. This means increased purchases of investment goods which will be accompanied by an increased flow of credit, ΔM, which will, in turn, bid up the price of investment goods still further. To quote Myrdal:

> As soon as the prices of consumption goods have increased, capital values increase *again*, since increasing prices of consumption goods necessarily make the entrepreneurs' price expectation more optimistic. If we now assume that the entrepreneurs continually, from each new moment, expect future prices to equal present prices of consumption goods, then the rate of increase of capital values will be roughly proportional to the rate of increase in the price of consumption goods. (...). The entrepreneurs are stimulated by it to start longer processes of production, again with the same effects on the direction and method of production, incomes, relative demand for and supply of consumption goods, prices of those goods, and finally, capital values once more, and so on. (Myrdal, 1939, p. 27)

Figure 10.1 tries to illustrate this process of expansion graphically. From the initial exogenous change in demand for investment goods (due to an increase in the natural rate), the upward evaluation both of the existing stock and of the newly-produced investment goods takes place by means

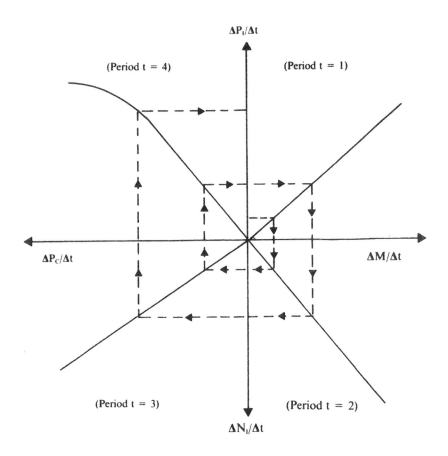

Figure 10.1   The neo-Wicksellian hypothesis

of an increased flow of credit during period t = 1. The relationship between ΔP_1 and ΔM is assumed to be both positive and linear. This is because, for a given output of investment goods, a disturbance in the original state of monetary equilibrium can only take place by means of an increased flow of credit.

During period t = 2, this financial flow will take the form of increased income for workers in the investment-goods sector. If we take their wage rate and the input–output relationship as given, then the flow of credit, ΔM, will lead to a proportional increase in employment in the investment-goods sector. The relation $\Delta N_I/\Delta M$ will become non-linear only to the extent that the increased employment is accompanied by a change in the wage rate or in average labour productivity in this sector. In any case, because of our assumption of full employment, the increase in employment in the producers' goods industries can only take place through a reduction in the resources employed in the consumers' goods industries.

By period $t = 3$, this shift in resources will give rise to shortages of consumption items and, consequently, to an upward movement in their prices. Here again, the element of non-linearity comes into play only to the extent that wages must rise as workers change sector.

Finally, and most critically, the cycle will follow its cobweb pattern of expansion depending on the way entrepreneurs react to the rise in the prices of consumption goods (that is, depending on the slope of the relationship $\Delta P_I/\Delta P_c$ in period $t = 4$). For instance, Lindahl (1939, p. 173) argues that 'a rise in the prices of consumption goods will cause a more immediate rise in capital values, so long as it is not considered to be only temporary'. Indeed, both Lindahl and Myrdal seem to suggest that the reaction of entrepreneurs is normally such that prices of investment goods will tend to expand at an increasing rate. As Myrdal (1939, p. 27) describes this: 'We have here a race of different "price levels": Of prices for real capital ... and consumption goods.'

There is, however, one effective brake to this cumulative process. Since for these neo-Wicksellian theorists the increase in prices was started by a rise in the natural rate (ρ) relative to the money rate (r), then the only effective check to this expansion can be a change in the relationship between these two rates. For instance, Lindahl argues that 'the price rise which is the effect of a lower rate of interest need not continue indefinitely, but comes to an end when the supply of capital has been increased until it corresponds to the new rate of interest' (Lindahl, 1939, p. 181). As Shackle (1967) emphasized, the relationship between the accumulation of capital and the level of the natural rate, to be found specified within these neo-Wicksellian models, resembles somewhat the Keynesian schedule of the marginal efficiency of capital. Indeed, as the above quotation describes it, the higher is the volume of investment, the lower is the associated value of the natural rate. Figure 10.2 depicts this relation for a given value of the money rate (r). An element of non-linearity is thus introduced into the relationship $\Delta P_I/\Delta P_c$. With every spurt in innovations affecting entrepreneurial expectations, a Schumpeterian cycle of expansion will take place which shifts the ρ schedule. However, the higher expected profitability will be ultimately mitigated by the increased accumulation of capital.

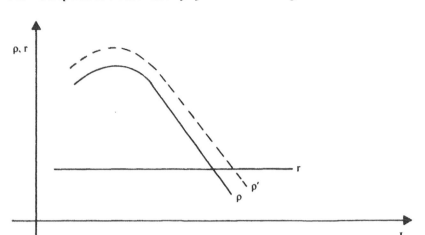

Figure 10.2   Lindahl's case

Hayek, on the other hand, placed greater emphasis on the behaviour of the banks in putting an end to the inflationary process of expansion. We have seen that the only means by which firms can undertake further investment is if the banks extend them credit. Following Wicksell, both Myrdal and Lindahl assumed a very elastic monetary system. Hayek, however, was to qualify their hypothesis that:

> so long as the banks go on progressively increasing their loans it will, there-fore, be possible to continue the prolonged methods of production or perhaps even extend them still further. But for obvious reasons the banks cannot continue indefinitely to extend credits; and even if they could, the other effects of a rapid and continuous rise of prices would, after a while, make it necessary to stop this process of inflation. (Hayek, 1931, pp.89–90)

Indeed firms, which may have initially invested on the basis of a given interest rate (r), now come to face a credit crunch as more and more entrepreneurs attempt to invest. To the extent that the slowdown in investment, due to higher interest costs, has an effect on the overall expectations of return, then the system could easily find itself engulfed in a situation shown in Figure 10.3. While point E is a stable position of equilibrium, point F is highly unstable in the downward direction owing to the downward shift in the expectations of return.

Numerous possibilities can be conjectured of the effects that changes in the parameter values may have. For instance, the simple linear functional relations shown in Figure 10.1, for periods t = 2 and t = 3, would become highly non-linear as soon as wages tend to change with the restructuring

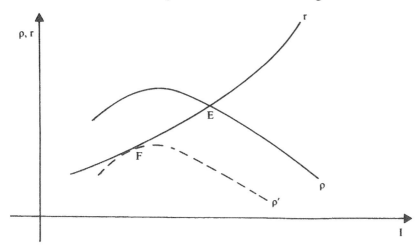

Figure 10.3   Hayek's case

of employment. In much the same way, if we were to identify more complex reaction functions on the part of the individual agents, the slope of the relationships described in Figure 10.1 would be further affected.

Thus far we have assumed full employment of factor resources. This assumption, however, can easily be disposed of without affecting the general conclusions of the theory. While both Myrdal and Hayek discuss cases where unemployed resources are available. Lindahl presented the most systematic analysis of the consequences of introducing unemployment as a variable.

If we suppose that unemployed resources are available and transferable between each sector, then an increase in the production of investment goods can occur without a corresponding decline in the output of consumption goods. The effects of this modification on the system, however, would not be fundamentally different. As soon as $P_i^d Q_i^d > P_i^s Q_i^s$, this will result in a rise in the prices of investment goods financed by an increased flow of credit, ΔM. As before, there will ensue an increase in employment in the investment-goods sector during period $t = 2$. Since the total wage bill increases initially without a corresponding rise in the output of consumption goods, then, during period $t = 3$, $P_c^d Q_c^d > P_c^s Q_c^s$ and the prices of consumption goods will be bid up. To the extent that the increase in P_c will encourage firms in this sector to expand their operations, a new cycle of expansion will begin in period $t = 4$. As a result, the crux of this theory remains intact under conditions of unemployment.

It may be argued that one cannot do full justice to Myrdal, Lindahl and Hayek in grouping their various theories as was done here. However, there are sufficient common characteristics to warrant this more aggregative approach. All three authors begin from the perspectives of a common tradition: that of Wicksell. These authors also tackle one crucial problem: price behaviour over the business cycle. Moreover, as was stated previously, they all reject the competing model: the quantity theory of money. A glance over this somewhat cursory survey of the process analysis employed by these writers will have conveyed to the reader the characteristic property of the neo-Wicksellian trade-cycle models. In a capitalist system of production, prices are condemned to follow an endogenous see-saw pattern of behaviour which must 'consist essentially in alternating expansions and contractions of the structure of capital equipment' (Hayek, 1931, p.101). In this respect, as Hayek (1933, pp.146–7) describes it, there is embedded an underlying general pattern of economic behaviour which '*must* always recur under the existing credit organization, and that it thus represents a tendency inherent in the economic system' (emphasis in original).

At any moment in time there exists a monetary equilibrium solution which will maintain the economic system on a steady-state path without price fluctuations. However, such a state cannot, by its very nature be a stable one. As soon as the *ex ante* values depicted in equation 5a come to diverge, prices will conform to a pattern of the type shown diagrammatically in Figure 10.4.

Figure 10.4 sketches a state in which, from the initial impetus in period $t = 0$, consumption-goods prices perpetually chase investment-goods prices (with a three-period lag) in a wavelike pattern over time. To quote Myrdal again: 'In the theory is implied not only certain causal relations between these sets of prices, but also a *given* order of sequence in their price movements' (emphasis in original) (Myrdal, 1939, p.27).

The extent to which there would be symmetry in the expansion and contraction phases of the cycle depends on the nature of the parameters in the system. For instance, on the technical level, the length of the upswing could be connected with the period of production of the investment goods, while the length of the downswing might be a function of the durability or rate of obsolescence of these same commodities. On the other hand, the degree of asymmetry in the behaviour of the banks, the degree of irregularity in the formation of expectations by entrepreneurs and the extent to which consumers are willing to accept an enforced restriction in their consumption would also be important dynamic factors in determining the actual timing and amplitude of the cycle.

The two streams of neo-Wicksellianism regarding policy matters
An attempt has been made to describe the convergent opinions of these various economists and to discuss at some length why these neo-Wicksel-

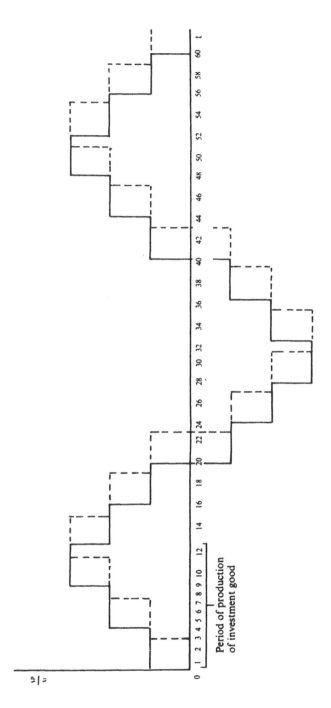

Figure 10.4 The neo-Wicksellian credit cycle

———— , investment-good prices.

– – – – , consumption-good prices.

lian theorists believed that the processes of inflation and deflation were real phenomena modifying the relative price and output structures. In particular, it was shown how, in this framework, inflation is the necessary consequence of a 'structural imbalance' in the system of production. It is a symptom of an underlying restructuring of output in favour of more roundabout methods of production. However, to enforce such changes, a shift in this structure cannot occur without the prior availability of credit. As Hayek (1933, p.88) put it, '[I]t is the existence of credit which makes these various disturbances possible'. Since inflation is the mark of a society living above its means (that is, living above what the community's savings would allow), then fluctuations in prices are an advance warning of an inevitable crisis. Hayek explains:

> By creating additional credits in response to an increased demand, and thus opening up new possibilities of improving and extending production, the banks ensure that impulses towards expansion of the productive apparatus shall not be so immediately and insuperably balked by a rise of interest rates as they would be if progress were limited by the slow increase in the flow of savings. But this same policy stultifies the automatic mechanism of adjustment which keeps the various parts of the system in equilibrium, and makes possible disproportionate developments which must sooner or later, bring about a reaction. (Hayek, 1933, pp.177–8)

The 'reaction' will normally take the form of higher interest costs accompanied by a severe retrenchment in demand for producers' goods. Any 'artificial' stimulus of both consumption and investment demands by the government can only provide the wrong signals that serve to prolong this structural maladjustment or crisis. Hence, the only effective long-term solution to this problem of misdirected investment must inevitably be the large-scale wastage of less productive capital made necessary by the higher interest costs. He thus proposes that banks follow a policy of 'neutral money' (as against 'constant money') in order to minimize the difference between a barter economy and a monetary economy. The lower the elasticity of the monetary system, the closer society is kept to living within its means. As certain writers of the period also understood it – including Hayek himself – the practical implications of this proposal to the banking authorities would be to follow a policy of cautious (but austere) *laissez-faire*.

Very few of the Swedish theorists accepted the Hayek-Mises policy option in favour of monetary austerity. Neither Lindahl nor Myrdal saw Hayek's policy conclusions as an ineluctable consequence of the neo-Wicksellian theory of the credit cycle. Although Lindahl (1939, p.183) did take up Hayek's concept of 'mal-investment', his approach evolved much more closely with that of Myrdal.

From an otherwise similar theoretical framework, Myrdal concludes, contrary to Hayek, that 'increased saving, *ceteris paribus*, necessarily intensifies a depression' (Myrdal, 1939, p.108). In the context of his analysis of monetary equilibrium, Myrdal proposes a policy based on the fundamental distinction between flexible and inflexible prices – a distinction which, for instance, Hicks (1965) was to adopt much later.

The underlying premise of Myrdal's monetary equilibrium is that, in order for the system to function smoothly along a more stable path, there must be a correspondence between the actual and anticipated course of events. Hence, a norm for monetary policy must be one that seeks 'to eliminate completely or at least to mitigate the "business cycle"' (Myrdal, 1939, p.178). This, consequently, opened the door to government stabilization policy in a style somewhat reminiscent of that of Wicksell. But Myrdal's notion of stabilization meant something quite different from what either Wicksell originally envisaged or what the modern economist is typically accustomed to. As it is essentially the flexible prices that disrupt the expectations of economic agents, the policy norm ought to be one that first tries to stabilize these latter prices by tying them to the inflexible ones and then by guaranteeing that these inflexible prices are themselves not violently disturbed. For instance, in discussing the situation of the Great Depression he writes:

> A situation like the present ... is obviously not one of monetary equilibrium. A depressive Wicksellian process has been in progress for several years with the result that even inflexible prices are slowly falling with some lag. In order to commence such a monetary policy, one must, naturally, increase prices to a level which restores monetary equilibrium at the existing level of sticky prices. Only by this means can the progressive fall of sticky prices, accompanied by continually deepening depression, be prevented'. (Myrdal, 1939, p.195)

Since the prices of factor inputs were seen to form the bulk of the 'sticky' prices during the 1930s, as shown by Hammarskjöld (1955, p.152) stabilization policy came to mean, therefore, income maintenance over the cycle.

The great debate over the importance of stabilization policies, which began in earnest among the Swedish writers, was to reach its peak during the late 1930s with the controversy between Hayek and the early Keynesians – a debate which, in many respects, continues to rage in slightly more modern guise. Hayek emphasized substitution effects and the more or less immediate reversibility in the structure of output as economic agents react to the changing price signals – 'a function which, of course [the price mechanism] fulfills less perfectly as prices grow more rigid' (Hayek, 1949, p.86); while Myrdal and Keynes came to lay greater emphasis on the gross income effects and on the possibilities of stabilizing actions by means of the public control of aggregate spending.

For Hayek, an 'artificial' increase in consumption demand in the midst of a recession would merely bid up the price of consumption goods relative to that of investment goods. The result would be a further distortion of the price signals that would otherwise return the system towards the natural equilibrium state in which household saving sets the terms for spending in the context of the neoclassical capital market. For Myrdal (and Keynes), instead, an increase in consumption demand will not only raise income in the consumption-goods sector but, through its impact on expectations, it will also increase demand and raise income in the investment-goods sector. In principle, a system can continue to expand over long periods by means of short-run supportive actions on the part of the public authorities so that the downward Wicksellian process need never occur.

Indeed, since investment was seen as the *primum mobile* of income determination, it was but a minor step to proceed from this distinct Myrdalian position of short-run income maintenance over the cycle, to the more radical Keynesian proposal for greater public control of investment spending. Yet, Myrdal was unable to take such a step in his early writings. Unlike Keynes whose revolutionary position in his *General Theory*, on the necessary and continual identity between aggregate investment and aggregate saving, provided no place for the neoclassical notion of a capital market (so dear to Hayek and Mises of the Austrian School), Myrdal was unable to shed this neoclassical assumption in his *Monetary Equilibrium*. In contrast with Hayek, however, who still retains the unenviable position of principal ideologue of austerity, Myrdal did nevertheless develop, together with Alva Myrdal, into one of the chief architects of the Swedish welfare state.

Acknowledgement
The author would like especially to thank R. Dimand and D. Laidler for their helpful comments at the June 1988 meeting of the History of Economics Society at the University of Toronto.

References
Akerman, J. 1955, *Structures et cycles économiques*, Presses Universitaires de France, Paris.
Bailey, R. E. 1976, 'On the analytical foundations of Wicksell's cumulative process', *Manchester School of Economic and Social Studies* 44(1).
Eagly, R. V. 1966, 'A Wicksellian monetary model: an expository note', *Scottish Journal of Political Economy* 13(2).
Haavelmo, T. 1978, 'Wicksell on the currency theory vs. the banking principle', *Scandinavian Journal of Economics* 80(2).
Hammarskjöld, D. 1955, 'The Swedish discussion on the aims of monetary policy', *International Economic Papers* 5.
Hansen, A. H. and Tout, H., 1933, 'Annual survey of business cycle theory: investment and saving in business cycle theory', *Econometrica* 1.

The Two Faces of Neo-Wicksellianism during the 1930s   153

Hansen, B. 1951, *A Study in the Theory of Inflation*, George Allen & Unwin, London.
Hansson, B. A. 1982, *The Stockholm School and the Development of Dynamic Method*, Croom Helm, London.
Hayek, F. A. 1931, *Prices and Production*, Routledge, London.
Hayek, F. A. 1933, *Monetary Theory and the Trade Cycle*, Jonathan Cape, London.
Hayek, F. A. 1939, *Profits, Interest and Investment*, Routledge, London.
Hayek, F. A. 1941, *The Pure Theory of Capital*, Macmillan, London.
Hayek, F. A. 1949, *Individualism and Economic Order*, Routledge & Kegan Paul, London.
Hayek, F. A. 1984, 'On "neutral money" (1933)', *Money, Capital and Fluctuations, Early Essays*, Routledge & Kegan Paul, London.
Hicks, J. 1965, *Capital and Growth*, Oxford University Press, London.
Honohan, P. 1981, 'A new look at Wicksell's inflationary process', *Manchester School of Economic and Social Studies* 49(4) (December).
Laidler, D. 1972, 'On Wicksell's theory of price level dynamics', *Manchester School of Economic and Social Studies* 40(2) (June).
Laidler, D. 1987, 'The Austrians and the Stockholm School – two failures in the development of modern macroeconomics?', *Research Report 8708*, Department of Economics, University of Western Ontario (July).
Lindahl, E. 1939, *Studies in the Theory of Money and Capital*, Rinehart, New York.
Lundberg, E. 1937, *Studies in the Theory of Economic Expansions*, P. S. King & Sons, London.
Lundberg, E. 1985, 'The rise and fall of the Swedish model', *Journal of Economic Literature* 23(1) (March).
Myrdal, G. 1939, *Monetary Equilibrium*, W. Hodge & Co., London.
Myrdal, G. 1960, *Beyond the Welfare State, Economic Planning and Its International Implications*, Yale University Press, New Haven, Conn.
Nell, E. J. 1967, 'Wicksell's theory of circulation', *Journal of Political Economy* 75(4) (August).
Ohlin, B. 1937, 'Some notes on the Stockholm theory of savings and investment, I & II', *Economic Journal*, 47 (185–6) (March and June).
Ohlin, B. 1960, 'The Stockholm School versus the quantity theory', *International Economic Papers* 10.
Ohlin, B. 1974, 'On the slow development of the "total demand" idea in economic theory', *Journal of Economic Literature*, 12(3) (September).
Palander, T. 1953, 'On the concepts and methods of the Stockholm School', *International Economic Papers* 3.
Parguez, A. 1988, 'Hayek et Keynes face à l'austérité', *Friedrich Hayek: philosophie, économie et politique*, ed. by G. Dostaler and D. Ethier, Editions ACFAS, Montreal.
Patinkin, D. 1952, 'Wicksell's "cumulative process"', *Economic Journal* 62(248) (December).
Patinkin, D. 1968, 'Wicksell's cumulative process in theory and practice', *Banca Nazionale del Lavoro Quarterly Review* 85 (June).
Patinkin, D. 1978, 'On the relation between Keynesian economics and the "Stockholm School"', *Scandinavian Journal of Economics* 80(2).
Seccareccia, M. 1987, 'Les courants de la pensée économique à l'origine de la *Théorie générale*: quelques éléments nouveaux d'interprétation', *La 'Théorie générale' et le keynesianisme*, ed. by G. Boismenu and G. Dostaler, Editions ACFAS, Montreal.
Shackle, G. L. S. 1967, *The Years of High Theory*, Cambridge University Press, Cambridge.
Uhr, C.G. 1960, *Economic Doctrines of Knut Wicksell*, University of California Press, Berkeley.
Uhr, C. G. 1985, 'Wicksell and the Austrians', *Research in the History of Economic Thought and Methodology*, Vol. 3.
Wicksell, K. 1907, 'The influence of the rate of interest on prices', *Economic Journal* 17(66) (June).
Wicksell, K. 1935, *Lectures on Political Economy*, Vol. II, Routledge, London.
Wicksell, K. 1936, *Interest and Prices*, Macmillan, London, [1898].
Wicksell, K. 1953, 'The enigma of business cycles', *International Economic Papers* 3.

Wicksell, K. 1954, *Value, Capital and Rent*, George Allen & Unwin, London.
Wicksell, K. 1958, *Selected Papers on Economic Theory*, George Allen & Unwin, London.
Wicksell, K. 1986, 'Preface to the 1922 German edition of Volume Two (Money and Credit) of the Lectures', *Political Economy* 2(2).

11 Early Mathematical Theories of Business-Cycles

Robert W. Dimand

'It is a notorious fact that investigators of business cycles have made little or no use of economic theory', complained Henry Schultz (Evans, 1931). 'Working in the field in which lack of equilibrium is the prevailing condition rather than the exception, and finding that the principal treatises on economics center around the notion of static equilibrium, they have refused to make their own theoretical ascensions in the captive balloon of the received theory.' This situation was changing rapidly at the time Schultz wrote. In the decade preceding the publication of Keynes's *General Theory*, a small group of mathematically-oriented economists in Europe and the United States attempted to replace verbal theorizing and atheoretical measurement of trade fluctuations with formal models of oscillating dynamic systems. While Tinbergen's (1939) simultaneous equations model of the US economy is well known, in part because of his debate with Keynes, earlier developments have been neglected in accounts of interwar macroeconomics such as Shackle (1967) and Backhouse (1985).

Early statistical work on business-cycles, notably that of Wesley Mitchell, Arthur Burns and their associates at the National Bureau of Economic Research and similar efforts such as the 'business barometer' of the Harvard Economic Society's *Review of Economic Statistics*, emphasized peridogram analysis of the length of cycles and atheoretical prediction based on leading indicators and on superimposed cycles of fixed duration. The work of Christopher Sims on vector autoregression has revived interest in atheoretical macroeconomics, but in the years 1926–35 a new trend in quantitative macroeconomics was away from 'measurement without theory' towards models grounded in economic theory. This trend was international: extending from Evans and Roos in the US to Frisch and Holme in Norway; Tinbergen and Koopmans in the Netherlands, Theiss in Hungary; Kalecki and Lipinski at the Institute for Business Cycle Research in Warsaw; Kondratieff and Slutzky at the Conjuncture Institute in Moscow; Amoroso, Bordin and Vinci in Italy; and the Statistical Institute for Economic Research in Sofia, Bulgaria. The Econometric Society provided a forum for international communication in this field.

A convenient starting point is Henry L. Moore's 'A Theory of Economic Oscillations' (1926). Moore announced that

> In the ensuing pages I shall carry the statical theory of general equilibrium elaborated by Walras and Pareto to the stage of a synthetic, realistic view of a moving general equilibrium: methods for determining numerically the necessary constants in the equations will be presented: and the conclusion will be reached that economic oscillations, other than periodic, are simply the results of perturbations in a system striving, under the influence of statical forces, toward a moving general economic equilibrium.

His article, although falling short of this ambitious programme, is an impressive achievement.

Moore proposed using least-squares regressions to obtain trend lines for each quantity supplied and demanded and for each price. He then replaced Walras's supply and demand equations with equations for the ratio of quantity supplied (or demanded) to its trend value as a function of the ratio of the price of each commodity to the trend value of that price. Deviations of quantities from trend-products could then be explained by the deviations of (relative) prices from trend-prices, together with the partial price-elasticities of supply and demand. Moore (1926, p. 25) argued that 'We have shown that the entire economic system oscillates about a general equilibrium moving along the lines of secular trends of prices and products. Trend-prices and trend-products are equilibrium prices and products.' He had, however, not shown, but rather asserted that equilibrium values could be found simply by computing trend lines.

Unfortunately, Moore's supply and demand functions were not identified, since they were functions of the same set of relative prices and he had no way of distinguishing quantity demanded from quantity supplied. This problem had plagued his earlier work on statistical fitting of demand curves, leading to his claim that demand curves for producer's goods typically slope upwards, a conclusion that was received with scepticism. Despite this, Moore's attempt to build a bridge between the theory of general equilibrium and statistical modelling of fluctuations provided a sharp contrast to the work of his Columbia University colleague, Wesley Mitchell, and stimulated further work.

Moore's work was built upon by Griffith Evans, a mathematics professor at the Rice Institute, and by Charles Roos, a Rice graduate teaching mathematics at Cornell. Roos is not widely remembered now but he played a crucial role in opening the economics profession to mathematical analyses of economic problems, as first secretary–treasurer of the Econometric Society, first research director of the Cowles Commission, and author of the first two Cowles monographs.

Evans and Roos were strongly influenced by Moore (1926) and by a series of lectures on integral equations delivered by Vito Volterra at Rice. To convert the Walrasian static general equilibrium system into Volterra integral equations, Evans (1930; 1931) and Roos (1927; 1930) assumed that demand and cost functions depend on both price and the rate of change of price, but offered little explanation of introducing the time derivative of price as an argument. This contrasts with their careful discussion of how production depends on profit-maximization by producers, given the cost and demand functions. Roos (1927, p. 634) mentioned, but did not stress, a possible empirical justification: Irving Fisher in 1923 had found a correlation of 0.77 between the volume of trade and a moving average of the rate of change of the price level. The strongest reason for adopting this modelling strategy appears to have been mathematical convenience. Evans and Roos differentiated the resulting Volterra integral equations to obtain first or second order differential equations.

Roos (1930) took the case of a monopolist maximizing the present discounted value of profits, who knew the demand function for his commodity, and whose cost function depended on the rate of change as well as the level of prices. Roos examined which changes in demand or cost coefficients would produce oscillations of diminishing, increasing, or constant amplitude around the trend price. Evans (1931) illustrated these cases for a single commodity with cobweb diagrams. Evans and Roos were vulnerable to criticism on the jump from relating adjustment of output of a single commodity to a change in its relative price to relating fluctuations in output as a whole to changes in the general price level. Roos (1930, p. 520) mentioned 'certain industries which contract for materials and which operate on a wage scale that remains fixed by agreement' as a reason why rising prices stimulate output, but admitted that 'It is not proposed that the reasons offered here are the only ones, and it is hoped that the reader will be able to supply others'.

Despite such weaknesses, the work of Evans and Roos on cycles culminating in the first Cowles monograph (Roos, 1934), was an important contribution. Instead of attributing cycles to irrational waves of optimism and pessimism or to exogenous forces such as weather or sunspot cycles, they showed how systems of equations could express theories in which shocks (taken as changes in coefficients, rather than in exogenous variables) generate oscillations around a trend, and attempted to ground business-cycle theory in a general equilibrium theory of rational optimizing agents.

Edward Theiss, of the Technical University of Hungary, Budapest, built on Evans (1930) and Roos (1930) in 'A Quantitative Theory of Industrial Fluctuations Caused by the Capitalistic Technique of Production' (1933), presented in Atlantic City in December 1932 to a joint session of the Econometric Society and the American Association for the Advancement of Science, of which Roos was permanent secretary. Following Aftalion (1927), Theiss noted that time is needed to turn raw materials and labour into output, so that quantity supplied depends on lagged prices and lagged rate of change of prices, while quantity demanded depends on current prices and current rate of change of prices. Equating supply and demand, Theiss showed that the solution for price would in general consist of aperiodic terms, which he interpreted as the secular trend, and a number of oscillatory terms, representing periodic fluctuations in prices. Theiss represented the cycle around trend as the summation of several sine curves of differing amplitude and period. He did not provide an explanation of why aggregate output should depend on the price level (let alone on the rate of change of prices) in the way that the output of a single good depends on the relative price of that good.

This representation of economic fluctuations as the summation of regular sinusoidal waves was in keeping with Eugen Slutzky's important 1927 paper. Slutzky, using the winning numbers in the Soviet government lottery loan as a source of random numbers, argued both that apparently irregular economic fluctuations can by analysed as the summation of regular cycles, and that the summation of random causes can explain the cyclic processes. Although Slutzky's article did not appear in English translation until 1937, the original 1927 paper in Russian had an English summary. The paper was discussed by Mitchell (1927) and expounded at length by Kuznets (1929). Although Theiss did not cite Slutzky, he was at the University of Chicago to work with Henry Schultz, a mathematical economist and econometrician who had studied with Moore, been the discussant for Evans (1931), and is credited in the first footnote of the English version of Slutzky (1927) with arranging translation of the paper. The prompt notice of Slutzky's article by Kuznets, Mitchell and Schultz in the United States is evidence of the rapid international transmission of ideas in mathematical business-cycle theory in this period. Additional evidence is that Theiss wrote his 1933 paper while working with Schultz in Chicago and his 1935 paper while working with Ragnar Frisch at the Institute of Economics in Oslo.

Like Theiss, Jan Tinbergen (1933), addressing the Econometric Society in Lausanne in September 1931, examined a system in which supply depended on lagged price but demand on current prices. Citing Evans, Roos and Luigi Amoroso as precedents, Tinbergen also made the rate of change, as well as the level, of price an argument in the supply and demand functions, and found that the solution for market-clearing prices would be the summation of a series of oscillatory terms.

Both Theiss (1933) and Tinbergen (1933) were presented to the Econometric Society, founded in 1930. Far more than the national economic associations and journals, the Econometric Society and its journal provided an opportunity for international discussion of formal modelling of trade cycles. The 1935 volume of *Econometrica* included papers on business-cycle modelling by Amoroso, Chait, Kalecki, Theiss, Tinbergen, and Frisch and Holme. More traditional, non-mathematical business-cycle theory lacked comparable institutions for international communication, and was far more subject to division into national schools, at least until political events led to the migration of Austrian and other Central European economists to Britain and the United States.

Not all the papers on cycle theory in *Econometrica* in the early 1930s appear, with the benefit of hindsight, to have been part of the mainstream of the development of macroeconomics. A 1934 paper by F. Creedy of Lehigh University approached economic fluctuations by means of a very rigid analogy to Newton's laws of mechanics. Creedy defined 'Effective Persuasive Force = Rate of Acceleration of Economic Action times a Constant', on the presumption that Newton's third law that force equals mass times acceleration must have a simple economic analogue, and used as a specific case of this law the assumption that a constant times the rate of acceleration of spending equals the unspent balance of income. Creedy made use of differential equations in his analysis, but his principle of economic inertia and principle of economic resilience lacked a basis in economic theory.

Far more important were papers by Ragnar Frisch and Harold Holme, by Michal Kalecki, and by Jan Tinbergen, presented to the Econometric Society in Leyden in October 1933 and published in *Econometrica* in 1935, representing the state of the art of formal theories of business cycles just before Keynes's *General Theory*.

A striking feature of these articles is the extent of the interaction among the authors. Frisch and Holme (1936) took as their starting-point the mixed difference and differential equation derived in Kalecki (1935b), and questioned as arbitrary Kalecki's imposition of the condition that the main cyclical solution be undamped (generate oscillations of constant amplitude). They investigated Kalecki's contention that although the characteristic solution of his mixed difference and differential equation would be transcendental and have an infinity of roots, all these roots would correspond to periods shorter than the 'gestation period' of investment, with the sole exception of a period of ten years that Kalecki had found. 'In the version of his paper, which will appear in *Econometrica*, Kalecki does not go into any further analysis of this matter, but has asked me to do so,' wrote Frisch in his introduction to his paper with Holme.

'One of the results which follows from the present analysis is that Kalecki's contention is right.'

Section 12 of Tinbergen's 1935 survey paper was a discussion of Kalecki (1935b), with a reference to Kalecki's (1933) pamphlet in Polish, followed by sections on other mathematical theories of business cycles, such as those of Frisch, Roos and Vinci (1934). The original Leyden versions of the Kalecki and Tinbergen papers were the subject of B. A. Chait's note (1935), and a less mathematical version of Kalecki's paper was published in French in the *Revue d'Economie Politique* (1935a). Thus, contrary to the widespread belief that Kalecki was an isolated figure in the early 1930s because he worked in Warsaw and wrote the first version of his business-cycle theory in Polish, his Econometric Society paper was published in English and French and more importantly, attracted the prompt attention of Frisch and Tinbergen, later the co-winners of the first Nobel Prize in economics. Publication in *Econometrica* meant that the paper would be circulated to (but not necessarily read by) such economists as J. M. Keynes, Fellow of the Econometric Society, member of the council of the Society, and member of the editorial advisory board of *Econometrica*.

The papers presented at the 1933 Leyden session were concerned with the periodicity and damping of oscillations derived from the summation of sinusoidal waves. Although relatively sophisticated mathematical concepts, notably integral equations and mixed difference and differential equations, were used, these were applied to simple and largely arbitrary postulated relations between output and investment decisions and such variables as prices, rates of change of prices, and interest rates. With the sole exception of Kalecki, none of the papers considered above recognized that the relation of aggregate supply and aggregate demand to the price level could not be dealt with by simple analogy to the case of a single commodity. Even Kalecki, who began his two 1935 papers with an account of the determinants of aggregate consumption and investment, did not deal with the theory of aggregate supply. There was nothing in the Leyden papers comparable to the analysis in Keynes (1936) of why the labour market might fail to clear, and nothing in the *General Theory* that paralleled the mathematical analyses showing how random shocks could generate economic cycles, rather than just random jumps in equilibrium values.

References

Aftalion, A. 1927, 'The theory of economic cycles based on the capitalistic technique of production', *Review of Economic Statistics* 9, pp. 165–70.

Amoroso, L. 1935, 'La dynamique de la circulation', *Econometrica* 3, pp. 400–10.

Backhouse, R. 1985, *A History of Modern Economic Analysis*, Basil Blackwell, Oxford.

Chait, B. A. 1935, 'Note sur les systèmes macrodynamiques', *Econometrica* 3, 472.

Creedy, F. 1934. 'On the equations of motions of business activity', *Econometrica* 2, pp. 363–80.

Evans, G. C. 1930, *Mathematical Introduction to Economics*, McGraw-Hill, New York.

Evans, G. C. 1931, 'A simple theory of economic crises', *Journal of the American Statistical Association* 26, pp. 61–8, with comment by Henry Schultz, pp. 68–72.

Frisch, R. and Holme, H. 1935, 'The characteristic solution of a mixed difference and differential equation occuring in economic dynamics', *Econometrica* 3, pp. 225–39.

Kalecki, M. 1935a, 'Essai d'une théorie du mouvement cyclique des affaires', *Revue d'Economie Politique* 49, pp. 285-305.

Kalecki, M. 1935b, 'A macrodynamic theory of business cycles', *Econometria* 3, pp. 327–44.

Keynes, J. M. 1936, *The General Theory of Employment, Interest and Money*, Macmillan, London.

Kuznets, S. 1929, 'Random events and cyclical oscillations', *Journal of the American Statistical Association* 24, pp. 258–75.

Mitchell, W. C. 1927, *Business Cycles*, National Bureau of Economic Research, New York.

Moore, H. L. 1926, 'A theory of economic oscillations', *Quarterly Journal of Economics* 41, pp. 1–26.

Roos, C. F. 1927, 'A dynamical theory of economics', *Journal of Political Economy* 35, pp. 632–56.

Roos, C. F. 1930, 'A mathematical theory of price and production fluctuations and economic crises', *Journal of Political Economy* 38, pp. 501–22.

Roos, C. F. 1934, *Dynamic Economics*, Principia Press for Cowles Commission, Bloomington, Indiana.

Shackle, G. L. S. 1967, *The Years of High Theory*, Cambridge University Press, Cambridge.

Slutzky, E. 1927, 'The summation of random causes as the source of cyclic processes', as revised and translated, *Econometrica*, 5 (1937), pp. 105–46.

Theiss, E. 1933, 'A quantitative theory of industrial fluctuations caused by the capitalistic technique of production', *Journal of Political Economy* 41, pp. 334–49.

Theiss, E. 1935, 'Dynamics of saving and investment', *Econometrica* 3, pp. 213–24.

Tinbergen, J. 1933, 'L'utilisation des equations fonctionelles et des nombres complexes dans les recherches economiques', *Econometrica* 1, pp. 36–51.

Tinbergen, J. 1935, 'Annual survey: suggestions on quantitative business cycle theory', *Econometrica* 3, pp. 241–308.

Tinbergen, J. 1939, *Statistical Testing of Business Cycle Theories*, 2 vols, League of Nations, Geneva; reprinted in one vol, Agathon Press, New York, 1968.

Vinci, F. 1934, 'Significant developments in business cycle theory', *Econometrica*, 2 pp. 125–39.

12 Hicks's Changing Views on Economic Dynamics[1]

O. F. Hamouda

Hicks has been consistently aware, since the early 1930s, of the nature of the problems of economic change and the difficult tasks facing economic theory in conceiving economic dynamics. He has insisted all along that a great deal of economics should deal with the problems of change. In the present paper, some discussion on development and the evolution of Hicks's notion of economic dynamics is presented. The focus of attention will be on the methods of analysis he proposed in approaching economic problems and the problems of change.

In *The Theory of Wages* Hicks began by reminding the reader that

> The problems of the nature of the market are almost entirely problems of change. ... There can be no full equilibrium unless wages of labour equal its marginal product. ... In actual practice changes in methods are continually going on; and resources are continually being transferred ... or new resources being put at the disposal of industry ... changes in tastes, changes in knowledge, changes in natural environment, and in the supply and efficiency of the factors of production generally. As these things change, so the marginal product of labour changes with them ... adjustments are not instantaneous. (Hicks, 1932, pp. 6, 18–19)

In *Dynamic Problems* he re-emphasized that 'In dynamic conditions, the events of one moment are ordinarily different from the events of another' (Hicks, 1935, p. 270). *Value and Capital (VC)* was an attempt to construct a dynamic theory in which he said 'The economic system has now to be conceived ... as a process in time' (Hicks, 1939, p. 116). He stressed that 'Economic dynamics ... pay special attention to the way changes in these dates affect the relations between factors and products ... and have not much in common with the distinction between statics and dynamics in the physical sciences' (ibid., p. 115).

In 'Methods of Dynamic Analysis' Hicks tried to build a relation between the Swedish *ex-ante/ex-post* method originated by Lindahl and the method of Keynes. Dynamics, he said, was 'the theoretical analysis of the process of economic change. So defined, the subject includes the study of fluctuation as well as that of growth' (Hicks, 1956, p. 140). After having reassessed his previous work ('Commentary', 1963), he noted 'I do not believe that a process of change can be analysed so statically. It cannot be analysed without explicit attention to expectations and uncertainties' (p. 315).

By 1965 in *Capital and Growth*, he fully realized the complexity of modelling dynamic relationships:

> No attempt is made in this book to present a Theory of Economic Dynamics...I do not think that there is such a theory; I doubt very much if there can be. The phenomenon that is presented by a developing (changing) economy is immensely complex. Any theory about it is bound to simplify, and at least in some ways, to oversimplify. (Hicks, 1965, p. v)

Capital and Time (CT) (1973) was another attempt to construct a theory in time descending from Böhm-Bawerk, where production had a time structure. Hicks realized afterwards (1975, p. 366), however, that, 'Convergence to equilibrium has been shown to be dubious; but it has also been shown to be unimportant...it will take a long time; and in most applications before that time has elapsed, something else will surely have occurred.'

In 1976, writing in honour of N. Georgescu-Roegen, Hicks emphasized the very simple principle: 'the irreversibility of time is that past and future are different' (p. 135). In *Causality in Economics (CE)* (1979) he again stressed that 'The more characteristic economic problems are of change and fluctuation ... For "dynamics", in its original sense, is a branch of mechanics; and the problems to which the economic counterpart refers are not mechanical.'

It is very clear from these few quotations that in most of his past work Hicks was concerned with *economic change, problems of change* and *economic dynamics*. Depending on which part of his work one is considering, differences in the manner in which he approached problems of change and developed theories become apparent.

In terms of the development of his ideas, one can identify three main periods in which his attitude towards economics is somehow distinct. The transition from one period to another is, however, not as clear-cut as the present suggested delineation. Even though these changes were part of a very slow and continuous process, the following stages can none the less be distinguished.

1. The first period was from 1929 through the mid-1950s, culminating in the publication of *A Contribution to the Theory of the Trade Cycle* (1950). Hicks was then a leading neoclassical figure. He refined and promoted the 'marginal productivity theory' and claimed that his work was *the* 'general theory'. Although he believed that he was

producing dynamic theories he none the less adhered to techniques that did not lend themselves to dynamic analysis. In this period, Hicks's economic theory was perforce a static theory. This part of Hicks's work will not be discussed in the present paper.

2. The second period, which is the concern of the present paper, extended from the mid-1950s up to the suggested neo-Austrian theory of the seventies. During this period Hicks became more critical of some of his own work and also more open-minded. He came to accept that there is more than one way of looking at the same thing and that many definitions of economic dynamics can coexist. He no longer claimed that his work was *the* method of approach, but simply one method among others. Although this period was characterized by moments of doubt about whether Economic Dynamics could be described by mechanical models, he none the less tried to produce a 'non-steady state theory of growth'. Hicks gave more consideration to integrating the time element into his models. The difficulties he encountered would lead him to reconsider in a third period his attitude towards mechanical constructions in economic theory.

3. Finally, there came a third period which will be dealt with very briefly here in the last section; in this period it was no longer a question of building models. In recent years, Hicks's economic theory has extended beyond the usual mechanical treatment of economic problems. This is the period during which Hicks ponders the significance of 'time' in Economic Dynamics. As a consequence Hicks's treatment of economic problems now incorporates his broad knowledge of philosophy and history enhanced by a long professional experience. His approach to economic theory has drastically changed.

One more clarification concerning the presentation of Hicks's work needs to be made. He pursued two objectives: on the one hand, a study of a 'pure economic theory' and, on the other hand, an almost separate explanation of monetary theory (see Morgan, 1981; Hamouda, 1985).

The second period – Hicks's new attitude towards economic dynamics
Evidence of a second period (beginning with 1956 up to the publications of 1973) in Hicks's work is demarked by his paper 'Methods of Dynamics Analysis' (1956) in which his concern about the development of his own ideas on Economic Dynamics is expressed. He began to reveal mixed feelings about whether mechanical approaches in general could describe the dynamics of a real changing economy. At a certain moment, he raised serious doubts about the relevance of building Economic Dynamic models (1965, p. v); nevertheless, since there was another attempt to build a

theory (Traverse II), which took time into consideration, in Hicks's own mind it seemed there was hope that such a construct is possible. The changes in Hicks's conception of economic dynamics were gradual. (Reference will be made to 1965, 1969, 1970, 1975 and 1976.) He was slowly moving towards the idea that there is not a general theory which can explain everything, but only several partial theories which capture certain aspects at certain times. This new perception permitted him to be self-critical about his previous work without having to reject everything he had written. Here and there he repudiated some elements, but overall he stood by nearly all of what he had written.

What motivated transitional changes in Hicks's attitude towards economics
During the earliest period, in Hicks's work the word 'dynamics' appears in almost every writing. The significance attached to it played a crucial role in the method of analysis he tried to develop. Indeed, in different places, he gave it different definitions and hence produced different methods of analysis.[2]

On different occasions, using different definitions of dynamics and the various methods of analysis, Hicks created some confusion among his readers. Some of his critics (for example, Kaldor), rejected his notions of dynamics, while others (for instance, Harrod and Samuelson) did not accept his dynamic methods. Partly as a response to critics and partly as a personal challenge, Hicks felt the need to clarify further the matter of dynamics and, as he said (1956, p. 139n), 'build a bridge between my own approaches'. The outcome of 'Methods of Dynamic Analysis' was to be the beginning of a change of attitude toward economic modelling in general. This change was significantly developed in *Capital and Growth* (*CG*) (1965).

Reconsideration of dynamics   To clarify the notion of dynamics which left him open to criticism, Hicks, in his 1956 article, focused on two alternative methods of analysis. One was provided by Lindahl, stressing the *ex-post/ ex-ante* distinction, the other provided by Keynes was based on the stock and flow relationship. Both of these methods dealt with plans, realizations and expectations. When analysing changes and economic processes it is possible, using either of these two methods to superimpose one upon the other time pattern. Hicks attempted to formulate a dynamics which took into consideration different time patterns:

> ... the comparison of what does happen with what is expected to happen becomes a key point of dynamic analysis. ... Dynamic analysis is not solely

concerned with the comparison of what happens in successive periods, so as to build up a story in terms of these *actual* changes; there is also a form, or phase, of dynamic analysis which concentrates attention upon a *single period*, being concerned with the difference between what happens in that period and what is planned to happen in it. (1956, p. 139)

Two important ideas emerge from this statement alone: the notions of *period* and *successive periods*, and the concept of *comparison*. First, the concept of time was introduced in the form of the single period; then came a concern with the way successive periods are linked together. Hicks referred to these analyses as single period theory and continuation theory respectively. Second, in dynamics according to Hicks, the emphasis should be on the comparison of what has happened and what is expected to happen. Plans and expectations are made for one period at its beginning, and actual facts become available either at the end of the period or at some future date. In this kind of dynamics there is a possible comparison simultaneously of different contemporaneous points of time or periods of time.

By 1965 Hicks fully realized that 'Dynamic theory is inherently difficult; we can never hope to grasp with our analysis all aspects of a dynamic process' (1965, p. 34), when attempts at modelling are made. Hicks, ultimately, questioned whether even growth theory was 'dynamic' enough; there are too many ways in which it remains 'semi-static' (1965, p. 14).

Market analysis   Although the terms 'fixprice' and 'flexprice' surfaced much later in Hicks's vocabulary, they can, however, be used to describe Hicks's early models. They had been given special meaning in models which were designed to accommodate only one type of change, either in price or quantity, not both.[3] In an effort to remedy and improve on these methods, Hicks suggested bringing together price disequilibrium and quantity disequilibrium in one model, based either on an *ex-post/ex-ante* distinction or on stock-flow relations.

In Hicks's model based on stock-flow relations, both stock equilibrium and flow equilibrium considerations in a changing economy were to be taken into account. Although he believed it worthwhile to go through the algebra of such models, he said, 'we can invent rules for their working, and calculate the behaviour of the resulting models; but such calculations are of illustrative value only' (1965, p. 83); thus he warns of the limitations of such approaches. He even went so far as to say, 'we are unable to "simulate" the behaviour of intelligent business management by any simple rule ... mechanical principles of adjustment do not offer a good representation' (1965, pp. 102–3).

There are, thus, enough indications in his writings to reveal that, by 1965, Hicks was getting more and more reluctant to use mechanical approaches in Dynamic Economics. This new attitude however, should not be interpreted as a rejection of his own early work or of mathematical models in general. Hicks believed simply that he could not rely on mechanical models alone to arrive at a reasonable understanding of economic changes. Nonetheless, he felt that these models could still be used as indicators, and with judgement exercised could allow some general conclusions to be drawn about the dynamic problems studied.

There was a smooth evolution in Hicks's attitude toward Dynamic Economics in general. There were not really any major new elements in his reconsidered views, since the *ex-ante/ex-post* distinction he got from Lindahl and the stock-flow relationship inspired by Keynes had already been used in his earlier models. Despite the new perspectives, Hicks was still looking at the same issues. Now he could look back and describe what he disapproved of in his macro-dynamic models and those already existing which related to his own work. He continued, however, to rely on models of Economic Dynamics even constructing new ones.

Hicks tried, during the second period, to construct 'a formal theory of an economy which is not in a steady state ... an economy which has a history, so that things actually happen' (1976b, p. 144). This attempt, which may be called Traverse I, was first tried in *CG*. It was static, too closely tied to a steady state method. In itself, it has no particular interest except to show the way Hicks formulated his model. A later more elaborate attempt, which may be called Traverse II, was developed in *Capital and Time*. Traverse II was more elaborate.

Hicks's growth theory and the idea of the Traverse
Although Hicks continued in *CG* (1965) to refer to his growth theory as *one particular* analysis of Economic Dynamics, this version of his theory was still closely linked to the concept of equilibrium.

The first attempt Hicks provided the model, Traverse I, which used classical assumptions. It was a steady-state growth equilibrium of discrete processes of production in which commodities were produced by means of commodities. A two-sector model, it used one consumption good and one capital good, modeled in the linear Sraffa system in which coefficients of production were fixed. Hicks referred to it as the classical system. He established three basic relationships: first, the rate of profit to the wage rate in the price equation, and then, the rate of growth to output and consumption in the quantity equation.To relate the rate of profit to the rate of growth, Hicks introduced a third relationship: a 'saving function'.[5]

In Traverse I, Hicks relied on the concept of equilibrium; his analysis was essentially static, thus, uninteresting for the present discussion. To achieve the idea of building a formal theory of growth which was not a steady state, Hicks made a second, more elaborate attempt.

The second attempt[6]   As in classical economics, Hicks focused his attention on the production side of the economy. In a very simple model, he called the production process, a process that converted a flow of inputs into a flow of outputs. He assumed one type of input (homogeneous labour) and one type of output (consumer good) in a process which was completely integrated (there were no references in his equations to intermediary transformations – for instance, in his system, machines would be produced but they would be absorbed within the process; thus capital does not appear in his model). To have homogeneous products and factors, he expressed input and output in their value terms. There was only one interest rate, one price and one input–output ratio, the wages being expressed in terms of the consumer good. Hicks also assumed a fixed coefficient production function and constant returns to scale.

Objectives   Hicks asked the old classical question about the short-run and long-run impact of technological change on employment and on the distribution of income. In doing so Hicks attempted to achieve many objectives. These goals are divided into two types.
   In terms of general theory he tried:

1.   to build a theory of *dynamics* which was in time (he claimed that this was in the Austrian tradition);
2.   to build a theory of *causal* analysis in which convergence and stability were not necessarily the ultimate purpose of the study;
3.   to build a theory of *capital* which accommodated both fixed and working capital.

In terms of consequences, he tried:

4.   to build a theory which could *explain* substitution of factors in an expanding economy where full employment was not always maintained, (here he revived the Wage Fund Theory);
5.   to build a theory *without money* to show that even a barter economy would have problems of equilibrium adjustment.

Some brief elaboration on these points:

(1) Hicks found the Böhm-Bawerk theory of capital very attractive: 'Production was a combination of Labour and Time. The Time that was taken in production was an identifiable figure – the degree of Roundaboutness. ... Roundaboutness was a measure of capital intensity' (1973b, p. 8). It was the link between Production, Time and Capital which was the appeal of Böhm-Bawerk's theory. To Hicks these were the basic ingredients needed to construct a theory in time.[7]

He believed, however, that, in a model designed to fit fixed as well as working capital (1973a, p. 193), 'there is no *period of production*; there is no *roundaboutness*', these concepts would have to be abandoned. When these concepts are suppressed, however, the whole Böhm-Bawerk model collapses. Hicks was not elaborating Böhm-Bawerk's model but suggesting to maintain only 'Böhm-Bawerk's true insights. ... Production is a process, a process in Time ... Capital is an expression of sequential production. Production has a time-structure, so Capital has a time-structure' (1973a, pp. 193–4). In fact, Hicks's new model cannot be considered identical to any modeling of Böhm-Bawerk. In Hicks's own words, 'I am writing in their tradition; yet I have realized, as my work has continued, that it is a wider and bigger tradition' (1973b, p. 12); he meant that 'the neo-Austrian theory cannot look like the old Austrian theory ... it has a closer resemblance to the growth theory ... evolved ... during the last twenty-five years' (1973b, p. 9). Obviously Hicks's neo-Austrian theory did not try to resuscitate Böhm-Bawerk's theory, but was, as he claimed, simply inspired by its spirit.

(2) Hicks thought that the Traverse analysis could not be made properly, if it did not pay attention to the cause-effect relationship. But what did he mean by causal analysis? He suggested that it must begin from a particular situation at a given date, assume everything that had happened before as given, and then compare two alternative paths which extend into the future of which one is affected by a disturbance (or a cause) but not the other:

> the difference between the paths is the effect of that cause. The difference itself extends over time, so that there are 'short-run' and 'long-run' effects. But merely to distinguish between short-run and long-run is not sufficient; it is the *whole* of the difference between the paths which is the effect of the cause. (1973a, p. 203)

Hicks was, thus, interested not only in the comparison of the initial and terminal positions, but also in the differences between and along the Traverses at every point in time.

(3) Any theory of capital cannot be adequately conceived, if it does not

seriously consider the time element. Conversely, an economic process which is in time cannot be conceived without taking into account at least some form of capital. Capital, however, is a difficult concept which gives headaches to many economists. Both classical and Austrian economists dealt with working capital only. According to Hicks, they did not know technically what to do with fixed capital. Aided by the work of von Neumann, Sraffa and the development of linear programming, Hicks believed that he had developed a method which 'accommodates both fixed and working capital with equal ease; it is competent to deal with both' ('The Austrian Theory', p. 195).

(4)   The economic message that Hicks wanted to deliver in *Capital and Time* was the short-run and the long-run impacts of technological change on employment and on distribution of income. The message itself was centred around one *Principal Proposition* 'the most important in all this book':

> the function of substitution, in an expanding economy, is to slow up the rises in wages that come from technical improvement; but the effect of the retardation is to stretch out the rise, making it a longer rise, so that a larger rise, than would otherwise have occurred, is ultimately achieved. (1973b, p. 115)

In his chapter on machinery, Ricardo discussed these rent and profit effects, while wages were not the issue because of the assumption of an elastic supply of labour. What Hicks seems to be trying to do was to analyse in the case of an improvement in technology both the employment impact in the situation of an elastic supply of labour (as in the case of fixwage), and the wage impact in the situation of an inelastic supply of labour (as in the case of full employment). Ricardo's discussion of Rent-Profit then became Hicks's Wage-Profits analysis. Although their approaches were different 'all that, in this place, is relevant, is that we are all of us – Ricardo, Mill and I – saying what in terms of economic principle is the same thing' (1973b, p. 123). It was the principal, not the method, of analysis which contained the similarities.

(5)   Finally, a question on which Hicks stood firm: was money the cause of economic fluctuations? The answer was 'money is not the cause of fluctuation; it is a complication, but no more than that' (1973b, p. 124). According to Hicks, many great economists, among them Hayek, believed that money was the cause. He thought they were deluded in assuming that, if money were to be removed from the scene, then there would be no fluctuations in the economy. It was with respect to this issue that Hicks delivered his second message: 'One of my objects in writing this book has

been to kill that delusion ... that there has been no money in my model, yet it has plenty of adjustment difficulties. It is not true that by getting rid of money, one is automatically in "equilibrium"' (1973b, p. 55).

Hicks preferred to work in real terms to show that money was not the primary cause of fluctuation. However, this did not mean that money was unimportant. Adhering to points (1) to (5), Hicks tried to construct a Dynamic Economic Model, Traverse II, in which he applied the classical principles in an Austrian tradition, using recently available mathematical techniques.

From the time that Traverse II appeared, to the present, as Hicks correctly observed, people in general 'have not known quite what to make of it' (1976b, p. 144).[8] This despite the fact that almost none of the elements contained in *Capital and Time* were new. Some of them had already existed (see *VC*, chapter XVII).

How, from Hicks's point of view, should his neo-Austrian theory be perceived? Hicks did spend too much time setting up a single mechanical model and proving technical details. The heavy emphasis placed on the technical aspects of the standard case in his neo-Austrian theory submerged any subtle remarks made here and there, which might have prevented the readers from relying too much on such mechanics. Hicks, nevertheless, would have liked his readers to have responded more to the principle underlying his theory in general terms, rather than focusing on the technicality of his model, which was what engaged most of his critics. Responding to Harcourt's review in 'Revival of Political Economy' (1975), he made the following points:

1. Challenged that his assumptions were unrealistic, he responded, 'they are meant to be unrealistic. I have deliberately removed a number of obvious obstacles to smooth the working of an economy ... cut out natural scarcities' (1975, p. 365). All these simplifications he claimed were made in order to discover the rules of convergence in the most elementary case.
2. Even in this elementary case, he said, 'results which emerge...confirm my suspicion that convergence may not be smooth at all' (1975, p. 365). This showed that the objective of his work was not to construct a model in which convergence was guaranteed, but to find out whether in the standard case convergence was possible. He then concluded that when one went beyond the standard case, 'the prospects for convergence look much less good' (1975, p. 366).
3. One positive result ensued from his work: he no longer believed that

convergence was a vital condition in dynamics analysis: ' "Convergence to equilibrium" has been shown to be dubious; but it has also been shown to be unimportant' (1975, p. 366). This conviction was due to the fact that in the real world changes take place unceasingly; adjustments never have sufficient time to be completed.[9]

The above arguments were compatible with the evolution of Hicks's second phase of thinking as explained in the first section. However, they were hardly transparent in *CT*. Why was this so?

In his neo-Austrian theory, Hicks had not totally succeeded in liberating himself from the equilibrium concept. Despite these obvious holdovers from his earliest thinking Hicks was, nonetheless, introducing a new approach. First, although Hicks, in Traverse II, still adhered to the mechanical consideration of the standard case, he clarified the issues in much more general terms. He referred to the non-standard case, to the irrelevance of convergence, and to the difficulty of isolating various effects due to different changes occurring simultaneously or overlapping through time. Second, Hicks dissociated himself from the neo-classical school and also from what he called the 'equilibrists'. Third, also in *CT*, for the first time he assumed that economic theory has a corresponding historical aspect, an assertion which could be found in his *A Theory of Economic History (TEH)* (1969). The two books, he said, go together.

The basic hypotheses underlying his historical explanation of the impact of English Industrialism are as follows: the supply curve of labour was of a reversed L shape, savings were made mainly out of profits, and there was a relationship between circulating capital and the demand for labour. These were precisely the basic hypotheses used in the standard case of his neo-Austrian theory. It was no surprise that Hicks wanted these two books read together. While in *TEH* the explanation of the impact of the substitution of factors was conducted in terms of historical facts, in *CT* Hicks used the same hypotheses to build a theoretical framework. In *CT*, he wanted to prove mathematically his Principal Proposition (i.e. that technical progress would eventually lead to higher wages), and provide historians with a definite answer to their unresolved questions of the economic impact of changes in technology. Hicks actually seemed more concerned with finding answers for historians than with the technicality of his work. He did not succeed, however, in diverting the critics' attention from the latter. In order to make his model manageable and mathematical, Hicks allowed too much distortion in the presentation of his theory, consequently transforming completely the picture of his initial investigation and changing the nature of the problem altogether. Therefore, the conclusions he found himself forced to draw from his neo-

Austrian theory could not be accepted as answers to the questions raised in *TEH*.

The explanation given in *TEH* provided a realistic approach to the question of the impact of technological change. This explanation remained, however, a historical interpretation and the general question of technological impact thus remained restricted to the events within *TEH*. Recognizing the limitation of history Hicks then turned to economic theory. Here in terms of saying anything about the real world, a mechanical approach did not lead him very far. His model did not succeed in eliminating the steady-state constraint. As it turned out, his mechanical approach was only compatible with hypothetical situations, and could not therefore prove or disprove any historical facts or events. After *CT* Hicks actually refrained from building technical models of Economic Dynamics, and tried to make economics 'more time-conscious'. He had come to believe then that 'as economics pushes on beyond "statics", it becomes less like science, and more like history' (1979, p. xi). This was quite a contrast to his view on dynamics in the 1930s and 1940s.

The third period and concluding note – Hicks the methodologist
No doubt, Hicks was aware very early in his career of the complexity involved in handling the economics of change. In the first phase of his work, however, he was very preoccupied with the ongoing academic debates, and his priorities were targeted at a specific objective, i.e. consolidating the marginalist revolution and defending the ideological neutrality of economic science. Owing to the force of circumstances, Hicks came to realize that the business of economics was to deal with Economic Dynamics in order to describe and explain a world in motion which had a past and a future, and in which facts were dated. Historical and social movements, he came to believe in phase two of his work, could not be represented accurately by mechanical models, no matter how complex they could be made. Most of such models were created for 'purely intellectual interest' (1979, p. viii). In his third period, he asserted that economic theory was ideology. He began to discuss fundamental questions such as what purpose economics has, and whether or not economics is a science. This discussion is found in many of his works written since 1976, the central piece being *Causality in Economics*. Hicks tackled the question of the role and purpose of economics from a broad philosophical perspective. The contributions of the work of Hicks's third period are today seen as an unconventional approach to the discipline; some (see Johnson, 1975) even think that he was sailing against the wind.

The changes in Hicks's approach to economic theory occurred slowly; when they did appear, they often came as a surprise to his readers. In his

Causality in Economics he wrote, 'the subject of this book is not one which I have kept in my cupboard, mulling over it for years; I came upon it quite recently, and rather suddenly' (1979, p. vii). He now believed that, on the one hand, 'Economics is more like art or philosophy than science' (1976, p. 207), and on the other hand, 'there is, there can be, no economic theory which will do for us everything we want all the time' (1976, p. 208). Hicks had travelled far from those days when he believed that economics is a branch of science, and that it is possible to build general theories which have answers for everything.

Hicks recalled that in his early training in economics he knew very little of Marshall. As his work evolved Hicks occasionally mentioned him; but Marshall was not given as much consideration as Walras, Keynes or the Swedish economists. Concerning Hicks's general attitude toward economics it seems that Hicks had more in common with Marshall[10] than with any other economist.

With respect to theory, Hicks believed that there were certain circumstances where an equilibrium theory could be accommodated and used safely, but that, overall, one would have to be careful not to rely too much on such constructions.

With regard to the relationship of economics to other disciplines, like Marshall, Hicks believed that because economics (a) deals with facts which cannot be known with precision (mainly at an aggregate level), (b) is concerned with the past, present and future, and with things in historical time, and (c) deals with making decisions which can have very profound implications, all these factors place economics on 'the edge of science and on the edge of history' (1979, p. 38).

Like Marshall, Hicks was conscious of the importance of time in economics. The handling of the concept of time gave him great difficulty and forced him to search for a better way of integrating it properly. 'It is because I want to make economics more human that I want to make it more time-conscious' (1976a, p. 149). Hicks arrived very close to Marshall's attitude toward economics. None the less, he remained open-minded and explored many ideas from various schools of thought. In an address to a neo-Austrian audience (179, p. 63), he said:

> I have been distributing prizes, but also a few slaps. You will, I fear, feel in the end that I am too open to be an Austrian; for I am an Open Marshallian, and Ricardian, and Keynesian, perhaps even Lausannian, as well. I put [sic] perhaps to the last, for I think I have shown why I now rate Walras and Pareto, who were my first loves, so much below Menger.

Hicks flirted with various theories cautiously and attentively; and by keeping ideas which suited him and reorganizing them his way, he created a body of economics all his own. His eclectic interest was, no doubt, of a great help to him in establishing a theory of Economic Dynamics.

Notes

1. I would like to thank B. B. Price, G. Giovannetti, G. C. Harcourt, J. R. C. Rowley and C. Sardoni for their helpful comments.
2. For instance, in *The Theory of Wages*, although there was no explicit definition of dynamics, there was a certain kind of dynamic analysis. It was more clear in *Value and Capital*: dynamics was defined as a situation in which variables were dated and the Temporary Equilibrium Model was the method of analysis used. In his theory of the trade cycle, the definition was extended to include the definitions of Frisch and Harrod, and Hicks constructed an altogether different method of analysis. Soon after, in a different context, he analysed the process of imperfect competition and came up with another method. He analysed (1954) a firm which tried to set up a new plant in an oligopolistic market. He assumed that time was divided into three periods: the construction period during which output was zero; a closed period in which the plant was operational, the firm being the only one producing this type of output because the competition had not yet completed similar plants; finally, the open period in which the market was open to competition. The closed period was of limited length while the open period was of an indefinite length. He then produced another dynamic analysis which was totally different from the previous one.
3. *Value and Capital* was a flexprice macro-model which consisted of several markets based on micro-analysis. Price determination was the main concern of the approach. Hicks did not question whether goods were perishable or storable or whether stocks were carried forward. He simply assumed perfect competition; his goods and services were to be sold in the market according to supply and demand, and their prices would be determined accordingly. According to Hicks, no distinction was made between stock and flow. This, he said, was a 'Stock-Flow equilibrium' (1965, p. 85). Any distinction, he added, was irrelevant (see 1965, p. 85n). In a completely different analysis, his trade-cycle was a fixprice macro-model based this time on a one product market – a highly aggregative model in which the focus was on the variation of output. Prices were assumed to be given exogenously, and their variations were simply ignored within the model. These two models were dealing with particular markets in which only one adjustment – price or quantity – was considered.
4. This model is to be found in *Capital and Growth*, chapter XII.
5. 'When we have (i) the price equations, (ii) the quantity equations, (iii) some saving equation, the system is complete. The equilibrium of the economy, at its given rate of real wages, is completely determined' (1965, p. 142).
6. This was a further development, with some alteration, of chapter XVI (1965) which later became the neo-Austrian theory (1973b). This second attempt was worked out in full detail (1973b).
7. Hicks admitted, like many other economists, that Böhm-Bawerk's theory was limited, that it could not be generalized nor handle fixed capital. However, he believed that even if Böhm–Bawerk's model was not satisfactory, there were elements in the method which could be valuable.
8. What annoyed most economists was that they could not determine to which school Hicks belonged. Unlike in the early days when his stand was clear, he now had each of his fingers in a different bowl. Many economists seemed dissatisfied and critical with how he tried to marry the Austrian tradition (not to be confused with the Austrian theory) to the classical theory, calling this neo-Austrian theory. As a consequence, his audience diminished considerably. Neo-classicals were almost pleased to point out that Hicks's return to the old theories had not brought him very far. Neo-Austrians denied that such an approach had anything to do with the Austrian tradition. Neo-Ricardians may have thought it a mistake to mix Ricardo with Böhm-Bawerk.

Hicks entered the Growth and Capital debates in an unexpected manner, a move from a neo-classical field to a Ricardian ground. The move by itself left many of his readers uncertain about his real intentions. His model and his method of approach raised a whole range of questions: some queried his fundamental theorem along the lines of the question of truncation (see Eatwell, 1975), some tried to show that his model was nothing but a special case of von Neumann (see Burmeister, 1974). Many wondered whether, besides the simple profile, anything could be done with such a model (see Steedman, 1973).

9. Arguments (i) to (iii) put forward are, we believe, some of the hidden positive parts of Hicks's work. These arguments, together with a well-thought-out article (1976b), constitute the new approach to Economic Dynamics in Hicks's third period.

10. It is perhaps worthwhile to repeat Marshall's definition: 'The main concern of economics is thus with human beings who are impelled, for good and evil, to change and progress ... the central idea of economics ... must be that of living force and movement' (1974, p. xiii). Hicks also was concerned with a close definition.

References

Burmeister, E. 1974, 'Synthesizing the neo-Austrian and alternative approaches to capital theory: a survey', *Journal of Economic Literature* 12(2) (June), pp. 413–56.

Eatwell, J. 1975, 'A note on the truncation theorem', *Kyklos* 28(4) pp. 870–5.

Hamouda, O. F. 1985, 'The evolution of Hicks' theory of money', *Bulletin of Economic Research* 37(2), pp.131–51.

Harcourt, G. C. 1975, 'Decline and rise: the revival of (classical) political economy', *Economic Record* 51(135) (September), pp. 339–56.

Hicks, J. R. 1954, 'The process of imperfect competition', *Oxford Economic Papers* (February), pp. 41–5.

Hicks, J. R. 1956, 'Methods of dynamic analysis', in *25 Economic Essays* (Festschrift for Erik Lindahl), Ekonomisk Tidskrift, Stockholm.

Hicks, J. R. 1963, (1st edition 1932), *The Theory of Wages*, Macmillan, London.

Hicks, J. R. 1965, *Capital and Growth*, Clarendon Press, Oxford.

Hicks, J. R. 1969, *A Theory of Economic History*, Oxford University Press, Oxford.

Hicks, J. R. 1970, 'A neo-Austrian growth theory', *Economic Journal*, (June), pp. 257–81.

Hicks, J. R. 1973a, 'The Austrian theory of capital and its rebirth in modern economics', in J. R. Hicks and W. Weber (eds), *Carl Menger and the Austrian School of Economics*, Clarendon Press, Oxford, pp. 190–206.

Hicks, J. R. 1973b, *Capital and Time*, Clarendon Press, Oxford.

Hicks, J. R. 1975, 'Revival of political economy: the old and the new' (reply to Harcourt), *Economic Record* (September), pp. 365–7.

Hicks, J. R. 1976a, '"Revolutions" in Economics', in S. J. Latsis (ed.), *Method and Appraisal in Economics*, Cambridge University Press, Cambridge, pp. 207–18.

Hicks, J. R. 1976b, 'Some questions of time in economics', in A. Tang, F. M. Westfield and J.S. Worley (eds.), *Evolution, Welfare and Time in Economics: Essays in Honor of Nicholas Georgescu-Roegan*, Lexington Books, Lexington, Mass., pp. 135–51.

Hicks, J. R. 1979, 'Is interest the price of a factor of production?, in M. J. Rizzo (ed.), *Time, Uncertainty and Disequilibrium*, Lexington Books, Lexington, Mass., pp. 51–63.

Hicks, J. R. 1979, *Causality in Economics*, Basic Books, New York.

Johnson, H. 1975, 'What is wrong with monetarism?', in *Lloyds Bank Review*.

Marshall, A. 1974, (1st edition 1920), *Principles of Economics* Macmillan, London.

Morgan, B. 1981, 'Sir John Hicks's contributions to economic theory', in J. R. Shackleton and G. Locksley (eds), *Twelve Contemporary Economists*, Macmillan, London, pp. 108–40.

Steedman, I. 1973, review of *Capital and Time*, *Manchester School of Social Science* (December).

13 Progress and Production: Three Episodes in the History of Production Economics

Robin Rowley and O. F. Hamouda

The area of production economics seems appropriate for illustrating the evolution of some important research interests and evaluating their tentative association with progress or rational science. First, the area is relatively uncluttered with side-issues if we focus our attention on the persistence of empirical neoclassical production functions over the last sixty years. Second, the area's controversies have generated some pronounced differences of attitudes among economists while revealing distinctive fashions for the conduct of research. Third, as any review of our textbooks will reveal, the production function and its contour counterpart, the isoquant or isoproduct line, are ubiquitous for both microeconomics and macroeconomics. Finally, we can identify three particular episodes that are simple to explore, have significant content for our purposes, and are distributed over the sixty-year period.

One episode involves the introduction of the Cobb–Douglas production function with its specific mathematical formulation in terms of aggregates, its reliance on data for estimates of coefficients, and its connection with notions of marginal-productivity theories and the intertemporal fixity of factor shares. This occurred at the beginning of the reference period but remained influential to the present time. The second episode arose as the heterogeneity of capital inputs provided a convenient focus for discussing significant problems of aggregation, the potential non-existence of production functions as descriptions of technological possibilities (since aggregate inputs might not be defined independently of prices and of the motivations of economic agents) and the emergence of a 'surrogate' function. We combine the outcome of this interest in the consequences of heterogeneity with the emergence of a (less sceptical) acceptance of the transcendental-logarithmic (translog) production function, other alternative flexible-form specifications and duality notions which are not free from the complications of heterogeneity. Both components of this second episode were prominent in the middle part of our reference period. The final episode is a current one of theoretical and econometric awkwardness. It emerged when empirical evidence from fitted cost functions and profit functions were often found to be incompatible with the assumptions for 'well-behaved' production functions so the empirical validation of production theories became questionable. It also involved the potential reconciliation of approximations, flexibility and theoretical constraints, which affects the reliance on empirical standards and statistical rules for model choice.

The empirical production function

In 1927, Douglas plotted aggregate data in logarithmic terms to obtain an empirical linear relationship that linked labour and capital with total product. This particular choice of mathematical specification had been suggested to Douglas by Cobb when the former was temporarily lecturing at Amhurst College. The results of their joint endeavour were subsequently reported to the American Economic Association and were then made available to a wider audience in a supplement to the *American Economic Review* in 1928. The Cobb formula was, however, not novel to economists. Douglas (1934, p. 224), for example, noted a slightly more complicated formula devised by Wilcox in 1926, while Samuelson (1979), Olsson (1971) and Velupillai (1973) point to various uses of the Cobb formula by Wicksell during the period that extended from 1896 to 1916. An English version of Wicksell's *Lectures on Political Economy* (1901) was published in 1934. This contained his 'Analysis of Akerman's Problem', which includes a use of the Cobb formula with the production function constrained to be linear homogeneous. Douglas was probably unaware of Wicksell's treatment but he acknowledged some awareness of major contributions to marginal-productivity theories and the use of Euler's relation for linear homogeneous functions by von Thünen, Clark and Wicksteed. See, for example, Douglas (1934; 1948) where some misstatements and significant omissions reflect a surprising illiteracy with respect to precursors for the components of the Cobb–Douglas framework but where this partial awareness is also clearly demonstrated.

The essential novelty of the Cobb–Douglas framework was its emphasis on *empirical verification* of the production function's coefficients. This verification had two elements; namely, the direct estimates of these coefficients or input elasticities and their indirect association, through a marginal-productivity connection, with constant shares of total product. The latter confirmed the stability noted by a number of earlier authors, such as Dalton (1920) and Bowley (1920), but added considerable vigour to the further investigation of intertemporal stability in distribution by moving research analysis from simple tabular displays of relative shares in total product to the search for least-squares estimates of production coefficients. Moreover, the leadership displayed by Douglas and his associates seemed to indicate how modest deviations from stability might be explored and perhaps 'explained' by inspection of least-squares residuals or by the inclusion of additional adjustments to deal with 'non-normal' utilization of capacity. Thus, for example, Douglas (1934, p. 204) could invoke the concept of a 'normal' relationship, approximately represented by an estimated regression line for time-series data:

> [Our] equation, while describing the 'normal' relationship between labor, capital, and product gives a computed product which is too high during years of depression and too low during years of prosperity. ... These discrepancies were mainly due ... to changes in the degree to which the available total plant capacity was utilized. The percentage of utilization was, of course, below the 'normal' proportion during the recession years and above 'normal' during the years of recovery and prosperity.

Clark (1928) also used a concept of normal labour, 'the labor employed when existing plants are working at normal per cent of capacity', but the scale of Douglas's use of data was considerably larger than that of earlier economists in this context.

The use of marginal-productivity notions also affected estimates based on cross-sectional data. Douglas (1976, p. 909–10), in reviewing a half-century of research on empirical production functions, noted the principles that guided his interpretation of cross-sectional discrepancies:

> We would expect positive residuals in industries characterized by (a) monopoly or highly imperfect competition or (b) expanding demand when the demand curve as a whole was shifting to the right. ... We concluded that a very large majority of the major positive residuals... were from precisely those industries that one would expect on *a priori* grounds. This strengthens the case for the production function as a description of normal competitive relationships.

Earlier, Gunn and Douglas (1940) listed the extra assumptions that had governed their cross-sectional studies.

The Cobb–Douglas framework quickly became the standard against which estimates should be confirmed. This is apparent from the attention given to the framework in early textbooks on econometrics, such as those of Davis (1941) and Tintner (1952). However, the spread of this framework is surprising for a rational economic science. The move to statistical estimation and to the appraisal of regression residuals in terms of deviations from various types of normality, for example, weakened the theoretical basis for the indirect approach using marginal-productivity theory although, in the hands of Douglas, these ingredients of research conduct were so attractive to economists. Also the presence of residuals eliminated the identification of the empirical production function with the *boundary* concept that underlies the common treatment in economic textbooks of productive efficiency and, hence, obscured the reliance on equilibrium. Compare, for instance, the empirical construct of Douglas, his associates and successors with the assertion by Brown (1968, p. 10) that the theoretical production function implies 'a technical maximization problem has been solved' and is 'defined such that the maximum product is obtained from each combination of factors'. This break between the empirical production function and its theoretical counterpart is especially significant. It led, after a hiatus of about three or four decades, to the recent interest in newer stochastic-frontier models and in decomposition formulae for inefficiency. As we indicate when discussing another illustrative episode, it also affects the role of theoretical constraints in evaluating the quality of particular empirical results for models that combine flexible-form specifications, approximations and duality. Clearly it weakens too the reliance on empirical standards to validate theoretical assumptions as repeatedly used by Ferguson (1969).

The assimilation of the Cobb–Douglas framework is also surprising in view of resistance to it that could be drawn from a number of sources. Knight (1921, p. 124), for example, in reacting to Clark's advocacy of marginal-productivity theory for aggregate 'factors of production' gave an elegent and unrestrained statement of the inadequacies of using aggregate factors. He insists on the 'absurdity of the two-factor analysis, as exemplified particularly in the work of Professor J. B. Clark', and noted:

> The same author falls into the closely related fallacy of measuring separate agencies by their productive contributions ... . It is to be observed that the fallacy is equally involved in all other distribution theory which makes use of 'factors' at all – the number is immaterial – and this includes most of the literature of the subject.

Thus heterogeneity means that the validity of marginal-productivity theories is restricted to microeconomic (perhaps) individual agencies. From this perspective, the indirect approach of the Cobb–Douglas framework (which uses distribution of total product among a few aggregate factors) is thoroughly misguided. Similarly the modelling of an aggregate macroeconomic system with neoclassical elements by 'analogy' (Ferguson, 1969, pp. 4–5) with a corresponding microeconomic one is to be dismissed.

A second source of resistance could be based on the inadequate variability of aggregate data; that is, on the problem of spurious correlation. Looking back at his own reaction to empirical production functions, Simon (1982, pp. 404–5), for example, points to excessive optimism (as he saw it) and dismissal of the functions on the basis of empirical evidence:

> It seemed to me just too good to be true that aggregate data could be fitted by simple production functions, much less that those functions should turn out to be homogeneous of the first degree and that they should make reasonably accurate predictions of labor's share in the total value of product.

By reference to Simon's papers in 1963 and 1979,

> [It] is shown that these results are a statistical artifact without economic significance. My skeptical conclusions are consistent with doubts that were expressed about the Cobb–Douglas function from the time of the first publications on it, in the 1930s. ... Since the Cobb-Douglas results have long been cited as one of the principal pieces of macroeconomic evidence for classical theory, their refutation makes the empirical foundation for that theory a good deal shakier.

Somehow, many economists failed to ask if the stability of relative shares was roughly consistent with specifications other than the Cobb–Douglas one. The conventional form of production functions was simply accepted and the values of its coefficients 'confirmed'. This is a very restricted form of statistical validation, markedly different from the exploratory 'model criticism' that has come to characterize the best-practice econometrics of today.

A final source of resistance could be based on the cardinality requirement for measurement of factors, the issue of replicants (that has often been associated with the specification of linear homogeneity), and the general avoidance of agent-specific productive characteristics. For much of its research life, the empirical production function has not been conducive to statistical analysis of elements that could not be put into the rigid format of the classical linear model or its simple generalizations. Special dummy-variable representations could be used to identify the average influence, for example, of managerial differences but the regression framework was an inhibiting one. It severely constrained what constituent elements could be embedded in the production function. Consequently, issues of inter-firm productivity differences and of optimal firm size were substantially downplayed even when the economic agents of production theory were linked with individual firms.' They were reduced to *ad hoc* parts of residual analysis for cross-sectional data and were often totally absent from macroeconomic models for time-series data.

Given these potential sources of resistance to the Cobb–Douglas framework, it is interesting to speculate why it was so widely assimilated and whether this assimilation should be viewed as a progressive step in the evolution of economics. Clearly, the framework is still with us in many of our textbooks and, often with very modest adjustments, in our research reports despite its evident flaws. Why have we not dismissed it? Answers to these questions can be put quite simply. The empirical production function is an excessive abstraction and the boundary conditions for its valid use are little understood but the function is easy to manipulate and can give straightforward inferences for some (unrealistic) economic environments. It is, that is to say, convenient for 'academic' purposes, for exposition, and for simplifying mathematical models that would otherwise be intractable. Given a commitment to mathematical models and statistical analysis, the empirical production function persists because it is instrumental in this sense and because we have failed to find an alternative approach that is equally convenient. Fashion was a major force in both its assimilation and longevity. As the comments by Stigler (1983) indicate, many economists are conservative in their choice of problems to explore, their choice of concepts and their research methods. Mistaken interests occur and persist because of the plurality of standards that plague the emergence of a consensus on the appropriateness of such choices. The empirical production function is fertile in a 'busy' sense, as attested by its ubiquity, but it may not be very fertile in other progressive senses. Its popularity has survived the introduction of 'vintage' concepts, adjustment technologies, innovation frontiers and other forms of technical progress because of this limited fertility based on mathematical tractability. Perhaps, too, we can point to the widespread illiteracy of flaws in the explication of formal empirical standards, incomplete specifications of model components (as in vague notions of competition and equilibrating forces), the emergence of a dominant establishment that *needed* the simplest formulations of production functions to discuss matters of economic growth, and the absence of sufficient advance in the development of alternative approaches (such as, for example, those stressing Schumpeterian visions or simulative modelling). On the other hand, the Cobb–Douglas framework was compatible with the fashionable shifts in economics that saw mathematics and statistics move from peripheral elements of theoretical accounts to 'mainstream' status. Not necessarily progressive in their impact, these shifts were certainly the concern of many economists who saw themselves as pursuing normal science.

Heterogeneity and flexible forms
Perspectives on progress that stress the interactions of economists within well-defined groups of skilful researchers fit the conditions of production economics in the middle of our reference period. Three particular groups can be distinguished. One stressed the 'enervating effect' of the production-function concept, which 'distracted attention from the more difficult but more rewarding questions of the influences governing the supplies of the factors and of the causes and consequences of changes in technical knowledge' (Robinson, 1953–4, p. 81), while being seriously flawed by problems of measurability. A second group addressed the consequences of aggregation over disparate capital inputs and sought means of keeping the production function as a convenient theoretical or empirical device. As represented by Solow (1966), their overall pragmatism was evident:

I have never thought of the macroeconomic production function as a rigorously justifiable concept. In my mind it is either an illuminating parable, or else a mere device for handling data, to be used so long as it gives good empirical results, and to be abandoned as soon as it doesn't, or as soon as something better comes along.

Here the choice of any particular functional form for the production function was 'a matter of no great significance' so the Cobb–Douglas framework was initially kept with the presumption that it provided 'a safe procedure as long as it is taken frankly as an approximation and no deep distributive meaning is read' (Solow, 1960, p. 90) into empirical results. This group became interested in 'vintage' concepts and in the feasibility of establishing a 'surrogate' production function as an aggregate relationship free from the realistic obstacles of 'Clark-like' measures of aggregate capital.

[A] new concept, the 'Surrogate Production Function,' can provide some *rationalization* for the validity of the simple J. B. Clark parables which *pretend* there is a single thing called 'capital' that can be put into a single production function and along with labor will produce total output (of a homogeneous good or of some desired market-basket of goods). (Samuelson, 1962, p. 194; emphasis added)

The focus on parables and its dependence on equilibrium (steady-state configurations of equilibrium real wage and interest rates) stimulated qualitative analysis and mathematical economics rather than confirmatory econometrics. However, they led to simulative computer studies on whose results the group's efforts floundered.

The third group chose to emphasize duality and the use of flexible-form approximations for production functions and their theoretical counterparts involving costs, profits, factor shares and input demands. Its origins are traced by Fuss and McFadden (1978, preface) to the activities of Uzawa, McFadden and Nerlove at Stanford during the beginning of the 1960s and to subsequent research at Berkeley somewhat later. The smooth neoclassical production function with a few aggregate inputs was retained (effectively ignoring the linear-programming elements of the surrogate approach, the complexities of disequilibrium, and the dismissal by the first group that we noted). Within a few years, successful advocacy by members of the third group and the attractiveness of duality concepts, which were developed by Hotelling (1932), Roy (1942), Samuelson (1947) and Shephard (1953), meant that duality and flexibile-form specifications became part of many graduate courses in economics. This development certainly reinforces the image of conservative conduct that was given by Stigler. Persistence of the production function (and, especially, the empirical production function in its new dual forms), models of optimization, aggregate measures and smooth substitutability between factors despite major criticisms of these ingredients indicates an overall preference for the convenience and 'fertility' of the familiar neoclassical approach. Further the absence of effective counter-responses to this approach during the last decade has led to these ingredients being embedded in the 'authority' of the dominant establishment.

To some extent, this persistence was anticipated by Robinson (1953–4, p. 81), perhaps the most influential critic for production theory:

> [The] production function has been a powerful instrument of miseducation. The student of economic theory is taught to write $Q = f(L,K)$.... . He is instructed to assume all workers alike, and to measure L in man-hours of labour; he is told something about the index-number problem involved in choosing a unit of output; and then he is hurried on to the next question, in the hope that he will forget to ask in what units K is measured. Before ever he does ask, he has become a professor, and so sloppy habits of thought are handed on from one generation to the next.

Her vision can readily be extended beyond its stress of capital measurement to the neglect of other expressions of troublesome consequences of capital heterogeneity as provided by prominent members of the second group. We can identify the plurality of standards across groups, their immanence within groups, the emergence of a potentially unscientific consensus after preliminary search, and the illiteracy and intransigence of research 'scientists'. We seem to have ignored the advice of Samuelson (1962, p. 194) that 'one need never speak of *the* production function, but rather speak of a great number of separate production functions, which correspond to each activity and which need have no smooth substitutability properties'. Similarly, we now often seem to disregard the experimental and theoretical results of Solow, Fisher and Sato which established the crucial micro–macro connection between heterogeneous capital and aggregate production function for members of the second group. See the surveys by Johansen (1972) and Sato (1975) in this context. Hahn (1971, p. ix), not a disinterested observer, drew out the strong conclusion of these results:

> It is indeed one's impression that the macro-models may have shed more darkness than light.... . It is now agreed that it will not in general be possible to justify rigorously a 'well-behaved' technological relationship between the aggregated inputs and outputs, such as is required by the macro-models which have been proposed.

Compare this conclusion with the widespread incidence of the hypothetical production relationship in our professional journals and research reports a decade later! The familiar conditions for well-behaved functions are absolutely crucial for duality and the attendant indirect exploration of production through dual formulations so the persistence of the macroeconomic production function is a startling fact with which to assess the rational evolution of production economics in a progressive sense.

One consequence of the re-emergence of the empirical production function in its flexible-form and dual representations is the stress of empirical standards and, especially, the use of statistical tests of significance. Robinson and one Cambridge group used logical consistency to assess the non-invariance of capital measures in a context of changing prices and thus seriously weakened the interpretation of the production function as a strict technological relationship. Samuelson, Solow and the other Cambridge group weakened the rigour of theoretical consistency by accepting approximation, simulative experimentation and other pragmatic elements. Neither group seemed to make much use of Neyman–Pearson tests for statistical significance. The third group, however, saw such tests as a means of adding information to empirical studies of production. They became means of validating homogeneity, concavity and symmetry constraints from production theory with duality and means of determining the level of aggregation among potential inputs. Alternatively, the tests presumed the validity of theoretical constraints and were used to validate particular sources of data or formulae for inputs' user-costs (shadow prices).

Use of statistical tests must be based on the careful specification of a suitable stochastic framework. Unfortunately, the (deterministic) production theory with duality has no stochastic errors so this framework is noticeably absent from economic models. Any reliance on empirical standards by members of the third group is thus somewhat tentative for there occur fundamental problems affecting the interpretation of test results and estimated coefficients. A typical procedure has a number of steps. The mathematics of the theory provides some dual representations which characterize production. These representations are approximated by particular choices of flexible-form functions, random errors are added to these approximations and then estimates are calculated for the coefficients of the flexible-form functions by use of the method of seemingly unrelated regression (SUR) or some other 'system' method, which can recognize the theoretical constraints of homogeneity and symmetry. After estimation, some data-points are examined to see if second-order conditions for optimality (concavity or convexity, depending on the choice of dual representation) are satisfied by the estimated functions. Explanations for the stochastic errors or disturbances, when they occur, are two-fold: namely, the consequences of approximations and non-optimal behaviour. Examples include the following:

> The rationale for the disturbance term is the recognition that the translog form is a second-order local approximation to the true function and the disturbance term captures the influence of all higher-order terms. This implies that the magnitude of the disturbance term will depend on the discrepancy between the point of evaluation and the point of expansion. (Burgess 1975 p. 114)

> Entrepreneurs plainly are not able to minimize costs in any exact sense. Under circumstances of varying input prices and technical innovation, to say nothing of employment and raw material contracts, capital in place, and sheer entrepreneurial *inertia*, we may expect further usage, to be *tending* toward optimal combinations. (Moroney and Toevs, 1979, p. 34; emphasis added)

> It is assumed that the observed input-output coefficients are distributed stochastically *around* the cost-minimising coefficients. (Woodland, 1975, p. 173, emphasis added)

These explanations do *not* imply that the errors have zero means or that they must be normally distributed and weakly stationary. Similarly they do *not* indicate that some variables in the approximations are exogenous in a statistical sense. Finally, even if such desirable properties were present, tests using system estimates have only asymptotic validity and the sparse data supplies that exist now hardly generate confidence on that score, while explorations of small-sample properties by Fiebig and Theil (1983) and Theil and Rosalsky (1984; 1985) are disconcerting for system estimates. Overall the prospects for testing are dismal! Tests are part of the rhetoric of the third group (and now also part of general discussion with the assimilation of their methods across a wide population of economists) but they are surely difficult to keep as part of a progressive economic science. Rather, reliance on them is a striking example of the immanence of standards, the persistence of mistaken interests, neglect of anomalies and plain illiteracy or ignorance.

Against this background, we can recognize that the use of duality satisfies aesthetic elements and offers the comprehensiveness found in Stigler's notion of 'fertility' while introducing practical difficulties which are generally overlooked. Perhaps the widespread acceptance of flexible forms and duality in the 1970s reflects the consequences of two significant preferences of economists. We seem to prefer the comfort of analytical solutions rather than simulative experimentation, even when the solutions themselves can only refer to somewhat unsatisfactory abstract problems. Further, we seem to prefer such solutions over the recitation of flaws in rigour and logical inconsistencies, which demonstrate their lack of realism or absence from history, without providing alternative simple models. The emergence of our third group in the 1970s despite the implications of the research agendas of the other two groups can be partially explained by reference to these preferences.

Before leaving the middle of our reference period, we should briefly note a development outside the activities of the three particular groups on which we have focused attention but affected by references to parables. Hicks (1965, pp. 183–4) introduced the notion of a 'traverse' between equilibria to permit a better treatment of change.

> [In] the real world changes in technology are incessant; there is no time for an economy to get into equilibrium (if it was able to do so) .... It follows that at any actual moment, the existing capital cannot be that which is appropriate to the existing technology; it inevitably reflects past technology; to existing technology it is more or less inappropriate. ... Once we turn our attention to the study of economies with inappropriate capitals, we shall (by that alone) have taken a big step nearer reality.

This view acknowledges the very limited value of production functions as efficient boundaries in disturbed times. It leads to the consideration of historical developments on a much larger scale than usually occurs in production economics. Unfortunately, although later pursued by Abramovitz and David (1973) and David (1977) in combination with production-function parables, the 'traverse' has not attracted much empirical attention. To some extent, this failure reflects the two preferences noted above and the conservatism indicated by Stigler. The 'traverse' has not attracted a group of advocates for its use and much of production economics has remained outside history.

Well-behaved production functions
One of the most puzzling aspects in the evolution of production economics is the apparent reluctance of economists to dismiss a popular theoretical approach even when its use leads to clear anomalies. Our third illustrative episode reveals a current problem in which empirical evidence is troublesome. This is succinctly described by Diewert and Wales (1987, p. 43):

> One of the most vexing problems applied economists have encountered in estimating flexible functional forms in the production or consumer context is that the theoretical curvature conditions (concavity, convexity, or quasiconvexity) that are implied by economic theory are frequently not satisfied by the estimated cost, profit, or indirect utility function.

There are several important features of the problem that are worth exploring. First, its severity needs to be clarified. Second, the issue of non-self duality has to be addressed. Then a distinction between theoretical functions and their approximation must be clarified in relation to the imposition of theoretical constraints. Finally, the responses of economists to anomalies and their reliance on testing and data adjustments should be identified. All of these features affect 'normal' scientific conduct.

For over fifty years, production economics has involved the assumption that economic agents normally operate in an 'economic region', which is characterized by the principle of increasing marginal rate of substitution or some other criteria for 'well-behaved' production functions. Often the purpose of this assumption is to permit the derivation of demand functions for productive inputs. See, for example, the exposition by Allen (1938, pp. 286, 503), where the criteria are linked to second-order conditions for optimization, or that by Ferguson (1969, p. 11) where the graph of the 'economic region' is displayed. Justifications for the focus on well-behaved production functions have ranged from the nature of 'free enterprise or the competitive system' in Knight (1921, pp. 101–3) to non-separability and empirical observations in Silberberg (1981, pp. 81, 181–3) whereby convexity of isoquants is seen as 'the only assertion about ... technology ... consistent with the simultaneous use of several ... inputs' and as compatible with the non-occurrence of 'intransigence and disconti-nuous hiring of factors in the real world'. When duality concepts were explored, the theoretical constraints in production economics grew for the homogeneity of various dual representations emerged and reciprocity or symmetry conditions were established. These constraints could then be expressed as significant features of cost, profit and share functions which were the basic ingredients of econometric models. Unfortunately, the mathematical theory needs to be supplemented, for regression models are more explicit than their theoretical counterparts. Several explicit flexible-form formulae were introduced to permit econometric estimation. Theor-etical constraints were then simply transferred from the mathematical theory to the empirical approximations using flexible forms. However, the theoretical constraints or 'regularity conditions' were not satisfied by flexible forms across all potential values of productive inputs and their occurrence in practice needed to be checked.

The outcome of such checks proved to be somewhat disturbing. Some examples include the following:

> The concavity of the cost function was checked at each observation point ... For Fishing local concavity was not attained at any sample period while for Forestry, Manufacturing, and Finance there were some observations for which concavity was not attained. (Woodland, 1975, p. 177)

> For four of eight manufacturing industries at the 2-digit SIC level, it was found they 'do not appear to satisfy the concavity condition and the performance of the model has to be considered suspect for these four industries'. (Halvorsen and Ford, 1979, p. 61)

> It is disappointing that the necessary condition for the concavity of the cost

function in factor prices ... was not explicitly satisfied by the data for most industries. (Mohr, 1980, p. 186)

Regularity conditions ... are often violated by the translog and the CES-translog. Both flexible functional forms tend to satisfy regularity at price situations near the center of the sample and to violate them at extreme observations. (Pollak, Sickles and Wales, 1984. p. 605)

For about 117 observations, four models (identified by mnemonics TL, EGCDI, EGCD2 and SGM) with flexible-form specifications were fitted. 'The TL violates concavity conditions only 3 times whereas the SGM model fails this test at 23 observations. Both versions of the EGCD model violate these conditions more than 100 times.' 'In this case, our experience suggested that the more "flexible" the form, the more difficulties we had in achieving convergence in an economically meaningful region.' (Kokkelenberg and Nguyen, 1987)

A more comprehensive survey of our literature reveals that such examples accurately reflect the frequent incidence of non-confirmation for well-behaved production functions. What should we make of this finding? One response is to search for computational software that imposes global flexibility (so curvature conditions always hold) when flexible forms are estimated. Diewert and Wales (1987) indicate how much has been achieved in pursuing this direction of activity during the preceding decade. Unfortunately, it seems that global flexibility can only be obtained if we add much computational complexity and other potential biases. A second response, illustrated by Mohr (1980, p. 186) and by Humphrey (1980, p. 237) in discussing this paper, is to reassess estimated coefficients perhaps in connection with use of statistical tests of significance. Another response, also illustrated by Mohr and Humphrey, is to adjust the observations themselves so that the theoretical constraints might be satisfied. For example,

It is difficult to know what to make of the empirical result that various Allen own partial substitution elasticities are positive and/or the price concavity condition is not met. ... [In] my own work, I have found the price concavity condition to be a very sensitive restriction, a restriction in which minor changes in the data set (through use of theoretical *a priori* information) will generate the correct theoretical result with only small changes in coefficient estimates. (Humphrey, 1980, p. 237)

Similarly, Mohr (1980, p. 127) points to 'improvement in raw source data and/or methods of data construction as a possible key to satisfying the curvature condition for cost-minimization'. Overall the problem of non-confirmation for theoretical constraints seems quite severe. None of these responses successfully resolves it. Certainly the post-estimation adjustment of data and estimates is contradictory to most views of testing or scientific checks.

One aspect of this situation stems from the paradigm-dependency of standards. Attitudes to testing and the choice of estimates, for example, are conditioned by the attractiveness of the duality framework. The absence of self-duality for flexible forms weakens this attraction and affects testing but, as yet, has not effectively modified the standards applied to evaluate empirical results. Houthakker (1960) seems to have introduced the concept of self-duality, while Samuelson (1965) further developed it. In our context, the absence of self-duality means, for example, that a translog production function is incompatible with a translog cost function. More generally, the choices among flexible-form specifications and dual representations for production are non-trivial. Estimates of fundamental productive characteristics (for substitution, scale and concavity, say) are sensitive to these choices and we have few grounds for making them. Hence estimates are, in some sense, arbitrary and the results of statistical tests or diagnostic checks are not invariant to the vagaries of research. After twenty years, the awareness of non-self duality should have considerably weakened both the dependence on empirical standards here and the fashionability of the duality framework involving flexible forms. Their persistence indicates the non-progressive nature of much research on production.

The situation is further complicated by the frequent use of language to suggest that flexible-form specifications are approximations. Suppose $f(x)$ is a theoretical function involving argument x, $g_n(x)$ is an approximation and $e_n(x)$ is the corresponding error of the approximation so $f(x)$ is $g_n(x)$ plus $e_n(x)$. For example, if $f(x)$ has a Taylor series representation, then $g_2(x)$ could be the first few terms in this representation including second-order ones. The subscript indicates the point of truncation in the approximation, which will affect its 'closeness' to $f(x)$. Irrespective of the degree of such closeness, theoretical constraints on $f(x)$ need *not* be satisfied by $g_n(x)$ so if the latter is identified with regression equations, the validity of imposing the same constraints on these equations is questionable! The approximation $g_n(x)$ may not be homogeneous or exhibit regularity of a required type even if $f(x)$ does. Thus the non-confirmation of concavity, say, by inspection of an estimated $g_n(x)$ can tell us little about its presence for $f(x)$. Although seeming severe, the problem of non-confirmation may simply be the unanticipated consequence of an inopportunistic use of particular fashionable standards. Responses to anomalies, therefore, may tell us more about intransigence and the commitment to a fashionable pursuit than about the validity of a theoretical approach.

Concluding remarks
Our three episodes are informative. Exploring them in their historical context can assist us to perceive when progress occurred in production economics and when it did not. The episodes reveal the continual interplay between fashion and science and between abstraction and realism. They also permit an evaluation of research methods and encourage meta-analytical comparisons of empirical results. We suggest there are adequate grounds for suggesting a preoccupation with mathematical theory and formal methods of analysis has often restricted progress rather than enhancing it. Further, we indicate significant inadequacies in the use of statistical tests. These and other considerations mean that there is much that is unsatisfactory and irrational in our conduct and evaluation of research. Fashion encourages complacency while science abhors it.

References
Abramovitz, M. and David, P. A. 1973, 'Reinterpreting American economic growth: parables and realities', *American Economic Review* 63, pp. 428–39.
Allen, R. G. D. 1938, *Mathematical Analysis for Economists*, Macmillan, London.
Bowley, A. L. 1920, *The Change in the Distribution of the National Income, 1880–1913*, Oxford University Press, London.
Brown, M. 1968, *On the Theory and Measurement of Technological Change*, Cambridge University Press, Cambridge.
Burgess, D. F. 1975, 'Duality theory and pitfalls in the specification of technologies', *Journal of Econometrics* 3, pp. 105–21.
Clark, J. M. 1928, 'Inductive evidence on marginal productivity', *American Economic Review* 18.
Cobb, C. W. and Douglas, P. H. 1928, 'A theory of production', *American Economic Review* 18, Supplement, pp. 139–65.
Dalton, H. 1920, *Some Aspects of the Inequality of Incomes in Modern Communities*, Routledge, London.
David, P. A. 1977, 'Invention and accumulation in America's economic growth: a nineteenth-century parable' in K. Brunner and A. H. Meltzer, (eds), *International Organization, National Policies and Economic Development*, North-Holland, Amsterdam, pp. 179–228.
Davis, H. T. 1941, *The Theory of Econometrics*, Principia Press, Bloomington, Indiana.
Diewart, W. E. and Wales, T. J. 1987, 'Flexible functional forms and global curvature conditions', *Econometrica* 55, pp.43–68.
Douglas, P. H. 1934, *The Theory of Wages*; reprinted Augustus Kelley, New York, 1964.
Douglas, P. H. 1948, 'Are there laws of production?' *American Economic Review* 38, pp. 1–41.
Douglas, P. H. 1976, 'The Cobb–Douglas production function once again: its history, its testing, and some new empirical values', *Journal of Political Economy* 84, pp. 903–15.
Ferguson, C. E. 1969, *The Neoclassical Theory of Production and Distribution*, Cambridge University Press, Cambridge.
Fiebig, D. G. and Theil, H. 1983, 'The two perils of symmetry-constrained estimation of demand systems', *Economics Letters* 13, pp. 105–11.
Fuss, M. and McFadden, D. (eds) 1978, *Production Economics: A Dual Approach to Theory and Applications*, Vol. 1: *The Theory of Production*, North-Holland, Amsterdam.
Gunn, G. T. and Douglas, P. H. 1940, 'Further measurements of marginal productivity', *Quarterly Journal of Economics* 54, pp. 399–428.

Hahn, F. H. (ed.) 1971, *Readings in the Theory of Growth*, Macmillan, London, 'Introduction'.

Halvorsen, R. and Ford, J. 1979, 'Substitution among energy, capital, and labor inputs in U.S. manufacturing', in R. S. Pindyck (ed.), *Advances in the Economics of Energy and Resources*, Vol. 1: JAI Press, Greenwich, Conn., pp. 51–75.

Hicks, J. R. 1965, *Capital and Growth*, Clarendon Press, Oxford, ch. 16.

Hotelling, H. 1932, 'Edgeworth's taxation paradox and the nature of demand and supply functions', *Journal of Political Economy* 40, p. 577–616.

Houthakker, H. 1960, 'Additive preferences', *Econometrica* 28.

Johansen, L. 1972, *Production Functions*, North-Holland, Amsterdam.

Knight, F. H. 1921, *Risk, Uncertainty and Profit*, University of Chicago Press, Chicago.

Kokkelenberg E. and Nguyen, S. V. 1987, 'Forecasting comparison of three flexible functional cost forms', *Proceedings of the Conference of the American Statistical Association, San Francisco.*

Mohr, M. F. 1980, 'The long-term structure of production, factor demand, and factor productivity in U.S. manufacturing industry', in J. W. Kendrick and B. N. Vaccara (eds), *New Developments in Productivity Measurement and Analysis*, University of Chicago Press, Chicago, ch. 2. Comment by D. B. Humphrey, pp. 229–38.

Moroney, J. R. and Toevs, A. L. 1979, 'Input prices, substitution, and product inflation', in R. S. Pindyck (ed.), *Advances in the Economics of Energy and Resources*, Vol. 1, JAI Press, Greenwich, Conn., pp. 27–50.

Olsson, C.-A. 1971, 'The Cobb–Douglas or the Wicksell function?', *Economy and History* 14, pp. 64–9.

Pollak, R. A., Sickles, R. C. and Wales, T. J. 1984, 'The CES-translog: specification and estimation of a new cost function', *Review of Economics and Statistics* 66, pp. 602–7.

Robinson, J. 1953–4, 'The production function and the theory of capital', *Review of Economic Studies* 21, pp. 81–106.

Roy, R. 1942, *De l'utilité: Contribution à la théorie des choix*, Hermann, Paris.

Samuelson, P. A. 1947, *Foundations of Economic Analysis*, Harvard University Press, Cambridge, Mass.

Samuelson, P. A. 1962, 'Parable and realism in capital theory: the surrogate production function', *Review of Economic Studies* 29, pp. 193–206.

Samuelson, P. A. 1965, 'Using full duality to show that simultaneously additive direct and indirect utilities implies unitary price elasticity of demand', *Econometrica* 33.

Samuelson, P. A. 1979, 'Paul Douglas's measurement of production functions and marginal productivities', *Journal of Political Economy* 87, pp. 923–39.

Sato, K. 1975, *Production Functions and Aggregation*, North-Holland, Amsterdam.

Shephard, R. W. 1953, *Cost and Production Functions*, Princeton University Press, Princeton, NJ.

Silberberg, E. 1981, *The Structure of Economics*, McGraw-Hill, New York.

Simon, H. A. 1982, *Models of Bounded Rationality* Vol. 1: *Economic Analysis and Public Policy*, The MIT Press, Cambridge, Mass.

Solow, R. M. 1960, 'Investment and technical progress', in Arrow, K. J., Karlin, S. and Suppes, P. (eds), *Mathematical Methods in the Social Sciences, 1959*. Stanford University Press, Stanford, Ca., pp. 89–104.

Solow, R. M. 1966, Review of *Capital and Growth*, *American Economic Review* 56, pp. 1257–60.

Stigler, G. J. 1983, 'The process and progress of economics', *Journal of Political Economy* 91, pp. 529–44.

Theil, H. and Rosalsky, M. C. 1984, 'More on symmetry-constrained estimation', *Economics Letters* 17, pp. 257–63.

Theil, H. and Rosalsky, M. C. 1985, 'Least squares and maximum likelihood estimation of non-linear systems', *Economics Letters* 17, pp. 119–22.

Tintner, G. 1952, *Econometrics*, Wiley, New York.

Velupillai, K. 1973, 'The Cobb–Douglas or the Wicksell function?', *Economy and History* 16, pp. 111–13.

Wicksell, K. 1896, 'Ein neues Prinzip der gerechen Besturung', *Finanztheoretische Untersuchungen.* Translated as 'A New Principle of Just Taxation' and reprinted in R. A. Musgrave and A. T. Peacock (eds) 1958, *Classics in the Theory of Public Finance,* Macmillan, London.

Wicksell, K. 1900, 'Marginal productivity as the basis of distribution in economics', reproduced in *Selected Papers on Economic Theory,* Allen and Unwin, London, 1958.

Wicksell, K. 1916, 'The "critical point" in the law of decreasing agricultural productivity', reproduced in ibid., London.

Woodland, A. D. 1975, 'Substitution of structures, equipment and labor in Canadian production', *International Economic Review* 16, pp. 171–87.

14 Realism in Friedman's *Essays in Positive Economics*

J. Daniel Hammond

Introduction

Through his essay, 'The Methodology of Positive Economics', Milton Friedman has had more influence on economic methodology than any other person in this century. His critics, both friendly and unfriendly, have disagreed over the interpretation of the essay as well as over the issue of how closely it hits the mark in identifying what the goal of economic theory is and ought to be. In light of the controversy over the interpretation of Friedman's essay it is curious that the secondary literature contains few references to other works by Friedman. It would seem natural, given confusion over what an author meant to say in one work, to read that work in the context of his other writings. But Friedman's critics by and large have not done that. Table 14.1 gives a list of twenty-four critiques of 'The Methodology' with their references to other Friedman works. Critics cite other methodological work, other critiques of the essay and works in philosophy, but very little of Friedman's other work.[1]

Yet 'The Methodology of Positive Economics' is by no means the only published expression of Friedman's views on methodology. Furthermore, Friedman wrote the paper as the introduction to *Essays in Positive Economics*, a book that itself includes four other chapters that are *primarily methodological*. Two of the methodological chapters, 'Lange on Price Flexibility and Employment: A Methodological Criticism', and 'Lerner on the Economics of Control,' which were originally published in 1946 and 1947, are grouped together under the heading 'Comments on Method'. The other two, 'The Marshallian Demand Curve' and 'The "Welfare" Effects of an Income Tax and an Excise Tax', originally published in 1949 and 1952, make up the 'Price Theory' part of the book. But they too are methodological arguments. Table 14.1 shows only two citations of any chapter of Friedman's book other than its Introduction.

Among the more recent critics there appears to be an emerging consensus that Friedman's point of view in the essay is instrumentalism. This is the interpretation of Wong (1973), Boland (1979), Caldwell (1980; 1982) and Blaug (1980). Caldwell modifies the label to methodological instrumentalism to reflect the fact that Friedman does not address the ontological status of theoretical entities.

Table 14.1   Secondary literature

Author	Publication	Friedman Citations
Mäki	RHET&M, 1986	'Marshallian Demand Curve' 'Lange on Price Flexibility' JPE, 1972 IEA, 1977
Caldwell	*Beyond Positivism*	JPE, 1977 AER, 1975 MF & Meiselman, 1963
Caldwell	SEJ, 1980	JPE, 1977
Blaug	*The Methodology*	None
Musgrave	*Kyklos*, 1981	None
Boland	JEL 1979	None
Rosenberg	*Microeconomic Laws*	Capitalism & Freedom
McClelland	*Causal Explanation*	None
Rotwein	JEI, 1973	None
Wong	AER, 1973	None
DeAllessi	JPE, 1971	None
Rivett	AEP, 1970	None
Bear & Orr	JPE, 1967	None
DeAllessi	QJE, 1965	PRICE THEORY
Massey	AER, 1965	None
Melitz	JPE, 1965	REStudies, 1963
Cyert & Grunberg	'Assumption...'	None
Nagel	AER, 1963	None
Samuelson	AER, 1963	None
Simon	AER, 1963	None
Rotwein	QJE, 1959	None
Archibald	BJPS, 1959	JPE, 1948
Klappholz & Agassi	*Economica*, 1959	None
Koopmans	*Three Essays*	None

The instrumentalism of which Friedman's essay is said to be an example is a particular form of anti-realism. Mäki (1988) marks Friedman's essay as the beginning of a turn away from realism in economic methodology:

> Before the 1950s, the 'realism' of economic theory used to be a shared concern of the majority of economists, especially among those writing on methodological issues, mainstream friends and foes alike. It is true that the methodological problem was often understood in narrow and even distorted terms, but, as I see the situation, a major issue was that of realism. It was Milton Friedman, together with Fritz Machlup, who challenged the relevance of this issue. They made their case in an obscure and partially misleading way, but in the twenty years that followed, their success was established within the mainstream of economics: realism was no longer a major issue in the 1970s. Realism was replaced by rules. (p. 90)[2]

Anti-realism regarding theory denies the importance of theory's truth or

falsity. Friedman's instrumentalism is said to be distinguished by the claim
that

> theories are best viewed as *nothing more* than instruments. Viewed thus, theor-
> ies are neither true nor false (instruments are not true or false), but only more
> or less adequate, given a particular problem. Just as a hammer is an adequate
> instrument for certain tasks, and not for others, theories are evaluated for their
> adequacy, which is usually measured by predictive power. (Caldwell, 1982, p.
> 178; emphasis added)

Instrumentalists emphasize the usefulness of theories (in allowing one to
make predictions) and do not worry about the truth of the theories. They
do not seek causal explanations.

Our purpose in this paper is to examine the neglected methodological
chapters from *Essays in Positive Economics* to determine if they show
Friedman as a realist or anti-realist. We pursue this question rather than
his instrumentalism because anti-realism is a broader and more fundamental outlook than instrumentalism. A negative finding on anti-realism
casts doubt on the instrumentalism interpretation while a negative finding
on instrumentalism would not necessarily cast doubt on anti-realism. We
shall find that Friedman is clearly a realist in the four chapters, which
should make us uneasy with the notion that his position in 'The Methodology of Positive Economics' is instrumentalism.[3] Finding that Friedman is
a realist does not imply that there was no difference in his methodology
and that of the critics of neoclassical theory. Realism is not a narrowly
circumscribed philosophical doctrine. In Ian Hacking's words, 'definitions of "scientific realism" merely point the way. It is more an attitude
than a clearly stated doctrine. It is a way to think about the content of
natural science' (1983, p. 26). The particular realist position of Friedman
in these essays can be circumscribed, however, in terms of methodological
rules or principles. But these are not the principles that until now have
been imputed to his methodology by his critics.

Friedman's own characterization of his methodology is Marshallian. In
the four chapters he compares Marshallian analysis with a type that he
initially called taxonomic theorizing (in his review of Lange) and later (in
'The Marshallian Demand Curve') labelled Walrasian. Friedman's Marshallian methodology can be summarized in terms of Lakatosian positive
and negative heuristics:

1. Centre analysis on real-world problems.
2. Begin analysis with a full and comprehensive set of observed and
   related facts.
3. Break the problem up into manageable portions in a way dictated by
   the problem itself.

4. Take account of the influence of real-world institutions.
5. Define terms within the context of the problem, rather than *a priori* and once and for all.
6. Do not allow mathematical considerations to dominate the analysis.

We shall test for realism in the four chapters by looking for explicit or implied answers to the following questions, with affirmative answers indicating realism. The first three questions are based on Mäki (1988; 1989).

1. Is there a reality independent of the economist's mind and theory?
2. Does the independent reality consist of unobservable as well as observable entities?
3. Should theory aim for this reality (for truth)?

We shall further expose Friedman's particular type of realism by seeking answers to two additional questions:

4. What is the best way to go about theorizing so as to get closer to reality (truth)?
5. What is the best way to handle unobservables?

We begin with the two chapters from the price theory section.

'The Marshallian Demand Curve'
Here, as Friedman challenges the standard interpretation of the Marshallian demand curve, we find clear, explicit answers to all but questions 2 and 5. Friedman uses Marshall's conception of the nature and function of economic theory as part of his evidence that the standard interpretation of Marshall's demand curve is wrong. Here also Friedman introduces the labels Marshallian and Walrasian for the two rival methodologies. His statement of introduction is 'We curtsy to Marshall, but we walk with Walras' (1953, p. 89).

Questions 1 and 3 are answered by Friedman (and Marshall as portrayed by Friedman) with a clear and direct 'yes'. Friedman uses a phrase from Marshall's 'The Present Position of Economics' (1885) to characterize economic theory as an 'engine for the discovery of concrete truth' (1953, pp. 56, 57, 90, 91). Here is the first hint that Friedman is a realist; for him truth matters. Furthermore, truth is to be discovered, not created, through use of economic theory. The realism of the position Friedman takes here stands in stark contrast to the instrumentalism whereby theory is seen *merely* as a prediction generator, and to the anti-realism of, for example, Nelson Goodman.[4] The methodological meat of Friedman's argument relates to our question 4, where he makes his Marshallian–Walrasian distinction and argues for Marshallian method.

The realism of Friedman's Marshallian position does make the usefulness of economic theory important:

> The primary emphasis is on positive economic analysis, on the forging of tools that can be used fairly directly in analyzing practical problems (1953, p. 56). Economic theory, in this view, has two intermingled roles: to provide 'systematic and organized methods of reasoning' about economic problems; to provide a body of substantive hypotheses, based on factual evidence, about the 'manner of action of causes'. In both roles the test of the theory is its value in explaining facts, in predicting the consequences of changes in the economic environment. (1953, p. 91)

Friedman believed that this practical focus had been lost in the Walrasian concern over 'abstractness, generality, and mathematical elegance' (1953, p. 91).

There is a realist side to Walrasian method but it is different from the realism of Marshallian method. Friedman's Marshallian realism, based on application of theory to explain facts, is the realism of working scientists. In contrast, the realism of the Walrasian approach, with its concern for "assumptions" as photographic descriptions of reality' (1953, p. 91), is more akin to philosophers' representational realism.[5]

The central question regarding the demand curve is whether the appropriate interpretation of Marshall holds *all* other prices constant along the curve or only the prices of 'closely related' goods. Friedman argues that Marshall meant to hold the smaller set of prices constant, allowing prices of unrelated goods to adjust so as to maintain unchanged purchasing power of money. This effectively restricts the number of variables to be accounted for, making demand analysis compatible with Marshall's preference for breaking complex general equilibrium problems into manageable portions. Friedman quotes from Marshall's 'Mechanical and Biological Analogies in Economics' (1898): 'Man's powers are limited: almost every one of nature's riddles is complex. He breaks it up, studies one bit at a time, and at last combines his partial solutions with a supreme effort of his whole small strength into some sort of an attempt at a solution of the whole riddle' (1953, pp. 56–7).

Friedman reveals here another dimension of his 'working scientist's' methodology – concern for matching economists' tasks and tools with their abilities and proclivities.

> The analyst who attacks a concrete problem can take explicit account of only a limited number of factors; he will inevitably separate commodities that are closely related to the one immediately under study from commodities that are

more distantly related. He can pay some attention to each closely related commodity. He cannot handle the more distantly related commodities in this way; he will tend either to ignore them or to consider them as a group. The formally more general demand curve will, in actual use, become the kind of demand curve that is yielded by my interpretation of Marshall. (1953, pp. 57–8)[6]

'The "Welfare" Effects of an Income Tax and an Excise Tax'

Friedman wrote this chapter primarily as a continuation of his methodological challenge to Walrasian method and only secondarily as an analysis of income and excise taxes (1953, p. 100 and n.3). He uses his criticism of the 'proof' that income taxes are superior to excise taxes to demonstrate that the 'essentially arithmetical and descriptive' Walrasian analysis is less useful than the 'analytical and problem-solving' Marshallian analysis (1953, p. 100). The problem Friedman finds with the proof is that it completely leaves out production possibility conditions. Friedman shows how these make a difference in the evaluation of the two taxes. But his point here is not simply that production conditions should be included in the proof, but rather that *any general proof* will in fact fail by not taking into account some relevant condition. And the conditions that are relevant vary from one problem to another.

As in 'The Marshallian Demand Curve' Friedman opposes once-and-for-all definitions, which go along with formal analysis. He points out that even if the proof of the welfare implications of a 'pure' excise tax and 'pure' income tax could be fixed up, the fact would remain that real world taxes which are our ultimate concern are not pure types. There is not in the reality of taxes prescribed by laws and paid by citizens a sharp difference between income and excise taxes. So, Friedman concludes, the proof based on once-and-for-all definitions of 'pure' taxes *inevitably* leaves out important parts of reality. Unlike maximization of predictive power, Friedman offers here no one rule for all problems and all situations. Theory is a tool the effective use of which requires skill and insight of its handler.

In 'The "Welfare" Effects of an Income Tax and an Excise Tax' and 'The Marshallian Demand Curve' alike Friedman makes a methodological argument that virtually presumes affirmative answers to our questions 1 and 3, and that has its primary focus on question 4. The two essays indicate that in Friedman's view there is a reality independent of economists' minds and theories; that theory should aim for this reality; and that because of its lack of empirical content and its distance from the particulars of real world problems formal analysis is not sufficient for 'hard problems'.[7]

'Lange on Price Flexibility and Employment: a Methodological Criticism'
Friedman's review of Lange's book is his severest criticism of formalism in
the sense that he portrays Lange's book as the very best of its type;
nevertheless he is highly critical. In this way Friedman clearly establishes
that his position is that the problems arise from the type of analysis, not
from avoidable faults in execution. In this, the earliest written of the four
chapters, Friedman refers to Lange's formal analysis as 'taxonomic theorizing'. Lange starts with many abstract functions without form (definition) or content (shape), but with relevance suggested by casual observation.[8] Then he 'largely leaves the real world and, in effect, seeks to
enumerate all possible economic systems to which these functions could
give rise' (1953, p. 284). The next step is to 'relate his theoretical structure
to the real world by judging to which of his alternative possibilities the real
world corresponds' (1953, p. 284).

In criticizing Lange's taxonomic theorizing Friedman forcefully
answers our questions 1 and 3 in the affirmative. There is an independent
reality and it is essential for theory to aim for this reality. It also becomes
clear here that Friedman believes that all economists have realist tendencies, though not all theoretical approaches are conducive to realist outcomes. Friedman gives the same answer we have found in other chapters
for our question 4 – how to go about the search for truth – though there is
less emphasis here on the strengths of Marshallian analysis. Something we
encounter only in this chapter is attention to the problem of unobservables.

Friedman argues that taxonomic theorizing is outside the conventions
of natural sciences in that it makes little use of facts of the real world. The
approach of physical scientists, according to Friedman, is to begin

> with some set of observed and related facts, as full and comprehensive as
> possible. He seeks a generalization that will explain these facts; he can always
> succeed; indeed, he can always find an indefinitely large number of generaliza-
> tions. The number of observed facts is finite, and the number of possible
> theories is infinite; infinitely many theories can therefore be found that are
> consistent with the observed facts. The theorist therefore calls in some arbitrary
> principle such as 'Occam's razor' and settles on a particular generalization or
> theory. He tests this theory to make sure that it is logically consistent, that its
> elements are susceptible of empirical determination, and that it will explain
> adequately the facts he started with. He then seeks to deduce from his theory
> facts other than those he used to derive it and to check these deductions against
> reality. Typically some deduced 'facts' check and others do not; so he revises his
> theory to take account of the additional facts. (1953, pp. 282–3)

Lange's approach is doomed to miss the mark of truth, according to
Friedman, because it omits the crucial first step of observing facts. Logic

and mathematical structure are emphasized and attempts to connect the theory to observed reality are cursory and haphazard.[9]

Friedman identifies two problems that are part and parcel of the *logic* of taxonomic theorizing: oversimplification and unsatisfactory classification. There is an ironic twist in his oversimplification argument. The more abstract the analysis is, the more variables and functions can be included. Yet, Friedman argues, the gain in generality is in appearance only, 'since, on the abstract level on which he [Lange] has chosen to operate, multiplication of variables and functions of the same kind is likely to mean simply the insertion of appropriate 'etc.s' into the argument; it is not likely to add any essential complication' (1953, p. 285). Lange's system – the best of its type according to Friedman – 'contains only four kinds of things and four kinds of functional relations. There is no room ... for such obviously important factors as lags in response, discontinuities in feasible investment undertakings, and physical limitations on the time that it takes for economic activities to be initiated and conducted' (1953, p. 286).[10] Friedman concludes this point with the observation that abstraction is necessary for any theorist, but not on the scale found in Lange's type of analysis.

His argument about unsatisfactory classification is that there is an inevitable clash between the urge to be theoretically comprehensive (the primary motivation for taxonomic theorizing) and the urge to connect the model to the real world. Classifications that are consistent with the theoretical structure have no 'direct empirical counterparts' and empirically-based classifications are incompatible with the model. So a compromise must be struck that inevitably is unsatisfactory on both counts.[11]

There are four other errors that Friedman considers based on the psychology of the analyst rather than the logic of the method: casual empiricism, invalid use of inverse probability, resort to *deus ex machina*, and unwillingness to accept logical implications of the theory that seem unreasonable. The first two are born of the urge to simplify the system by cutting down the number of admissable possibilities, and the second two of the urge for realism.[12]

On the use of unobservables Friedman bypasses the issue raised by our question 2 (does the independent reality consist of unobservable as well as observable entities?) to focus on how economists should treat unobservables (our question 5). His answer, simply put, is that they should not deal with them. We find this in the first and third steps of his description of the way theory is produced in the physical sciences: 'the theorist starts with some set of *observed* and related facts. ... He tests this theory to make sure ... that its elements are susceptible of *empirical* determination' (1953, pp. 282–3; emphasis added). Friedman continues: 'the ultimate check of deduced against observed facts is essential in this process. A theory that has no implications that facts, potentially capable of being observed, can contradict is useless for prediction: if all possible occurrences are consistent with it, it cannot furnish a basis for selecting those that are likely' (1953, p. 283). Friedman rejects the classification scheme of formal analysis because its classifications have 'no direct empirical counterparts'.

Here Friedman rules out theories without observable *implications*, which would seemingly leave a place for unobservable terms elsewhere in the theory, such as in its *premises*. Yet he criticizes Lange for his use of unobservable price expectations, an element that occupies the place of premise rather than implication in the theory.

It may appear, with his insistence on restricting the entities of theory to observables and on connecting theory to the 'real world', that Friedman is answering question 2 in the negative (treating unobservables as unreal). But this need not be the case. He gives no indication whether unobservables are part of the independent reality, but only insists that they have no place in theory. Why rule out the use of what may be real entities? Because of his concern that formal analysis has extremely little empirical content and his belief that observed facts must be the ultimate check on theory. Also we find that while Friedman insists on the primacy of observation in science, he offers nothing here in the way of determining what counts as observation.[13]

'Lerner on the Economics of Control'
Friedman's criticisms of Lerner's book, *The Economics of Control*, offer more of the same type of evidence of his realism. Again, we find that Friedman's target is formal analysis without 'a *realistic* appraisal of the administrative problems of economic institutions or of their social and political implications' (1953, p. 319; emphasis added). He characterizes formal analysis ('strictly mathematical exposition') as 'abstract and artificial' (1953, p. 303). He criticizes Lerner for drawing policy prescriptions from this analysis without any attention to the real institutional context (economic, political or social) within which policy would be (or would fail to be) carried out. The important factors that Lerner ignores include the incentive structure faced by officials, and far from perfect information on shadow competitive prices and timing of business cycles and policy lags.[14]

Friedman emphasizes the importance of information and measurement in this review. He suggests that Lerner's Board of Counterspeculation would, in fact, have difficulty producing accurate counterfactual estimates of competitive prices for monopolistic industries. He rejects Lerner's 'proof' that equal income shares maximize social welfare because the proof depends critically on two assumptions: that it is impossible to determine individuals' capacities to enjoy income, and that those capacities are equal. Since it is conceivable that such capacities are unequal, for the 'proof' to prove Lerner must offer 'at least a conceptual possibility' of measuring capacities, which is ruled out by assumption.[15] Another point at which Friedman stresses the importance of measurement of real world phenomena is where he compares formal Keynesian 'business cycle analysis' with the dynamic (and more realistic) analysis found in Burns and Mitchell's *Measuring Business Cycles*:

> Though much of it [Lerner's analysis] is worded in terms of the 'trade cycle' or 'business cycle', there is no real discussion of the business cycle. ... To make this into a prescription to 'produce full employment', Lerner must tell us how to know when there is 'insufficient total demand', whether this insufficiency is a temporary deficiency in the process of being corrected or the beginning of an increasing deficiency that, if left alone, will lead to drastic deflation. He must tell us how to know what medicine to use when a diagnosis has been made, how large a dose to give, and how long we may expect it to take for the medicine to be effective. ... A glance at a few monthly time series depicting the movement of important economic magnitudes, preferably subdivided regionally and by industries, and a brief review of attempts at retrospective identification, current diagnosis, and forecasting suggest that they [these questions] are anything but simple. (1953, pp. 312–14)[16]

Conclusion

We have found a realist foundation under these four chapters of *Essays in Positive Economics*.[17] For Friedman the subject-matter of economics is a reality that exists independently of the economist and his theory. The economist going about his business is involved in a search for truth. To that end some approaches are more fruitful than others. In particular, Friedman thinks Marshallian analysis is a superior 'engine for the discovery of concrete truth' than Walrasian analysis. The Marshallian approach is better suited to the realities of the world around us and of our capacities as flesh and blood economists.

What do these views indicate about Milton Friedman at the time he put *Essays in Positive Economics* together and wrote its introductory chapter? Unless we are willing to attribute to him a change of mind between that time and the earlier times when he wrote the chapters we examined, and a blindness to fundamental inconsistencies between the introduction and these four chapters, we must conclude that there is a problem with the interpretation of Friedman's position as instrumentalism. He must not be an instrumentalist, for anti-realism is the foundation of instrumentalism.

If Friedman is a realist, why has instrumentalism seemed to the critics to be the best typing of his methodology? The answer here on one level is not too difficult; it is because of what Friedman wrote in 'The Methodology of Positive Economics'. After all, he wrote that it matters not that a theory's

assumptions are unrealistic, that theories should be evaluated on the basis
of their predictive power. But as has been noted many times, what he
meant by unrealistic assumptions is not clear. Also Friedman uses the
term prediction without offering a definition that would help us see how
his use of the term might fit with philosophical analyses of prediction and
explanation.[18] Instrumentalism is a problem-oriented pragmatic approach
to science. In Caldwell's description of the view, 'theories are ... more or
less adequate, given a particular problem' (1982, p. 178). Friedman's
Marshallian method is also problem-oriented and pragmatic. Therein lies
a similarity. But instrumentalism is anti-realist, and as we have seen,
Friedman's Marshallian view is realist.

Surprisingly, interpretive problems have not led critics of 'The Methodology of Positive Economics' to use Friedman's other writings on methodology as part of their context. But pre-Kuhnian twentieth-century
Anglo-American philosophy has been an important part of this context,
and this may be another key to the critics overlooking Friedman's realism.
In particular, economic methodologists have been especially influenced by
Karl Popper's philosophy.[19] Popper, whom Ian Hacking has called 'the
most theory-oriented philosopher of recent times' (1983, p. 145), held a
representational realism. He formulated and rejected the anti-realist
instrumentalism of which Friedman's essay is said to be an example.[20]
From the Popperian representational realism perspective good theories
provide accurate pictures of the world, so Friedman's assertion that good
theories can have unrealistic assumptions made him seem to be an anti-
realist. Instrumentalism, as formulated by Popper, seemed to be the apt
label for Friedman's view.

'Friedman's methodology is seen more clearly for what it is in the
context of a different tradition, that of the working scientist, represented
in philosophy most closely perhaps by C. S. Peirce's pragmaticism or Ian
Hacking's realism.[21] Friedman's background, after all, was thin on philosophy and thick on applied economics and statistics. In the context of the
working scientist, theory is not so much representation as recipe. The
scientist is not merely an observer and describer; he is an observant doer.
For the scientist engineering, not theory, is the basis for realism. By
contrast, in the philosophical tradition epitomized by Popper, engineering
is placed on a plane below science.[22]

An example of economic methodologists' bent towards the Popperian,
or representational, philosophical tradition is seen in a passage that Blaug
quotes from Archibald's 'Reply to Chicago' (1963). He considers a situation in which two theories, A and B, each predicts some of an economic
entity's behaviour, but for situations where A predicts correctly B would
not, and vice versa. Archibald says, and Blaug assents, 'My view is that

the correct predictions of both A and B constitute part of our stock of useful knowledge, available for what I call [*sic*] engineering purposes, but that both A and B are, as scientific hypotheses, refuted' (Blaug, 1980, p. 107, n. 25; Archibald, 1963, p. 69). This distinction betrays a 'philosophical' rather than a 'scientific' bent. The practical problem orientation of Marshallian economics that motivated Friedman's realistic critique of the standard interpretation of Marshall's demand curve, of the income-excise tax 'proof', and of Lange's and Lerner's books would not make such a distinction between engineering and scientific purposes.

Acknowledgments

The author would like to thank Bruce Caldwell, Paul Diesing, Daniel Hausman, Abraham Hirsch, John Lodewijks, Uskali Mäki, Kenneth Rivett and Eugene Rotwein for comments on an earlier draft, and Warren Samuels for comments at the HES meeting. Preparation of the paper was supported by grants from the Earhart Foundation and the Wake Forest Graduate Council.

Notes

1. Diesing (1971) is a notable exception. Though Friedman's essay is not a major subject in the book and Diesing does not treat directly other works by Friedman, he argues that Friedman's critics have gone astray by reading the essay within their contexts rather than within Friedman's. See pp. 58–60, 299–303. Hammond (forthcoming) is an historical analysis of the contexts used by critics of Friedman's essay.
2. Mäki (1989) characterizes Friedman's methodological position regarding the theory of the firm in 'The Methodology of Positive Economics' as 'a mixture of ontological and semantic realism, on the one hand, and methodological instrumentalism, on the other' (p. 185).
3. Two other chapters fit well into the realist methodological position that Friedman sets out in the four we examine, without adding to his methodological argument. 'The Effects of a Full-Employment Policy on Economic Stability: A Formal Analysis' illustrates Friedman's idea of correct use of formal analysis, and 'A Monetary and Fiscal Framework for Economic Stability' examines the institutional and informational constraints on policymaking. See also Friedman (1955) for a later use of the Marshallian–Walrasian distinction.
4. See Goodman (1978) and Breit (1984) for a 'Goodmanian' interpretation of Friedman's economics.
5. See Hacking (1983) for an extensive discussion of these two different perspectives on realism: intervention realism and representational realism.
6. Friedman's concern here closely parallels that behind his constant money growth rate rule. Central bankers should not attempt, nor should advisers encourage them to pursue, a policy strategy that requires better knowledge and information than they can in fact have. The rule for the use of theory that he emphasizes here is also unlike the one rule given so much attention by his critics – maximizing predictive power. In advising economists to hold only prices of closely-related products constant along a demand curve, he is not providing nearly so complete and specific an instruction on how to make best use of theory.
7. The proper role for formal analysis, according to Friedman, is 'to suggest the considerations relevant to an answer and to provide a useful means of organizing the analysis' (1953, p. 113).
8. See 'The Marshallian Demand Curve' (1953, p. 73) for the Marshallian interpretation of these terms.

9. Freidman's n.2 contains a long quotation from Pigou's *The Economics of Welfare* in which Pigou contrasts the *pure type* of economic science patterned after mathematics with the *realistic type* patterned after experimental physics. Friedman's argument closely matches Pigou's.
10. The list continues.
11. Friedman gives as an example of a classification without a direct empirical counterpart Lange's positive, negative and neutral monetary effects – an interesting choice in light of Friedman's own subsequent work.
12. Invalid use of inverse probability is the use of mathematical probabilities to eliminate possibilities, but without evidence drawn from experience.
13. Shapere (1982) provides an instructive comparison of philosophers' and scientists' conceptions of the nature of observation.
14. '[T]he hard fact that neither government action nor the effect of that action is instantaneous' (1953, p. 315).
15. Another realistic twist in Friedman's criticism at this point is his suggestion (pp. 310–11) that Lerner's 'proof' is in fact rhetorical window-dressing.
16. See also Friedman's assessment of Mitchell's contributions in (1950).
17. Hammond (1986; 1988) gives a treatment of the causality in Friedman's monetary economics that is consistent the realist tendencies we have found here.
18. He uses the term predict throughout the essay in reference to the use of economic theory, as in: 'Its task is to provide a system of generalizations that can be used to make correct predictions about the consequences of any change in circumstances' (1953, p. 4). He also uses the term explain for the same reference, but with quotation marks, as in: 'Viewed as a body of substantive hypotheses, theory is to be judged by its predictive power for the class of phenomena which it is intended to "explain"' (1953, p. 8).
19. See de Marchi (1988).
20. See Popper (1965).
21. See Hacking (1983).
22. See Wible (1984) for a discussion of the differences in the Popperian tradition and the American pragmatism tradition, and for an interpretation of Friedman's methodology as a special case of John Dewey's instrumentalism. On this last point see also Hirsch and de Marchi (1984).

References

Archibald, G. C. 1959, 'The state of economic science', *British Journal for the Philosophy of Science* 10 (May), pp. 58–69.

Archibald, G. C. 1963, 'Reply to Chicago', *Review of Economic Studies*, 30 (February), pp. 68–71.

Bear, D. V. T. and Orr, D. 1967, 'Logic and expediency in economic theorizing', *Journal of Political Economy* 75 (April), pp. 188–96.

Blaug, M. 1980, *The Methodology of Economics*, Cambridge University Press, Cambridge.

Boland, L. A. 1979, 'A critique of Friedman's critics', *Journal of Economic Literature*, 17 (June), pp. 503–22.

Breit, W. 1984 'Galbraith and Friedman: two versions of economic reality', *Journal of Post-Keynesian Economics* 7 (Fall), pp. 18–29.

Caldwell, B. J. 1980, 'A critique of Friedman's methodological instrumentalism', *Southern Economic Journal* 47 (October), pp. 366–74.

Caldwell, B. J. 1982, *Beyond Positivism: Economic Methodology in the Twentieth Century*, Allen & Unwin, London.

Cyert, R. M. and Grunberg, E. 1963, 'Assumption, prediction and explanation in economics', in R. M. Cyert and J. G. March (eds), *A Behavioral Theory of the Firm*, Prentice-Hall, Englewood Cliffs, NJ.

DeAllessi, L. 1965, 'Economic theory as a language', *Quarterly Journal of Economics* 79 (August), pp. 472–7.

DeAllessi, L. 1971, 'Reversals of assumptions and implications', *Journal of Political Economy* 79 (July), pp. 867–77.

de Marchi, N. (ed.) 1988, *The Popperian Legacy in Economics*, Cambridge University Press, Cambridge.

Diesing, P. 1971, *Patterns of Discovery in the Social Sciences*, Aldine, Chicago.

Friedman, M. 1950, 'Wesley C. Mitchell as an economic theorist', *Journal of Political Economy*, 58 (December), pp. 463–95.

Friedman, M. 1953, *Essays in Positive Economics*, University of Chicago Press, Chicago.

Friedman, M. 1955, 'Leon Walras and his economic system', *American Economic Review* 45 (December), pp. 900–9.

Friedman, M. 1962, *Capitalism and Freedom*, University of Chicago Press, Chicago.

Friedman, M. 1962, 'More on Archibald versus Chicago', *Review of Economic Studies* 30 (1), pp. 65–7.

Friedman, M. 1962, *Price Theory: A Provisional Text*, Aldine, Chicago.

Friedman, M. 1972, 'Comments on the critics', *Journal of Political Economy* 80 (September–October), pp. 906–50; reprinted in R. J. Gordon (ed.), 1974, *Milton Friedman's Monetary Framework*, University of Chicago Press, Chicago.

Friedman, M. 1975, 'Twenty-five years after the rediscovery of money: what have we learned? Discussion', *American Economic Review*, 65 (May), pp. 176–9.

Friedman, M. 1977, *From Galbraith to Economic Freedom*, IEA, London.

Friedman, M. 1977, 'Nobel lecture: inflation and unemployment', *Journal of Political Economy*, 85 (June), pp. 451–72.

Friedman, M. and Meiselman, D. 1963, 'The relative stability of monetary velocity and the investment multiplier in the United States, 1897–1958', in Commission on Money and Credit, *Stabilization Policies*, Prentice-Hall, Englewood Cliffs, NJ.

Friedman, M. and Savage, L. J. 1948 'The utility analysis of choices involving risk', *Journal of Political Economy* 56 (August), pp. 270–304.

Goodman, N. 1978, *Ways of Worldmaking*, Hackett Publishing Co., Indianapolis, Ind.

Hacking, I. 1983, *Representing and Intervening*, Cambridge University Press, Cambridge.

Hammond, J. D. 1986, 'Monetarist and antimonetarist causality', *Research in the History of Economic Thought and Methodology*, W. J. Samuels (ed.), JAI Press, Greenwich, CT.

Hammond, J. D. 1988, 'How different are Hicks and Friedman on method?', *Oxford Economic Papers* 40 (June), pp. 392–4.

Hammond, J. D. forthcoming, 'The problem of context for Friedman's methodology', *Research in the History of Economic Thought and Methodology*, W. J. Samuels (ed.), JAI Press, Greenwich, CT.

Hirsch, A. and de Marchi, N. 1984, 'American pragmatic instrumentalism and the methodology of positive economics', mimeo.

Klappholz, K. and Agassi, J. 1959, 'Methodological prescriptions in economics', *Economica* 27 (February), pp. 60–74.

Koopmans, T. C. 1957, *Three Essays on the State of Economic Science*, McGraw-Hill, New York.

McClelland, P. D. 1975, *Causal Explanation and Model Building in History, Economics and the New Economic History*, Cornell University Press, Ithaca, NY.

Mäki, U. 1986, 'Rhetoric at the expense of coherence: a reinterpretation of Milton Friedman's methodology', *Research in the History of Economic Thought and Methodology*, W. J. Samuels (ed.), JAI Press, Greenwich, CT.

Mäki, U. 1988, 'How to combine rhetoric and realism in the methodology of economics', *Economics and Philosophy* 4 (April), pp. 89–109.

Mäki, U. 1989, 'On the problem of realism in economics', *Ricerche Economiche* 1–2 (June–July), pp. 176–98.

Marshall, A. 1885, 'The present position of economics'; reprinted in A. C. Pigou (ed.), *Memorials of Alfred Marshall*, Kelley & Millman, New York, 1956.

Marshall, A. 1898, 'Mechanical and biological analogies in economics', reprinted in A. C. Pigou (ed.), *Memorials of Alfred Marshall*, Kelley & Millman, New York, 1956.

Massey, G. J. 1965, 'Professor Samuelson on theory and realism: comment', *American Economic Review* 55 (December), pp. 1155–64.
Melitz, J. 1965, 'Friedman and Machlup on the significance of testing economic assumptions', *Journal of Political Economy* 73 (February), pp. 37–60.
Musgrave, A. 1981, '"Unreal assumptions" in economic theory: the F-twist untwisted', *Kyklos* 34, pp. 377–87.
Nagel, E. 1963, 'Assumptions in economic theory', *American Economic Review*, 53 (May), pp. 211–19.
Popper, K. 1965, *Conjectures and Refutations*, Harper & Row, New York.
Rivett, K. 1970, '"Suggest" or "entail"? The derivation and confirmation of economic hypotheses', *Australian Economic Papers* 9 (December), pp. 127–48.
Rosenberg, A. 1976, *Microeconomic Laws: A Philosophical Analysis*, University of Pittsburgh Press, Pittsburgh.
Rotwein, E. 1959, 'On "The Methodology of Positive Economics"', *Quarterly Journal of Economics* 73 (November), pp. 554–75.
Rotwein, E 1973, 'Empiricism and economic method: several views considered', *Journal of Economic Issues* 7 (September), pp. 361–82.
Samuelson, P. A. 1963, 'Problems of methodology – Discussion', *American Economic Review* 53 (May), pp. 231–6.
Shapere, D. 1982, 'The concept of observation in science and philosophy, *Philosophy of Science* 49 (December), pp. 485–525.
Simon, H. A. 1963, 'Discussion', *American Economic Review* 53 (May), pp. 224–31.
Wible, J. R. 1984, 'The instrumentalisms of Dewey and Friedman', *Journal of Economic Issues* 18 (December), pp. 1049–70.
Wong, S. 1973, 'The "F-twist" and the methodology of Paul Samuelson', *American Economic Review* 63 (June), pp. 312–25.

Author Index

Subject Index

entrepreneurs, 139–43, 145–6, 148
Eponymy, Law of, 50
Equal Rights Party, 26
equal weights, 4–5, 6–7, 10, 12
'equilibrists', 172
equilibrium
    convergence to, 163, 171–2
    intertemporal, 127, 128
    lack of, 155
    unemployment, 105–6
    see also general equilibrium theory
'Equilibrium and the Trade Cycle'
        (Hicks), 127, 128–30, 132
'equivalent certainties', 79
Essays in Positive Economics
        (Friedman), 194–205 *passim*
ethics, 61
Ethics (Moore), 75
ex ante values, 140, 141, 148
ex post values, 140, 142
    distinctions, 162, 165–7
excess aggregate demand, 41–3
exchange economy, real, 85
exchange rate, 113, 114, 115
exchange relations, 125
excise tax (welfare effect), 199, 205
expansion, 138, 142, 143, 145, 147
expectations, 108–9, 129, 138, 148, 152
    mathematical, 77, 78
    rational, 114, 116–21 *passim*
    speculator, 113–14, 115, 116–17
expected values, 141

federal charters, 21
feedback effect (price changes), 41, 49
'fertility' notion, 186
financial intermediation, 133
First Bank of the United States, 21–2
'fixprice', 166
flexible-form function, 182–7, 189, 190
'flexprice', 166
forecasting (by speculator), 115, 116, 119
formal logic, 62, 65
formalism, 200, 202–3
Foundations of Mathematics (Ramsey), 55, 73
fraudulent banknotes, 24, 25
free banking, 20–26, 29–35

Free Banking School, 23, 25, 27, 28, 33, 34
free trade, 20, 21, 31
frequency theory, 53–5, 57–8, 64–5, 67–70, 75, 77, 78, 80
'frictions', 31, 131
Friedman-Baumol-Telser model, 114–19
Friedman-Tobin model, 120–21
full employment, 203
    cumulative process model, 41, 42
    Keynes's taxonomy, 86–9, 91–6
    neo-Wicksellianism, 141–2, 145, 147
    wage-rigidity, 104–5, 107–9
'fundamental' fluctuations, 115, 119–21

Gayer's index, 5–6, 8, 11, 13, 15
general equilibrium theory, 127, 130, 133, 139, 156, 157
General Theory (Keynes), 129, 152
    business cycles, 159, 160
    logical relations, 73, 77–8, 80, 82
    probability theory, 57–61, 63, 66–8
    remarks on Keynes's taxonomy, 85–98
    speculation theory, 113, 115
    wage-rigidity, 103–5, 108–11
generalizations, 200
geometric index, 4–6, 7–8
Gibson paradox, 50
gold, 44
    prices, 3, 6, 9–11, 14, 15, 16
    reserves, 29, 40, 42, 48, 49
    standard, 63
goods
    capital, 107, 127–8
    consumption, 127–8, 138, 140–43, 145, 147–9, 152
    cumulative process models, 40–51
    investment, 127, 138, 140–44, 147–9, 152
    producers', 140, 145, 150, 156
Great Depression, 151
growth theory, 167–71

hard money, 21, 22, 27, 29, 31
Harvard Economic Society, 155
Hayek, F. A., 29, 170
    neo-Wicksellianism, 139–40, 142–3, 146–8, 150–52

Printed and bound by CPI Group (UK) Ltd, Croydon, CR0 4YY

23/04/2025

14660984-0001

second-order conditions, 185–6, 188, 190
Second Bank of the United States, 21, 22, 26, 33
security prices, 114
seemingly unrelated regression, 185
self-duality, 187, 190
self-regulation, 23–7 *passim*, 31, 33–4
semi-neutral economy, 92–3, 96
sequence analysis, 139
SGM model, 189
short-run effects, 169
simultaneous equations model, 155
sine curves, 158
sine wave, 114, 115, 117–18
single period theory, 166
sinusoidal waves, 158, 160
specie-flow mechanism, 23–4, 27–9, 34
specie-redeemable money, 23–4, 27
speculation, theory of (methodology)
  motives of speculators, 114–17
  nature of the market, 119–20
  speculators and other participants, 117–19
  world-views (comparisons), 120–22
speculators
  other market participants and, 117–19
  motives, 114–17
Spiethoff-festschrift, 85, 86
spontaneous-order principle, 20
stabilization policy, 151
standards, 189–90
Statistical Institute for Economic Research, 155
statistics, 80, 155–6
steady-state models, 167, 173
stock-flow relations, 166, 167
strong rationality, 66, 67
subjective probability, 53–8, 60–62, 64–5, 67–70, 79, 81–2
substitution effects, 151, 170, 188
substitution of factors, 172, 184
successive periods, 166
supply function, 156, 158
  see also aggregate supply
surplus profit, 142
surrogate production function, 177, 183
Swedish School, 137–47

policy options, 148–52

tariffs, 31, 63
taxation, 199, 205
taxonomic theorizing, 200–201
taxonomy of economies (Keynes), 85
  obsolete nature of, 96–8
  reconstruction, 86–8
  Say's Law, 94–6
  tacit assumptions of orthodox theory, 88–9
  'truly decisive' assumption, 89–94
technological change, 170, 172–3
technology, 187, 188
Theory of Economic History, A (Hicks), 172–3
'Theory of Economic Oscillations, A', 155–6
Theory of Unemployment (Pigou), 98
Theory of Wages (Hicks), 127, 162
Thoughts and Details on the High and Low Prices of the Last Thirty Years, 2, 3
'Tilton Laundry Basket', 85
time
  Economic Dynamics, 164, 166, 169–70, 174
  -series data, 116, 179, 181
  structure of production, 127–8
TL model, 189
Tobin's model, 114, 116–17, 119, 132–3
Tooke, Thomas, *see* price changes (Tooke)
trade-cycle models, 140–41, 148, 159, 203
trade unions, 111, 127, 130
transaction costs, 131, 132
translog production function, 177, 186, 189, 190
'traverse' notion, 187
Traverse I, 167–8, 169
Traverse II, 165, 167, 169, 171–2
Treatise on Money (Keynes), 66, 86, 94–7, 109, 131
Treatise on Probability (Keynes), 53–4, 59–60, 62–70, 73, 78, 81
trend prices, 156, 157
true model, 117–19, 121
true propositions, 59